PLENTY OF TIME WHEN WE GET HOME

"Kayla Williams's intimate and honest portrayal of marriage after the tragedy of war is a must-read for military spouses, caregivers, and anyone hoping to gain an understanding of the challenges faced by soldiers coming home. Kayla and Brian's perseverance is a tribute to the power of the human spirit to not only survive but to thrive."
—Marie Tillman, author of *The Letter: My Journey Through Love, Loss & Life* and founder of the Pat Tillman Foundation

"This book stings. The back jacket says *memoir*, but to me, this is a love story. A brutally honest, real-life, painful, painful love story . . . anyone who reads this book will be better off for doing so."
—Don Gomez, *Carrying the Gun*

"In her second book, *Plenty of Time When We Get Home*, Kayla Williams's raw, honest, and take-no-prisoners prose gives service members and families scarred by war the greatest gift of all: hope."
—Tanya Biank, author of Lifetime TV's *Army Wives* and *Undaunted: The Real Story of America's Servicewomen in Today's Military*

"*Plenty of Time When We Get Home* is a powerful testimony to the power of love and the failings of the military to address veteran issues. It should be in every military collection."
—*Midwest Book Review*

"Searing and brutally honest—should be required reading for everyone in health care and government agencies."   —*Booklist*

"The emotionally raw, disarmingly candid saga of [Williams] and her fellow veteran husband returning to civilian life psychologically and physically wounded. . . . Superb storytelling. A perfect complement to David Finkel's *Thank You for Your Service*."

—*Kirkus Reviews*, starred review

"Powerful [and] unbelievably frank."

—Bob Brewin, Nextgov

"Williams' honesty and openness . . . not only compels readers to listen, but also helps shed new light on the aftereffects of the wars in Iraq and Afghanistan."   —Rebecca Forbes, *Avenue Varietal*

"Rising above recent memoirs by celebrated female soldiers, Williams's account is ruthlessly raw and objective, aiding our greater understanding of the obstacles faced by veterans stateside."

—*Publishers Weekly*, boxed review

PLENTY
OF TIME
WHEN
WE GET
HOME

PLENTY OF TIME WHEN WE GET HOME

Love and Recovery in
the Aftermath of War

Kayla Williams

W. W. NORTON & COMPANY

New York · London

For information about permission to reproduce selections from this book,
write to Permissions, W. W. Norton & Company, Inc.,
500 Fifth Avenue, New York, NY 10110

For information about special discounts for bulk purchases,
please contact W. W. Norton Special Sales
at specialsales@wwnorton.com or 800-233-4830

Frontispiece courtesy of Lynne Wilson Hass.

Manufacturing by Courier Westford
Book design by Ellen Cipriano
Production manager: Anna Oler

Library of Congress Cataloging-in-Publication Data

Williams, Kayla.
Plenty of time when we get home : love and recovery in the aftermath of war /
Kayla Williams. — First edition.
pages cm
ISBN 978-0-393-23936-2 (hardcover)
1. Williams, Kayla. 2. Iraq War, 2003–2011—Veterans—United States—Biography.
3. Iraq War, 2003–2011—Women—United States—Biography. 4. Women
veterans—United States—Biography. 5. Military spouses—United States—
Biography. 6. United States. Army—Non-commissioned officers—Biography. 7.
McGough, Brian. 8. Post-traumatic stress disorder—Patients—Biography. 9. Brain
damage—Patients—Biography. 10. Disabled veterans—United States—Biography.
I. Title.
DS79.767.V48W55 2014
956.7044'33730922—dc23
[B]
2013041185

ISBN 978-0-393-35062-3 pbk.

W. W. Norton & Company, Inc.
500 Fifth Avenue, New York, N.Y. 10110
www.wwnorton.com

W. W. Norton & Company Ltd.
Castle House, 75/76 Wells Street, London W1T 3QT

1 2 3 4 5 6 7 8 9 0

for Sonja, Duncan, and Alayna—who keep
Brian and me fully grounded in the present
while firmly focused on the future

CONTENTS

PLENTY OF TIME WHEN WE GET HOME

1.

THE INJURY

———— ★ ————

It happened partway through the first year of Operation Iraqi Freedom: October 17, 2003. Brian remembers only flashes of the day itself, and has had to piece the rest of it together based on what others have told him.

What's firm in his head is that he had not wanted to go home, even though he was due for a break. "Sergeant J," he said to Jacubiak, his platoon sergeant, "I do not want to go on mid-tour leave. Send one of the Joes."

"Sergeant McGough, this is not your call. Soldiers who were in Afghanistan and guys with children are first on the list. You're in both categories."

"I don't want to go. I need to be here to lead my soldiers. Send one of the guys who is married and has kids."

"McGough, you have been deployed three times in four years— Kosovo in 2002, Afghanistan in 2003, now you're here in Iraq. Go see your little girl."

"But my ex is barely talking to me!" Brian considered how depressing it would be to go home to a house that echoed with memories and broken dreams. His ex-wife had been Army too; they'd split up after his first deployment, and she'd taken their daughter

Sonja with her when she moved away. "Now she's in Washington State," Brian told his platoon sergeant. "I don't even know if I'll get a chance to see my daughter."

Jacubiak was having none of it. "You can't refuse! You are going. That is a direct order."

"Sergeant J," Brian was nearly begging now. He knew he had a reputation for being difficult, for struggling with authority—early in his military career he'd been denied promotions for disciplinary problems—but this was different. "I have a bad feeling about this. It's not a good idea. I don't need to leave—send someone else."

"Relax, Mac." Jacubiak couldn't believe this guy. "Go drink some beers and get a piece of ass. Get your mind off this shithole for a couple weeks."

Impossible, Brian knew. An Army lifer, he was closing in on ten years of active duty, and with his wife and daughter gone, it was his troops who counted most. Despite his early rebellion in the ranks, he'd risen to become a leader, earning a Bronze Star in one of Afghanistan's roughest battles, Operation Anaconda. Like many fellow Rakkasans (the nickname of our brigade in the 101st Airborne Division), he was confused about why they'd been pulled out of Afghanistan and sent to Iraq. Brian was particularly disillusioned about the shift in focus—he'd lost family in the 9/11 attacks and felt a personal stake in tracking down Osama bin Laden. Who cared about Iraq, a country with no connection to al-Qa'ida?

But orders were orders. Brian had gone to Iraq, and now, reluctantly, was going on mid-tour leave. Just as he'd suspected, he was unable to see his daughter. He spent his fifteen days home doing what he'd been told—drinking beer, getting some ass. And impulsively trading his pickup (he owed more on it than it was worth) for a new red sports car.

"Why not?" he asked himself. Debt was meaningless. Sure, he'd get fat paychecks while in Iraq—being exempt from paying taxes while overseas and getting hazardous duty pay in a combat zone bumped up our pay—and there wasn't anything to spend money on during a deployment. But that wasn't the reason. It was more his nebulous future. Would you be thrifty if you weren't sure you'd be coming back alive? Being in a war gives soldiers a sense of a fore-shortened life. Why quit smoking when you might get shot tomorrow? And this was his third deployment in four years—it seemed impossible to even imagine a normal life anymore.

Brian returned to Mosul still hungover. Crammed like a sardine in the military plane's belly, he and the other troops dozed off in webbed seating arranged in double rows facing each other. Suddenly the C-130 did a combat landing, coming in steep and fast. The men jolted awake, looking at one another with raised eyebrows: Iraq was supposed to be in SASO (stability and support operations), and Bush had landed on an aircraft carrier and declared "Mission Accomplished" months ago. What was going on? Brian's internal alarm flared.

After the plane landed, the ramp eased down, letting in a blast of astonishingly hot dry air, redolent of acrid jet fuel and the smell of burning trash and shit. "Mmm, smells like Iraq all right! Good to be back in the shit," someone joked. Most Forward Operating Bases (FOBs) lacked plumbing, and modern porta-johns were just being rolled out. The norm was a makeshift "shitter," a plywood structure with a toilet seat affixed to a platform, beneath which was a half-barrel. When it got full, a soldier would add jet fuel and set it alight, stirring the foul mess until it all burned up.[1]

At the Division-Rear airfield, he and his friend Bobby were in for a shock. No one from their unit was there with their gear. They'd been told that when they got back, they'd get their weapons

---

1. Although this disposed of the solid and liquid mess, who knows what it left in the lungs of everyone who breathed the disgusting smoke . . .

and PPE (personal protective equipment) back, but nothing was there for them—it was uncoordinated as hell. Without body armor or weapons, they would be unprotected on the trip back to Tal 'Afar, where our brigade's FOB was located. Another alarm tripped in Brian's head: if he hadn't gone on leave, he wouldn't be in this mess.

He, Bobby, and other guys from their unit managed to link up with the brigade convoy headed back to Tal 'Afar and borrow flak vests and Kevlar helmets from the guys heading out on leave. But it all felt wrong. There wasn't enough gear to go around, and what there was didn't fit properly. The worst thing, though, was to be without a weapon. He felt naked and helpless. You were never able to control when or if the enemy attacked, but you could control your response if you had a weapon. Now even the ability to return fire had been taken from him.

His anxiety intensified when he was ordered into a bus instead of a Humvee. Bad enough he wouldn't be driving and be in control, but at least in a Humvee he could monitor his sector of fire and watch for threats and IEDs (improvised explosive devices). The Humvees hadn't been up-armored yet,[2] but that meant the doors had been taken off and you could maneuver easily. Stuck in a bus, with windows that were impossible to open and aim out of even if he had a weapon—he felt terribly insecure.

Brian threw his duffel bag by a window on the right side of the bus a few rows back and sat down next to it. "Clusterfuck," he thought. "Fucking typical." Guys with PPE were in the window

---

2. This was the Rumsfeld era of "You go to war with the Army you have"—lots of the Humvees had canvas doors that offered no protection whatsoever. (Hell, I didn't even have plates for my flak vest for the first few months!) Our unit started having the locals build metal plates to reinforce them. It would be a few more years before Mine-Resistant Ambush Protected vehicles (MRAPs) showed up.

seats, while those without sat next to them, on the rationale that they'd be less at risk there.

When Bobby got on, the bus was almost full. To make room for him, Brian grabbed his duffel bag, ran off the bus and threw it onto the LMTV (light medium tactical vehicle) in front of the bus, then got back on and sat back down by the window. Bobby sat down next to him and they talked about leave, their kids, and what they were going to do—this part was strictly theoretical—when, if, the deployment was over.

The convoy drove through Mosul. In recent months the people there had become less and less friendly toward Americans. The kids used to wave at our convoys when they drove by, but they'd stopped. Now they flipped their middle fingers and spat as Americans passed. When the convoy neared a tall blue intricately painted arch on the outskirts of the city—the Gates of Mosul—Brian got even tenser. It was sunny and clear, locals milled around, kids and chickens picked through the trash that littered the roadside. Just ahead was what our unit called Ambush Alley—every area of operations had one, the place where the most attacks took place, where troops were most likely to get hit—this one was ours.

It was on that stretch of road that everything went to shit.

An IED went off on the right side of the bus, and the explosion blew out the front door and window. Pieces of glass flew everywhere. "We're hit, we're hit!" someone shouted. The bus kept rolling, and a rocket-propelled grenade (RPG) fired from an alley on the right missed the back of it by inches. Other attackers were shooting small arms at the convoy. "We're taking fire from the left!"

The LMTV in front of them was towing a fuel pod of JP-8 (jet fuel). The fuel pod had been hit, setting the canopy above the LMTV on fire, and soldiers jumped off to get away from the flames as it slowly pulled to the side of the road.

The outside of the bus was on fire, too. "Keep going! We have to get clear!" The driver of the bus, a young soldier who was the battalion mail clerk, kept his foot pressed on the gas, trying to get out of the attack zone as quickly as possible. Burning rubber disintegrated off the tires until they were down to steel scraping on pavement.

Immediately, the troops who had escaped the burning LMTV confiscated a local pickup truck. The Iraqi driver tried to argue, but they dragged him out and shoved him aside, commandeering the vehicle. As many guys as could fit crammed into its bed and the cab; two more rode on the hood as it took off after the bus, trying to stay with the convoy.

On the bus, troops were checking themselves and those around them for injuries. One guy sitting near the front had an injured arm. "I need a knife!" Bobby called; a Leatherman was quickly passed up from the back. Bobby cut away the sleeve to assess the injury. It was ugly, but didn't look life-threatening.

Brian said, "I think I hit my head," and tried to stand up.

There was metal sticking out of the back of his head.

"Sit down, man," Bobby said.

"Give me a cigarette," he mumbled.

"Is there a CLS bag?" Bobby called. Any Humvee would have had a combat lifesaver bag on it with sterile dressings, IV fluids, scissors, and more. But there wasn't one on the bus.

Another NCO from their unit passed up a clean T-shirt from his assault pack. "Let me take a look," Bobby said. The right side of Brian's face was wounded, one gash several inches long near his temple bleeding profusely. "Let me bandage this," he said, using the shirt to craft a makeshift bandage, carefully avoiding the piece of shrapnel protruding about an inch from Brian's skull behind his right ear, under his Kevlar. "Dude," Bobby said, "you gotta see a medic."

"No, man, I'm cool." Brian had no idea. "I just need a fucking cigarette! My head is killing me from this hangover and hitting it on the window."

Bobby pulled the left side of Brian's head down to his shoulder and held him to ensure he didn't accidentally drive it in deeper as he moved around, moaning. He didn't tell Brian about the shrapnel, not wanting him to panic or try to touch it.

The driver of the bus never took his foot off the gas, pushing forward until they got to the next American outpost.

Everyone got off the bus. First the most severely wounded, who were clustered near the front of the bus. One of the last guys off turned to thank the driver, but the words froze in his mouth when he saw the blood dripping down the mail clerk's head, forehead, face . . . despite his injuries, the driver had pushed through, getting them all to safety.

Brian was walking and talking but disoriented.

The MPs called for volunteers to go back and make sure no one was still out there. A staff sergeant from my unit, who had been riding on the LMTV and was bloodied and burned, stepped forward. They loaded up and headed back out—never leave a fallen comrade behind.

Bobby called a medic over to Brian: "We got to get him on a bird, get him outta here."

Brian tugged at Bobby: "Where's the cigarette?"

The medic evaluated Brian briefly. He was walking, making eye contact, talking. "We'll just bring him to the Battalion Aid Station. It's not life-threatening."

"Are you out of your mind?!" Bobby said, trying to keep his cool. It was obvious to him that an injury as severe as Brian's needed advanced medical treatment. "Get him on the bird. He needs to be evaced. He needs surgery!"

"Who do you think you are, a doctor?" the medic sneered. "Look at him—he's talking, asking for a cigarette. He's ambulatory. He doesn't need to be evaced."

Bobby wouldn't give up, arguing until a medevac helicopter had landed and the medic relented. "Come on, man, let's get you on the bird," one of his friends said, leading Brian forward. Brian tried to climb into the pilot's door.

"No, dude! Wrong door," his friend said, pulling him back.

The crew helped him onto a stretcher in the back and got him strapped down. Bobby's last glimpse of Brian was of him lying down, his head propped on a Kevlar. "Fuck!" he said. "What if he's pushing shrapnel in deeper?!"

The helicopter lurched upward. Brian was on his way to the Combat Support Hospital in Baghdad. He couldn't know that his battle wasn't ending; it was only beginning.

2.

FIX ME SOME COFFEE

———— ✶ ————

Brian and I met in Iraq. It was May 2003 on the side of Sinjar Mountain up north near the Syrian border. The Signals Intelligence team I was on made up the listening post part of an LP/OP; Brian was in charge of the COLT (combat observation and lasing team) guys that made up the observation post. My four-man team used our equipment to scan for enemy communications while theirs watched for enemy movement. Brian was in charge of all the brigade's COLT teams, so he only came up to the LP/OP to bring them resupply or replace one of the guys who needed to go down to the FOB or head out on leave.

He was a tall man—6 feet 6 inches, a foot taller than me—handsome, with a strong jaw, brown hair in the typical Army cut, and brown eyes that seemed to take in everything. His tattoos hinted at his background (the word "punk" bleeds into a skull) and sense of humor ("your name" is inked on his ass—literally). I was immediately attracted to him, and I sensed he felt the same. Why else our overly gruff verbal sparring? "Fix me some eggs, bitch!" he said many mornings. "Fix me some coffee, asshole!" I shot back.

This may not sound like much of a flirtatious exchange, but Army-speak can be a harsh and vulgar code. It isn't like we could go on a date—living out on the side of the mountain, we all slept on cots under the open sky. There were just eight of us at the first mountain site, and we didn't even have a generator to provide electricity, so all our entertainment came from books, battery-powered CD players, and each other. Our barbed exchanges were a playful form of bonding, and the way we did it signaled something I'd long been looking for, without even admitting it to myself.

After months in Iraq, it was common for men to stare at my boobs and blatantly hit on me. Brian did not. He expressed no physical interest in me—itself a refreshing change—but he did seem interested in what I had to say.

I am a woman who has often been told, "You intimidate men." I was born in the midst of the skyrocketing divorce rate of the 1970s, and the thought of relying on a man to take care of me seemed ridiculous; growing up poor taught me I would have to work for what I wanted. The nagging fear of poverty—food stamps and the threat of eviction, thrift store clothes and repressed dreams—pushed me to work harder, always strive for the next step. So I graduated cum laude from college at twenty, bought my first house at twenty-two, joined the Army, learned Arabic. I was not soft or girly, and I was not necessarily "nice." Several past boyfriends had asked me, "When are you ever going to just be happy with what you have?" This baffled me. "Never! Stagnation is death; you should always be seeking improvement." Independence and ambition were core components of my personality, but they clashed with the image many had of what a good girl should be like. I'd even been married briefly, to a civilian man who hadn't meshed with the military lifestyle. By the time I met Brian, I was used to men finding me off-putting.

But he did not.

Here was a man who was not at all in awe of me, who respected me the way only someone supremely confident in his own abilities could. He not only knew his job but also understood the military and how to motivate troops. Such experience and expertise gave him an easy self-assurance that meant he didn't see others as threats; he was happy to serve alongside those that many combat arms troops still thought didn't belong, like gays and women, as long as they did their jobs well. Though he joked easily, he knew what to take seriously: when I was sexually harassed and others said, "Don't ruin some man's career just because you can't take it," he alone encouraged me to report what had happened.

Out there on the mountain, there was nowhere to go, nothing to do but talk shit. So we did, trading stories about how we ended up in the Army and what we'd done during the initial invasion, debating music and politics, revealing what miserable failures our past relationships had been.

After college, I'd spent a few years working in the nonprofit world, doing fund-raising for PBS and NPR stations, living briefly in Denver before ending up in Florida. My responsibilities had been heavy for my age, and when I got a new boss with a terrible management style, I hadn't coped well with the pressure. After I cried at the office a few times and wasn't able to demonstrate my professional abilities effectively to the new manager, I'd been fired. When I had enlisted in the Army, I already had a bachelor's degree and was seeking money for graduate school, an escape from the deepening ruts of my daily life, a new challenge. And I figured that if nothing else, dealing with drill sergeants in basic training would teach me some emotional control, how to not cry when someone screamed in my face.

Sure, I knew the Army went to war—but it seemed so unlikely in the year 2000. I jumped at the chance to learn a new language for free, signing up to be a cryptologic linguist. Since the Army assigned languages somewhat at random, it was pure chance that I didn't end up in a Korean or Chinese class. On 9/11, my entire Arabic class knew that our military careers would be profoundly different than we might have imagined—it no longer seemed to be a question of whether or not we would go to war, simply when and where. After language school and Advanced Individual Training (AIT), my assignment was the 101st Airborne Division (Air Assault), a rapidly deployable unit with a proud and rich history—war was inevitable for me. I'd gotten to the unit's home base, Fort Campbell, Kentucky, just a few months before we began preparing to deploy and had been in the Army for less than three years, two of them spent in training, when we invaded Iraq.

Brian had majored in drinking during a couple of semesters at college and enlisted in 1995 rather than going home. Fort Campbell was his first assignment after he completed basic training and AIT to become a forward observer at Fort Sill, Oklahoma. Brian had gotten married when he was in his early twenties, still junior enlisted, to another female soldier, and their daughter Sonja had been born within a couple of years. They split up after his first deployment, to Kosovo in 2000, when Sonja was only a couple of years old. He didn't get reassigned to a new duty location after his first three years, and instead had stayed at 3/320th Field Artillery Regiment for six years.[1]

He finally left for Recruiter School in 2001, and was in training there on 9/11. Brian was pulled back to the 101st and sent to Afghanistan with the rest of 3rd Brigade, known as the Rakkasans. Six months after the brigade got back, they turned around and went to Iraq. So he had deployed three times in four years, and was burnt out and bitter from spending so much time away from his kid. Wherever he went, he carried a stuffed toy pig his little girl had given him, and his love for her was touchingly apparent. I've always had a soft spot for men who adore their children.

---

1. This is somewhat unusual—most soldiers have a permanent change of station (PCS) move about every three years.

We had both worked hard to get where we were, but early child-hoods spent with struggling single mothers had also given both of us a deep appreciation for the value of a social safety net: in a mili-tary still dominated by vocal conservatives, we were a relatively rare pair of open progressives. It was refreshing to talk to someone who largely shared my values, knew the facts, and was willing to speak up in debates about controversial issues. When troops would grouse about "those damned protesters," Brian or I would jump in with: "But isn't freedom of speech one of the core American values we're willing to die to defend?" If someone implied that everyone on food stamps was just lazy and should be forced to join the military, one of us might bring up our own childhood and the fact that most people are only on them temporarily. And when one of the guys would voice wholehearted acceptance of the death penalty, Brian and I were equally likely to bring up concerns about flaws in the justice system.

I was chafing in the military rank structure that forced me to be subordinate to people who seemed less competent than I was, but didn't see any way to change the situation. Bitching to Brian about how I'd had a couple of shitty team leaders in a row, he laughed. "When I was squad leader, the other squad leader in our platoon treated me like shit because I never polished my boots and I was more lax on my guys than he was when it came to appearance and formality. That guy and his squad always looked like hot shit, per-fect uniforms and everything. So I told the platoon sergeant, 'Test all of us on job-related knowledge.' He did—and all my guys scored above 80 percent, while the other team all scored below 70 percent. I said, 'Don't fuck with me. We focus on what's important, not this petty shit.' And he left me alone after that."

That willingness to push back against someone giving him shit struck me. Like many women—even those willing to join the Army—I was reluctant to get into open confrontations. It would never have occurred to me to stand up for myself that way, to get into it with someone and insist on being judged based on my merits. Brian's story threw my situation into a new light and offered a whole new world of possible responses.

Not that his entire military career had been smooth. He'd lost his promotable status a few times as he moved up in the ranks for not conforming to the military structure: showing up late or mouthing off one too many times. Right after they got back from Afghanistan, he'd been accused of fucking another guy's wife. "We weren't sleeping together, but everybody believed it, and I was constantly getting called into the commander's office and getting chewed out. Eventually we said fuck it—if we're going to pay a price for it anyway, we might as well. So we did start sleeping together."

"Really? That seems . . . weird," I said.

"Fuck them. They're all assholes. My battalion commander told me he hopes I don't make it home."

"Are you fucking kidding me?! That's a horrible thing to say before a war."

"Yeah. Fuck 'em. I'm sick of this shit. Why the hell are we here, anyway? We were hunting for Osama bin Ladin in Afghanistan— that asshole is responsible for 9/11, and it's personal for me. Two of my cousins died when the towers came down. They pulled us back just so they could send us here, and for what? Hussein had nothing to do with 9/11. What the fuck are we doing in Iraq? I just want to take care of my guys, do my job, and get everyone home safely."

His guys respected him. He didn't make them do bullshit tasks, didn't insist that they stand on formal military protocols with him, but always insisted that they knew how to do their jobs and were combat-ready.

"He was in Anaconda," one of the team leaders under him told me. I hadn't followed the news from Afghanistan very closely, so this didn't mean anything to me. "So?" I said.

"It was serious shit," the sergeant explained. "They were out there on a mountain taking fire with no resupply for days. They got no support. He never talks about it, but he got a Bronze Star." And though my unit seemed to have handed out Bronze Stars like Halloween candy to every staff sergeant or above who crossed the berm into Iraq, combat arms units weren't as generous with them. For the infantry unit Brian had been in combat with, to award him a Bronze Star was meaningful. He was tough, strong, and a good soldier—not in the picture-perfect Soldier of the Quarter way, but a soldier's soldier, the kind of non-commissioned officer (NCO) who was loved by troops and considered suspect by senior officers.[2] A man who had enough of a bad-boy image to excite me, tempered by enough tenderness (carrying that stuffed pig through three deployments!) to lure me in emotionally.

One night, after drinking a couple of illicit beers we got from the locals, I confessed that I wanted to get to know him better. My heart was pounding, and I was possessed by an uncharacteristic desire to be enveloped in his arms: he was tougher than me, capable of protecting me, making me feel safe. He looked around and shrugged: "This isn't the place for it. Don't worry, though. There's plenty of time when we get home."

A FEW MONTHS LATER, I was down at our FOB for resupply when news came in that the convoy had been hit. The NCO from

---

2. An urban legend in the Army was that an old officers' manual said, "Enlisted men are stupid, but extremely cunning and sly, and bear considerable watching"—and enlisted troops of a certain type wear this description like a badge of honor.

our unit who had been injured was going to be Return to Duty (RTD). I helped wash the blood out of his gear and was grateful no one had been killed.

Later that day I ran into Sergeant Jakubiak. He looked stressed. "Did you hear about the convoy?" he asked. "McGough got hit pretty bad." He shook his head and looked at me sympathetically. "Sorry, Williams. I know you liked him. But it doesn't look like he's going to make it. He took shrapnel to the head."

My insides twisted, and my earlier relief turned bitter. The spark of attraction had been so strong that even though we had never even kissed, I had a feeling deep inside that Brian and I would be together. No other man had ever made me feel quite as he did, not even my ex-husband. Only when faced with the prospect of losing him did I realize the depth of my longing to know him fully. His words echoed in my mind: "There's plenty of time when we get home"—suddenly they seemed like ironic foreshadowing of what was to come; there might be no time to get to know him at all. But the thought that he might die was unfathomable, unacceptable; I couldn't—or simply wouldn't—believe it. Each day I walked over to the bunker his unit was living in and asked for news, and each time I was told it was touch-and-go. I walked around with a perpetual knot in my gut.

BRIAN WAS STILL CONSCIOUS for the helicopter medevac. It stopped to refuel in Balad and took off again, then landed in the Green Zone. He was vomiting. "Knock me out," he said. "I fucking hate puking." And that's when his memories stop.

The 207th Neurosurgery Team, led by Lieutenant Colonel (LTC) Rocco Armonda, had been operating out in the desert for five and a half months, lugging all their equipment, drills, and cranial access kits around with them in big metal ISU-90 containers and operating

in extremely trying conditions. They didn't have their own generator and had to rely on other units to get power.

Now, they were settled in Baghdad, working out of a building
instead of a tent, in a fully operational standard operating room (OR)
with a reverse-pressure environment, just like you'd have back in the
States. All their gear and equipment was up to par, including a CAT
(computer tomography) scanner. To function, the CAT required
a room under 84 degrees with no vibrations. Out in the desert, it
was 120 degrees—and for a while they worked next to an ammo
dump; periodic controlled detonations would shake the whole area.
Finally, they were in a more controlled environment. Now the only
limit on the machine's operability was bodily fluids dripping in and
shorting it out.

The commander took his responsibilities both as a doctor and
as a leader very seriously, and did whatever it took to take care of
his team and his patients. After living and working together for
months, their small unit was tight-knit and efficient. There were
scrub technologists and NCOs from Walter Reed Army Medical
Center (WRAMC) in D.C. that LTC Armonda had worked with
before, and though it was his first deployment, many of the others on
his team had been deployed before. They had come prepared to deal
with privation and uncertain conditions. The other neurosurgeon on
the team had gone back to the U.S. to fulfill mandatory continuing
education requirements; so on that day in October, LTC Armonda
was the only American neurosurgeon in Iraq.

He approached his newest patient. Brian was still awake but
no longer lucid or able to follow commands. He was deteriorating
fast. Everyone was completely focused on the major laceration near
Brian's right eye, which was horrific—a huge, deep gash that was
bleeding heavily.

"That's an exit wound," LTC Armonda said. "Where's the entry
wound?" No one had turned him yet. When they did, they found

a hole in the back of his skull. The shrapnel Bobby had seen was gone—it had either dislodged in transit or someone on the helicopter had removed it. "That's the trajectory. You have to get the whole zone of injury so you know what tissue is involved."

Brian's legs were hanging off the operating table. "This guy is tall! Get a table to prop his feet up on." The team got him better situated and shaved his head around the wounds. The extent of his injuries was becoming clearer.

Shrapnel from the IED had entered below Brian's Kevlar helmet behind his ear, tearing through the scalp and skull and going through the cortico-temporal lobe in a guttering injury before exiting close to the eye orbit. The dry medical records detail it as "right temporal depressed open skull fracture, right temporal hemorrhagic contusion with severe right temporal laceration."

LTC Armonda did a reverse-question-mark incision, and once he turned back the scalp to take a better look, they could see Brian's brain herniating out through a portion of the fracture. "The underlying brain is all pulped." There was a hemorrhagic contusion—bleeding into bruised brain—and fragments of bone could be seen in the brain. But that was just the tip of the iceberg, the surface injury.

More dangerously, inside the skull, the middle meningeal artery was torn. It could have been from the shrapnel itself, or from tiny shards of skull that became secondary projectiles, extremely sharp bone fragments driven into the brain by the blast. Blood from the lacerated artery was building up and putting pressure on the brain—Brian had an acute epidural hematoma causing life-threatening brainstem compression.

The actress Natasha Richardson later died from an epidural hematoma resulting from a fall on the ski slopes; she, too, was initially lucid and later crashed. Luckily, the open-skull injury and Bobby's persistence had gotten Brian medevaced immediately. He was in front of a neurosurgeon within hours. In earlier eras of conflict, forward medical personnel would have merely focused on stopping the bleeding from the visible lacerations and he would almost certainly have died—and even if they'd sent him back for more advanced care, there's no telling how long it would have taken. But Brian had been rushed by helicopter to a top-notch (if portable and still somewhat makeshift) OR and was being seen by a talented neurosurgeon within the "golden hour," that window after traumatic injury when advanced medical treatment is most likely to prevent death.

The team didn't go after the deeply embedded metal—the portions of the brain affected, the right temporal and parietal areas as well as the posterior aspects of the right frontal lobe, are responsible for visual fields, movement to the left hand, memory, problem solving, judgment, and more. The surgeon didn't want to muck about deep in the white matter. The priorities were to clean the wound, stop the hemorrhaging, and repair the membrane.

To raise up the plates that were plowed into the brain and be able to start work, LTC Armonda created a series of burr holes around the circumference of the fracture, connected them with a router, and moved the whole skull plate up.

Once they had access to the brain, debridement was first: they irrigated out all the superficial fragments, tiny shards of bone that had splintered off like bits of eggshell and any pieces of metal, then went in with forceps to remove whatever hadn't washed away.

Then LTC Armonda followed the bleeding down and coagulated the severed artery, stopping the bleeding that was coming from inside. This prevented further damage from additional pressure building up.

Duraplasty was next, repairing the protective membrane that surrounds the brain. Whatever was salvageable from his remaining dura was used, supplemented by some of the fascia (connective tissue) surrounding nearby muscle that was used to form a patch.

Then they reconstructed the skull fragments like puzzle pieces, re-elevating the big plates that had been displaced, putting them back together with tiny micro-titanium screws and plates, and adhering the reassembled bone plate to the cranial vault. The scalp was put back in place and stapled closed. The medical team had peeled back Brian's scalp, removed parts of his skull, picked out bits of debris, stopped life-threatening internal bleeding, and then put the pieces back together.

"He'll probably survive," the doctor mused to his team once the surgery was complete, "but I doubt he'll ever be back to a point of total functional independence. This soldier will probably have paralysis in his left arm and leg; he'll need a wheelchair or a walker at a minimum. He won't be gainfully employed or able to work at any real level. Based on the severity of this injury, he won't have all his cognitive capabilities. The executive functioning will be too damaged in terms of planning, organization, concentration, and the ability to prioritize tasks for him to ever be fully independent."

The next day he was medevaced to Germany, sedated and intubated. By then he was opening his eyes and responding to commands; there had been some neurologic improvement. At that point, LTC Armonda was sure he would live. But his prognosis for long-term recovery was unchanged.

WHEN BRIAN VISITED HIS family on mid-tour leave, his parents (his mother Peggy had remarried when he was young, and his stepfather Gene had adopted him) thought he looked and sounded great. He explained his perspective on what was going on in Iraq, and how the chaos that erupted after Hussein was out of power would doubtless remain for a long time to come. Brian told his mom he was very proud of what he and his buddies were doing and felt the need to go back and finish the job. "Can't you tell us where you are, honey?" his mother asked.

Brian put her off by talking about the need for OPSEC, or operational security. But in reality he was trying to protect her. Peggy was a worrier, and he knew she already watched the news obsessively while he was gone, always wondering if he'd been injured or killed. Any more details would just give her an enhanced ability to fret. For the same reason, he didn't call home on a regular schedule (a habit we shared): if your family always expects a call at 6 p.m. on Sunday and you're out on mission or communications are down, you risk sending someone into a needless tailspin. Better to keep it unpredictable. "How will I know if something happens to you?" she asked for what seemed like the hundredth time. This was Brian's third deployment, and her concern for her son never ratcheted down a bit.

"If someone calls, it's not that bad," he said. "They'll send someone in person if I'm dead. Don't worry—I'll be fine."

But of course she worried.

Every time the phone rang, at home or at work, Peggy's heart stopped, thinking it might be *the* call. When the call finally came, there was almost a sense of relief... Now, though their fears had been realized, the waiting was over.

It was early on a weekend morning. Both Brian's parents jumped out of bed when the phone rang—no one called this early. Gene grabbed the cordless and started walking around the house talking. All Peggy overheard was bits and pieces, just enough to be terrified. When he hung up, they held one another. Desperate to take some sort of action, neither one knew what to do.

Gene was told that Brian had been hurt in an IED explosion that hit his bus on the way back to his camp. He had a head injury, lots of bleeding, but was going to be okay and they shouldn't worry. Brian was on his way to the U.S. Army hospital in Landstuhl, Germany, and his parents could get more info from staff there. They were told that Brian would call when he got to the hospital, and to contact the Red Cross because they could help: one of the services the Red Cross provides is to send confirmed emergency communications from families to deployed troops, and they have established systems for facilitating communications between troops and families during times of crisis.

When Brian's parents called, the Red Cross said they would try to get information and get back to Peggy and Gene. Unwilling to wait, his sister Shanna found the phone number for Landstuhl online. Peggy started calling to see how Brian was—but they kept telling her that he wasn't there and they weren't expecting him. The Red Cross still had no information. Increasingly frantic, his parents tried to call someone at Fort Campbell, but couldn't reach anyone.

Dread was setting in. Perhaps they hadn't been told the whole truth; maybe Brian was really badly hurt, dead. "How have they lost my son? How can you call a mother and tell her that her child is wounded and then not know where he is?" Peggy raged at anyone who would listen.

There was nothing to do now but wait and worry.

SLOWLY, CONSCIOUSNESS RETURNED. Fluorescent lights. White sheets. Antiseptic smell. Fuzzy thoughts began to crystallize: "I'm in a hospital." Pain surged. "My head is fucking killing me! I must have hit it hard. The bus! What the fuck happened?"

A nurse came in and started talking.

Panic.

"I can't understand him! Not a single word. Oh shit! I'm so fucked up that I can't even understand language anymore."

The nurse brought Brian some pureed food to drink through a

straw since he couldn't open his jaw to eat. It was so disgusting that it made him gag, tasting vaguely of sour pork.

Brian drifted in and out of lucidity, swimming in a sea of pain, painkillers, and sedatives.

The next time he was fully conscious, an Army doctor was there. "I wanted to check on you and let you know what's going on. You've been here at a civilian hospital in Homburg because your case was critical and the U.S. Army at Landstuhl Regional Medical Center doesn't have the ability to handle a neurological case of this degree. Now that you've stabilized somewhat, we're going to transport you back to Landstuhl, and then once you're more stable we'll ship you back to Walter Reed."

Relief flooded through him. The nurse had been speaking German.

IT WASN'T UNTIL BRIAN was back at Landstuhl on October 21 that his parents were able to learn what had happened and how the Army had "lost" him for a couple of days. They were able to talk to him every day. He was lucid and coherent but very tired, and complained of severe headaches that were not helped by medication. He would never stay on the phone long, not in itself unusual. Luckily, there was a very helpful male nurse who would then take the phone and try to explain what had happened and how Brian was doing that day. The nurse told Peggy and Gene about the surgery in Baghdad and tried to describe what Brian's injury looked like and what the results would be. He also warned them that Brian was very severely wounded and would have a long recovery, even though Brian was downplaying it to them. "Don't come to Germany," he urged them. "Brian will be coming back to Walter Reed or Bethesda as soon as a flight is available."

AT LANDSTUHL, JUST FOUR days after the injury, Brian was up and walking. The medical team had cut his clothes off when checking for other injuries and he was evacuated with nothing but his dog tags, so he needed a new ID, new everything. He was able to acquire a pair of donated sweatpants and a sweatshirt from a Red Cross closet.

Longing for real food, he dragged himself to the tiny Burger King in the hospital one day. It was minuscule, holding only half a dozen tables. After he got his burger and sat down, he realized that everyone was staring at him. "Why wouldn't they?" he realized. When he walked, he clung to the IV stand for balance. His head was swollen and misshapen, a caterpillar-like row of staples held his scalp together.

When the day came to send him back to the States, they told him he'd be traveling in a C-141, a military plane similar to the C-130s he'd been on many times before. Dreading the long flight in an uncomfortable plane, he asked, "Can you just knock me out?" They sedated him.

FINALLY THE RED CROSS called Brian's parents to tell them to get to Walter Reed because he was on a plane home. The call came on Friday, October 24, while they were at work, and they both headed home immediately. Peggy had to wait for Gene, whose office was farther away, for what seemed like an eternity. She fretted during the entire drive from their home north of Philadelphia to the Army hospital in Washington, D.C. "What will it be, what will it be...?" They got to WRAMC at night and were directed to a Red Cross waiting room with four or five other families.

The Red Cross representative told them that the soldiers were being brought in, but the families couldn't go to greet them yet and had to wait until they were settled in their rooms. Only the very seriously injured would have a quick visit beforehand.

Five minutes later, a man came and called for the McGough family.

They were petrified. Gene had to physically support Peggy as they walked down the hall, imagining Brian in very bad shape.

However, as they got closer, there was Brian: standing, skinny and pale, with a shaved head and a big wound on his face, wearing odd mismatched clothes—but also sporting a huge smile and saying, "Hey, Mom." Relief flooded through them.

The three of them were taken to a hospital room and the nurses settled Brian in. They received very little information that night and didn't stay long; Brian complained of being tired and wanted to sleep after getting some medication.

His parents checked into the Malogne House, a hotel on the Walter Reed campus. They went to see Brian every day. His only complaints were exhaustion and a very bad headache. He didn't eat very much and wasn't hungry.

The third day of his hospital stay, Brian and Peggy went down to see his neurologist. He showed them the CAT scan from the day before: a beautiful, perfect brain. Then he pulled up the CAT scan taken on his arrival at Landstuhl, in which the whole right side of Brian's brain was pushed into the left side. "This is usually a very bad thing," the doctor said. "I cannot explain how this change happened. It rarely does. I can only say it was a miracle." He expected that Brian would need a lot of physical therapy (PT) and occupational therapy (OT). "I have to warn you both: he may never be the same." The neurologist suggested Brian and his parents attend traumatic brain injury (TBI) meetings, but when they did, Brian was the odd man out, seeming relatively normal compared to more severely impaired soldiers.

Brian did not want to talk much about what had happened. All he would say to his parents was, "There is not enough money in the world to get me to go back to Iraq!" They didn't push him, knowing it had been traumatic and that he probably didn't remember much due to shock and the injury. He was, however, happy to tell them about his helicopter ride from Mosul to Baghdad: "I had the most beautiful nurse, she was so beautiful and so nice. She had such a beautiful voice; it was just like an angel."

Before long, Gene went home to go back to work. Peggy moved out of Malogne House and stayed with her sister Padi, who lived nearby with her husband Jim and their son, who was the same age as Sonja. Every day, Peggy went in to sit with Brian in his hospital room. After trying to work remotely a couple of hours a day for a couple of weeks, Peggy gave up and went on emergency family leave.

Other than family, only one other person came to see Brian while he was an inpatient at Walter Reed: a woman he had been dating before he deployed. They'd met when he was on a trip to Florida, and she'd come up to Fort Campbell to see him a few times before he left for Iraq, then they'd stayed in touch by email; she'd sent care packages. Right before he left on mid-tour leave, he'd told me he planned to break up with her and wasn't even going to see her on his trip home: "Long-distance relationships just don't work. It isn't fair to her; I don't know when I'll be home or what I'll want then." She was also in touch with Brian's friend Phil, and contacted Peggy once she learned of Brian's injury to ask if she could visit. Brian seemed ambivalent about it, but she came up. Once she got there, he wanted nothing to do with her. He avoided her, and on a couple of occasions when they were both in the room he turned his head away, refusing to talk to her or even look at her. After a couple of days, she gave up and went home early.

Before long, they were ready to release Brian from inpatient status, but only if Peggy would stay with him at Malogne House. He protested, not wanting to stay with his mother as a grown man, but the doctors insisted that he could not yet stay by himself.

—

IN IRAQ, I HEARD only snippets: Brian had brain surgery in Baghdad; it didn't look good. He was evacuated to Germany; don't expect much. Brian was sent on to Walter Reed; he was stable. When it was clear he would in fact survive, that knot finally eased. Even if I never saw him again, at least he was alive. I didn't want to admit it, but in the back of my mind was the hope that we would meet again.

3.

HOMECOMING
HONEYMOON

I t turned out to be hard work to nurture that hope. I was stationed in a camp completely cut off from instant communication, so I couldn't get updates on Brian's recovery. I wondered constantly if he ever thought of me, but there was nothing I could do to find out.

At last I was sent to a new location, one that had electricity, running water, and Internet access—absolute luxury. One day I logged on and was astonished to see a message from him:

> I am guessing this is your email. And by now you probably know what happened to me with getting blown up and all. I am ok, I am in DC at Walter Reed and will go on convo [convalescent] leave pretty soon, so I guess that is ok. I got some big ass scars on my head but oh well. Take it easy and be safe over there.

I was ecstatic to hear from him and immediately sent a lengthy response. His short answer came back soon:

> I am doing good. I got some nasty scars but Oh well. I dont much care if people dig em or not. Some scars are made to be worn with pride. Congrats on your E-5. Its good they fixed

your foot. I remmeber you getting shots into it. I got my e-6 but never got my orders yet.[1] They are in Iraq. Well stay safe and hang in there. My number is ### or ###. I'll still have them both when you guys return. Later.

I was so happy to hear from him that I barely even noticed the repetition or how short and choppy the sentences were compared to how articulately he had always spoken. And I assumed the spelling and punctuation errors were a result of the laziness many slip into in email. After all, I knew next to nothing about traumatic brain injuries (TBIs), and when he told me he was going to be okay, I took that at face value. Even when he wrote that they were considering additional surgeries to put a plate over the hole in his skull, it didn't fully register with me how seriously he had been injured.

Our messages got shyly flirtatious, and I gushed about it to my best friend Zoe, my roommate back home. "Do you remember McGough, from the mountain? He emailed me from the hospital! He's going to be okay! I think he's flirting with me."

"That's awesome! Do you think you'll hang out with him when we get home?" she asked.

"I hope so, if he's home from the hospital," I answered. "This probably sounds ridiculous, but I feel like a teenager. Twenty-seven fucking years old, and whenever I see an email from him, I feel all giddy and excited." I covered my face with my hands, blushing.

"Dude, he's hot! And super smart. I don't blame you at all. Hope it works out."

---

1. E-5 is the fifth enlisted rank, sergeant, in the Army; E-6 is the next rank up, staff sergeant.

IN JANUARY 2004 Brian bumped into one of his case managers in the hall at Walter Reed. "Why are you still here?" she asked.

"I don't know," he said. "Shouldn't you know?"

His mom had gone home weeks before. The doctors didn't see any reason for her to stay, and Peggy had to get back to work. Brian was going to appointments by himself and seemed to be doing well. President Bush had presented him with a Purple Heart. But despite how well he had been doing, Brian's parents were still surprised at what came next: he was released from Walter Reed and sent back to Fort Campbell.

The only explanation he got was, "Well, you can walk, talk, and wipe your own ass—you don't belong here." After a couple of months getting occasional art therapy sessions, hanging out with other patients (including amputees who called the sex they had "bumping stumps"), going out in D.C. to drink, going to follow-up appointments, and showing that he could indeed wipe his own ass, he was being sent home. He never got the other surgeries they had mentioned earlier. He still had a hole in the back of his skull where the shrapnel had entered and later where a shunt had been placed to relieve pressure and drain fluid, but they had decided it wasn't worth patching, telling him instead to just avoid activities that seemed dangerous. He couldn't ride his beloved dirt bike anymore, and was discouraged from skiing or snowboarding, too. He wasn't sent to an inpatient TBI rehab center—in fact, he never got any PT or OT to speak of. Without rehabilitation or a coherent plan for consistent follow-up care, without confirming there would be any kind of support system in place after he left, they simply cut him orders back to Fort Campbell and sent him off.

Brian got home not long before the rest of our division returned from the Middle East. I'd called him a few times while we were in Kuwait, awkwardly chatting in a room full of other troops talking to those they missed back home, trying to flirt without assuming too much, hoping he felt as excited as I did, not wanting to read too much into anything.

Zoe and I sat together on the plane back to Fort Campbell, clutching each other in a combination of nervousness and elation. Neither of us had family there waiting for us, but we had each other. We'd both asked our families to stay away to allow time for decompression, but it still ached a bit to be alone in a sea of joyous reunions.

She got the battery in her car hooked back up, got a jump, and we drove home, giddy and a bit overwhelmed. Every store—every Burger King and mattress store, everything—had signs up saying "Welcome Home, Troops!" Fluorescent lights, cars following traffic laws—everything seemed a little surreal. "Shower, pizza, beer—those are the top priorities!" we agreed. But there was one more for me: Brian.

The house was spotless when we walked in. My father had come to get it ready, and had even washed Zoe's laundry and folded it neatly. It was our house, but not as we'd left it . . . familiar, but strange. I'd let a couple of people stay there when they redeployed before us to PCS or because their enlistments were up, and the garage was full of furniture I'd never seen before.

Our phones couldn't be reactivated immediately. While Zoe was showering, I walked over to the house next door and rang the bell. A big dude with dreadlocks opened the door and stared at me. I tripped awkwardly over my words. "Um, hi, I'm your neighbor, I guess you moved in while I was gone? We were in Iraq, you know, and we just got back." He just stared at me, so I pushed on, "Well, anyway, I called Sprint and they can't get my phone turned back on until tomorrow, but I really want to call my friend, he got blown up over there and I want to make sure he's okay." Still just staring at me silently, no smile, no nod; my heart pounding as I started wondering if someone would really be this rude to a soldier just off the plane coming home from war. Deep breath: "Anyway, can I just use your phone for a minute?" After a long beat, he pulled out his phone and handed it to me. "Sure."

I thanked him and called Brian. "Hey! It's Kayla. We're back! I just got home. My neighbor let me use his phone; mine won't be on until tomorrow. Um, do you want to hang out?" My neighbor stood in his doorway watching me.

"Oh, yeah, cool, but you'll have to come pick me up; I don't have my car—it's at my parents' house. Can you come get me?"

"Sure, how do I get to your house?" I asked, eyeing my neighbor, who by now looked impatient.

"Take 41A past Gate 4, take the first right after Pancho Villa and then the first three lefts; my house is the one with a dumpster in the driveway," Brian said.

"What?!"

"You know 41A? From that, drive past Gate 4, take the first right after Pancho Villa and the convenience store, and then turn left on the next three streets, and my house is the one on the left with a dumpster in the driveway."

"You don't know the street names?"

"Nope."

I wasn't sure if he was fucking with me, giving those vague and weird directions. A dumpster? Was he putting me on? "Okay, I'll come over as soon as I take a shower."

The water was hot, unlimited, and in my own private bathroom, not a shared facility. It was heaven. If it weren't for the desire to eat and drink—and see Brian—I might have stayed there all night.

My mom had brought my car back just a couple of weeks previously, and it started immediately. The directions Brian gave me landed me in front of a house with a dumpster in the driveway. Nervous and excited, I rang the bell. Brian looked totally nonchalant when he answered the door. "Hey," he said, "I'm already a little drunk. Hope you don't mind."

"No, that's cool. I would be if I weren't driving. Um, we ordered a pizza, you want to come back to my place?"

"Sure. Let me grab some beer."

Zoe and Matt—one of the COLT guys from the mountain and our new roommate—were at my place, and we had pizza and beer, all of us laughing and joking, the three of us who had just gotten back getting drunk on very little after not having had much alcohol for so long.

When everyone else had crashed, Brian and I went into my room and got in bed. He kissed me, tenderly, gently, and held me in the dark. A tension in my shoulders I hadn't even known was there started to unknot. I felt tiny and delicate in his long arms, protected, safe, home. For the first time in an eternity, I relaxed. It was refreshing and a bit astonishing that he didn't push me to have sex, was content to keep getting to know me now that we could actually be alone together. I was so used to men only wanting to fuck; Brian's patience made this hint of a relationship feel special. We lay in my bed talking and kissing until I had to get up and head in to work for an accountability formation. Even if they were going to release us immediately after, since we weren't on leave yet our chain of command had to make sure we were all still alive and in the area.

I didn't sleep at all.

FOR THREE DAYS, we "worked" half-days—basically the unit's way of making sure we didn't do anything completely stupid while we readjusted a little bit. We got medical checks—several people came up positive on their tuberculosis tests and were put on six-month regimens of antibiotics during which alcohol was banned. "Dude, they are fucking crazy if they think I'm not going to drink for the next six months," I overheard. "A year in Iraq without beer, and they think I won't drink now that I finally have a chance? Yeah, right."

We also had to fill out the Post Deployment Health Assessment (PDHA) form. Along with questions about physical health concerns, it included a series of questions clearly aimed at seeing if we were fucked up in the head from the deployment, including:

Did you see anyone wounded, killed, or dead during this deployment? (mark all that apply)

☐ No   ☐ Yes—enemy
                        ☐ Yes—coalition
                        ☐ Yes—civilian

Were you engaged in direct combat where you discharged your weapon?

☐ No   ☐ Yes

During this deployment, did you ever feel that you were in great danger of being killed?

☐ No   ☐ Yes

Are you currently interested in receiving help for a stress, emotional, alcohol, or family problem?

☐ No   ☐ Yes

Have you ever had any experience that was so frightening, horrible, or upsetting that, IN THE PAST MONTH, you . . .

Have had any nightmares about it or thought about it when you did not want to?

☐ No	☐ Yes

Tried hard not to think about it or went out of your way to avoid situations that remind you of it?

☐ No	☐ Yes

Were constantly on guard, watchful, or easily startled?

☐ No	☐ Yes

Felt numb or detached from others, activities, or your surroundings?

☐ No	☐ Yes

As I read the questions, my mind instantly snapped to the worst experience of my deployment, when I translated as U.S. troops provided medical care to three Iraqis wounded when unexploded ordinance (UXO) went off. The memories forced their way, unbidden and unwelcome, into my mind. I could hear the screaming, see the fly landing in still-flowing blood, picture a man feebly trying to cover his exposed genitals to preserve his modesty as I tried to reassure him that didn't matter. I remembered the man who didn't survive writhing in agony, vomiting as they tried to give him CPR, calling out to God, and eventually not moving at all.

Just as quickly, I tried to push the sounds and images from my mind, tamp down the emotional responses that automatically swelled—first fear, followed quickly by guilt that we hadn't been able to save him—and control the physical reaction that ensued—tightness in my chest, spastic clenching of my muscles, faster breathing, pounding heart. It was widely understood that the "wrong" answers might prevent you from being released for block leave. I could hear people around me joking about it, telling each other they were lying as they filled in their answers. But I answered truthfully. We'd gone through this right before we left Iraq, too, and one of the guys on my team had ended up with a prescription for some kind of meds. What the hell—maybe I needed some, too. Might as well tell the truth.

When my form was reviewed, I was pulled aside. Someone skimmed the paper and perfunctorily asked, "Are you planning on hurting yourself?" "No." "Are you planning on hurting anyone else?" "Nope." She scribbled something and sent me on my way. I was reminded of a *Simpsons* episode where Homer is handed a certificate saying NOT INSANE after being released from a mental institution. Apparently I, too, was considered NOT INSANE and could be trusted to roam freely in society. I felt a little crazy, buzzing from lack of sleep and disconcerted by the sudden change in environment. But if the fact that I wasn't an immediate danger to myself or others was good enough for the Army, it was good enough for me.

EVERY MINUTE I WASN'T at work, I spent with Brian. My body and brain could not readjust to America—the time zone, the safety, the civilian clothes, the food, not carrying a weapon, any of it—and I didn't sleep at all the first three nights, just stayed up with Brian. He had brutal insomnia and didn't fall asleep until five in the morning anyway—and that's when I started to get ready for work. When I got home, he'd be waking up and we would spend the afternoons together.

We drank a lot. Everyone did. Groups of us who had deployed together would head out to the bars in town. Inevitably, in those early days, the bouncer checking IDs at the door would yell, "Hey,

these guys just got back from Iraq! Somebody buy them a round!"
And there would be cheers and applause and someone would buy a
round of beers, or the bartender would say "On the house" when
they tried to pay.

But the "guys" part of that was taken very literally. And on one
hand, it's hard to blame them: all the men had standard military haircuts, ramrod-straight posture—they looked the part, looked exactly
like the image everyone has in their head of what a soldier is. Zoe and
I didn't. Even though we showed the same military ID cards when
we walked in, we were overlooked. We could have been wives, girlfriends, sisters. We paid for our own drinks, shaking our heads and
rolling our eyes. "Fucking civilians." They didn't understand, didn't
think about the fact that women were in the Army too, didn't think
of us at war, didn't step beyond their automatic assumptions and ste-
reotypes to recognize our service and sacrifice. We were invisible.

———

ZOE AND I HAD already made reservations to spend our first
weekend home at the only five-star hotel in Tennessee, down in
Nashville. We wanted to get pampered—massages, manicures, pedi-
cures, drinking without having to drive. When we checked into
the room, there was an enormous bouquet of flowers on the table.
"Oh, wow, this is a fancy hotel!" I declared, assuming they were in
every room.

"Look, there's a card," Zoe said.

I opened it. "Oh my god, they're from Brian!" I exclaimed.

"Wow," she smiled, "he must really like you!"

I blushed like a teenager.

The first night, we went out drinking and got wildly, ridicu-
lously drunk. The first bar we went into, a couple of guys across the
bar bought us beers after they heard us telling the bartender we'd

just gotten back from Iraq. It felt great to finally be recognized as veterans—and then we noticed their haircuts and realized they, too, were freshly home.

It was around Mardi Gras, and we ended up in a New Orleans-themed blues bar in Printer's Alley. A big group of male soldiers came in, and they got a round of drinks on the house. I was already wasted, and this time I got pissed off and started yelling. "We were there too, goddamnit! We were in the same war! Where's my fucking beer? Just because we're chicks, you think we don't count?! We're fucking troops too, goddamnit! You assholes!" Shortly after I lapsed into sullen mutterings, the waitress came over with a round for us.

When I thanked her, assuming it was on the house, she pointed out who had sent it over: Kid Rock, who lived in Nashville, was in the bar and had heard my drunken rant. "That's so cool!" I said. "He did a USO tour, didn't he? That's fucking awesome." I raised my glass to him. "Thanks for supporting the troops!" I yelled.

We ended up back in the hotel room with Mardi Gras beads and masks, stumbling and laughing. Zoe was smart enough to puke. I refused, and spent most of the next morning nursing a brutal hangover.

THE SECOND NIGHT, Matt and Brian were coming down to have dinner with us at a fancy restaurant—and I had nothing to wear. None of my clothes fit; I'd gone from a size 10 to a size 2 during our deployment. Zoe and I went shopping. It was an entirely new experience for me: for the first time in my life, I could afford to buy brand-new clothes and had a body that looked good in everything I tried on. As a teenager, I'd been fit but poor; later I'd had more disposable income but had gotten insecure about my figure after gaining some weight. But I didn't know what to buy—a year in uniform in Iraq had left me with no idea how to dress myself in civilian clothes. Zoe helped me pick an outfit.

Then we went to a MAC store, where the clerk had to convince me to buy makeup—after a year of just sunblock and ChapStick, lipstick made me wail, "I look like a whore!" By the time we left, I'd been convinced that I absolutely had to own an eye shadow brush made from real goat hair that was apparently lovingly hand-plucked from free-range animals eating an organic diet in an idyllic pastoral wonderland. Since the goats had seemingly been living better than I had over the past year, it seemed impossible *not* to spend an inordinate sum supporting their happiness. Zoe bought the brightest, most vibrant shade of red lipstick she could find. "If all of it makes me feel like a hooker anyway, I might as well go all in."

AFTER THAT WEEKEND, I had an entire month of leave. In Iraq, I'd dreamed up countless things to do during that month, places I wanted to visit: New York, California, Hawaii, Europe. Anywhere. Everywhere. I went to see my parents for a few days, planning to drive on to visit other friends after that. But I was overwhelmed by the desire to be with Brian again, and wanted to go straight back to him.

Besides, being away from a military community felt too weird. In Clarksville, every mattress store and fast food joint had a sign up saying "Welcome Home, Troops!" Sure, maybe local businesses just missed the money we spent, but they knew we'd been at war. No one in the rest of the country seemed to remember. Cable news relegated the stories about troops getting killed to the ticker at the bottom of the screen, focusing instead on the celebrity du jour. It was infuriating—didn't they know what was important? Didn't anyone care that we were at war? My aunts had told me that during WWII they'd used eyeliner to draw lines up the backs of their legs so it looked like they were wearing stockings, because nylon was rationed—it was needed for parachutes. Where was the rationing now? Why were troops the only ones being asked to sacrifice for this war?

Civilians asked me stupid questions like "Were you allowed to carry a gun, since you're just a girl?" or "Were you in the infantry?"—or horrifyingly tone-deaf ones like "So did you ever kill anyone?" My mind still felt half in Iraq, and if I couldn't be there, at least I could be around people who had been there with me. I could be with Brian.

We spent most of the next month together, cramming a year's worth of dates into four weeks: hiking, going to movies, drinking, shopping, cooking, going to bars. Flush with deployment money, I could finally do things I'd always dreamed of but been unable to afford, and Brian went with me down to Nashville to hear the symphony, watch the ballet, dine at fancy restaurants, wander through Nashville's tiny art museum.

Sometimes I felt as if we were playing at being grownups. At dinner one night, I ordered the special, not quite paying attention to the description. When the waiter brought the plate, a whole fish was posed there as if it were swimming. Trying to keep my cool and act adult, I gaped at it silently. Brian grinned at me, "You okay? You look horrified."

"I don't know if I can eat a meal that's looking at me!"

He reached across the table and knocked it over with his fork, then put the lemon slice over its eye. "There you go," he said. "Now it can't see you."

I smiled at him. Through the gentle teasing, he was taking care of me.

Neither of us quite knew how to handle romance. The day after

Valentine's Day, just weeks into our fledgling relationship, he shyly gave me a necklace with tiny diamonds—he'd been too nervous to give it to me on the day itself. The next day, he gave me the jewelry box that accompanied it; in the slots for photos he had put printouts of some of the art from the show we'd seen at the museum. It was the most romantic gesture anyone had ever made toward me, and though I am a long-term cynic about romantic love and have never believed in "love at first sight," I knew I was already deeply involved. He talked of introducing me to his daughter, and admitted he had never let any other woman he had dated meet her.

I FLEW OUT EAST with him to pick up his car and drive it home, meeting his parents for the first time. We spent time at his parents' vacation home in St. Michael's, Maryland, and then headed in to D.C. to visit Smithsonian museums and go to a follow-up appointment Brian had at Walter Reed before stopping in Philadelphia to spend time with Brian's sister. While we were in D.C., I was excited about getting to have Ethiopian food again—in Clarksville, Tennessee, the Olive Garden was practically considered ethnic food.

"I have a confession to make," Brian said. "Remember how when I was at Walter Reed, you suggested I go eat Ethiopian and I told you I did and it was good? Um, I wasn't being entirely honest. I did go into an Ethiopian restaurant. But it looked weird. So all I had was the carrot cake."

I laughed. "Really? Why did you lie?"

"I didn't lie! I just wasn't telling the whole truth."

"Okay. Why weren't you telling the whole truth?"

"I don't know. I guess . . . I guess I wanted to impress you. I didn't want to admit that it freaked me out, since you said you liked it."

"That's okay," I said. "Let's go try it together now."

He didn't like it, especially the spongy, slightly sour crepe-like injera bread. But he tried it. And we were happy, being there together.

We were wonderful together that month. As long as I was with him, another combat veteran, I felt normal: *of course* loud noises made us jump, crowds were uncomfortable, trash in the road might be an IED and could not *possibly* be driven over. We stayed up late together, often drinking, and slept half the day away—it was a long, lazy, relaxed vacation. Brian was infused with a heady gratitude for being alive and having a second chance. If there were signs of his cognitive and psychological injuries, I didn't let myself see them. It was a glorious honeymoon period; everything seemed perfect. Within weeks, we were practically living with each other, spending nearly every night together at either his place or mine.

4.

BREAKDOWN

When my month of block leave was over, I went back to work. I'd enjoyed the respite and reveled in getting to know Brian with no responsibilities or distractions, but getting back into a routine was also a relief. It felt good to spend time with people I'd been to war with, get up early to do physical fitness training (PT), have a purpose. I was a team leader, responsible for two junior soldiers with less experience—we all knew another deployment was probably only a year away, and I felt confident in the skills and experience I'd gained in Iraq: I would be able to get them ready to go, I wouldn't let them go to war as unprepared as I had been. The heavy drinking and smoking had been taking a toll on my body, and now I had a reason to reimpose order on my lifestyle.

Brian's unit, however, was not making him come back to work. I'd vaguely assumed he was on block leave like the rest of us, but in fact they just weren't really keeping track of him. Most of his unit had gone on block leave, and those who remained weren't quite aware that he was back from Walter Reed. Now, they didn't even want him to come in. "Just stay home," he was told. "You can't wear headgear. You can't carry a weapon. And frankly, you're freaking out the new guys because you're so fucked up." His raw visible scars, obvious jumpiness, and frequent bouts of confusion made troops who hadn't deployed yet afraid of what might happen to them. Brian's chain of command didn't make him come in for the accountability formations that are mandatory throughout standard military units in the morning—an astonishing lack of leadership in my mind. How would they even know if something went wrong, if he had a seizure or other crisis and needed medical attention? His roommate was also a staff sergeant in the same unit, and I supposed Phil would give them a heads-up if there was any real problem. But I almost couldn't believe we were in the same Army.

My first day back, I came over to Brian's house for lunch—he lived just minutes away from the main gate to Fort Campbell. He was sitting on the couch, smoking, looking bleary-eyed. I'd been up for seven hours already, and was bouncily energetic. "Hey, can I grab something to eat?" I asked, heading into his kitchen.

As my hand closed on the refrigerator door, he called, "Don't open that!"

"Why not?" I asked.

"You don't want anything in there. This guy was renting my house while I was deployed, and when he moved he had the power cut off but didn't empty out the fridge. It's full of the nastiest, moldiest shit I've ever seen. The smell alone is enough to knock you on your ass."

"Seriously? That's fucked up." I jiggled the handle, and was greeted by a sudden rustling sound. "What the hell was that noise?" I yelped, jumping back.

"Mice," he answered.

"Excuse me?"

"Mice. There are mice living in the refrigerator. Some chick the guy knew decided to paint in here, and she took off all the outlet covers and painted, but never put them back on. No one mowed the grass, so it got really overgrown in the backyard—and then the mice came inside. Sometimes I see them poke their heads out of the holes near the outlets. Now some are living in the refrigerator."

"Why haven't you done anything about it?" I asked, wandering back into the living room.

He shrugged. "I don't know. Just haven't gotten around to it. Anytime I opened the door I started gagging, so I just gave up. We've been eating out or at your place, so it didn't seem like a big deal."

"Well, I'm getting my kitchen remodeled, and I have to go buy new appliances, too. Why don't we go together, and you can just buy a new refrigerator."

That night, we headed to an appliance store and completely baffled some poor clerk. Clearly we were a couple, intimately involved in picking things out together—but buying two refrigerators and having them delivered to two separate houses.

I was at Brian's house when they came to deliver his new refrigerator and take away the old one.

"Put a strap around it so it doesn't accidentally open," he said. "Don't open it."

The delivery guys raised their eyebrows. "Um, okay..."

"Seriously," I affirmed. "Do NOT open it. Ever."

While they carted it out to their truck on the dolly, we could hear the mice rustling around, and I couldn't help giggling. Once they were gone, I said to Brian, "Dude, I can't believe we just sent a refrigerator full of rotten food and a family of mice off to the dump. Now let's get those outlet covers back on and call an exterminator."

My garage had been full of someone else's furniture when I came home. You never knew what would happen when you let someone stay at your house while you were away. I felt lucky that my dad had come and checked my place while I was gone, cleaned up for us.

Refusing to deal with a problem in hopes it would just disappear made sense to me, too. Right before we deployed, every time I ran the dishwasher there would be a *squish* sound when you walked in front of it. I'd stared at the floor, thinking it needed to be taken care of—and then just deployed. When I got my kitchen remodeled and the contractor pulled up the linoleum, he found that the dishwasher had been leaking. While I was gone, rot had spread through the subfloor, requiring extensive repairs.

So who was I to judge Brian for having mice in his walls and refrigerator? "There but for the grace of God go I" and all that. I brushed it off. These things happen when you go to war and there's no one to take care of everything for you.

As my routine normalized, I started sleeping at night again.

Brian, on the other hand, still stayed up all night. Now that I wasn't staying up with him because I had to get up early to go in for PT, it started to become clear that there was a problem. He wasn't staying up to party; he was plagued by terrible insomnia. When we spent nights together, I often fell asleep on the couch with my head on his lap and later stumbled off to bed; when I'd wake in the morning, he'd still be sitting in the same place watching TV, an empty bottle of Jameson in front of him, empty beer bottles littering the table, and an ashtray overflowing with cigarette butts.

When Brian did sleep, nightmares stalked him, though he refused to tell me about them. "I don't want to talk about it," he invariably said. "Don't worry about it." I'd wrap my arms around him, holding his head to my chest until his breathing slowed and the tension slowly left his muscles, wishing I could carry some of his burden.

I didn't remember my own dreams, though I assumed they were bad: I often woke up drenched in sweat, my heart pounding, the sheets tangled around my legs.

ONE NIGHT WE WERE eating lasagna I made when I noticed an envelope with a telltale red stamp on it: "Warning! Final notice!"

"What's that?" I asked. I'd been poor plenty of times—I knew what those envelopes meant.

Brian mumbled something incoherent.

"Seriously. What's up?" I pressed.

He sighed. "They're going to cut off my water. I haven't paid the bill."

"So pay it!" I said.

"I can't."

"Why not? We just got paid a couple days ago."

"I don't have any money left," Brian admitted, poking at the food on his plate.

"Really?" I asked, shocked. He outranked me and had been in the Army longer than me, so his salary had to be higher than mine. And his roommate paid rent and half the utility bills. How had he blown through an entire paycheck in a couple of days?

"Yeah, well, I bought that stuff for my computer. And I was buying everybody rounds at the bar. And I was a couple months behind on my car payment so if I didn't pay that they were going to repossess it. So . . ." he trailed off.

"Here, give it to me," I said. "I got this."

"I can't let you do that," he protested.

"Don't worry about it," I said. "Since my kitchen is being remodeled I'm over here using yours all the time. It's better than using the microwave in my garage and washing dishes in the bathroom sink. And I shower over here half the time, too. So, really, it's only fair—I'm using plenty of your water." He was too proud to accept my help, I knew—so we had to invent a reason that it wasn't charity.

What the fuck was going on? Brian was older than I was, had been living on his own for years. He'd been responsible for planning and executing multi-day missions in Iraq, properly equipping all his guys with food, water, ammunition, and other supplies in life-or-death situations. How did he now run out of money within a week of getting paid? How was he suddenly unable to balance his checkbook or pay his own bills?

The next month, it was the electric bill.

———

"YOU WANT TO WATCH a movie?" I asked. "I brought over this French film called *Amélie*."

Brian shrugged. "I guess. I don't really like foreign movies. They're boring."

"This one is different. It's kinda quirky and fun," I said. "I'll make popcorn!"

Twenty minutes into it he turned off the television.

"What's the matter?" I asked, disappointed.

"I can't," he said, then paused. Sighed. Started again. "I can't follow what's going on. I can't read the subtitles and watch the action. It's frustrating." He downed his beer, opened another immediately. "And that book you lent me, that you wanted me to read? I can't keep track of who the characters are. Can't remember what happened the next time I pick it up. Every time I put it down, the next time I open it I have to reread the previous chapter. I'll never finish it at this rate. It's driving me crazy."

He got up and started pacing the room, lit a cigarette, grabbed a bottle of Jameson from the kitchen.

"What the fuck am I supposed to do? I can't even read this book. I read *War and Peace* before we deployed. Because I got blown up, I can't even watch a fucking movie and follow what's going on. I can't pay my bills. I can't do my job. I was going to make a career of the Army, I'm almost at the halfway mark—now what? I'm broken. I'm fucked up." He opened the door and threw his empty beer bottle into the dumpster that was still in his front yard.

"You're not broken," I said, going to him and laying my hand on his forearm. I was sure the cognitive deficits he had from the brain injury were temporary, and would heal the way a broken bone would, knitting back together over time. We just had to be patient.

He pushed me away.

"You don't understand! You'll never understand. I don't even know who I am anymore. I'm not what I used to be. My head—it doesn't work right anymore. I have a goddamned brain injury, and I can't do anything anymore." He punched the wall. "I have no fucking future. None."

My heart ached for him. "We can have a future together," I offered.

"Get the fuck out," he said.

"What?" I asked, astonished.

"Get. Out. Go away. Go home. I don't want to see you. I don't want to talk to you." Brian was yelling. He took a deep draw on the bottle of whiskey, then glared at me from slit eyes. "Just leave me the fuck alone."

Shaken and confused, I left. As I drove home, my heart pounded and my mind raced. "This is my fault. My fault. I tried to get him to watch a stupid foreign movie, and it was too much. It's hard for lots of people to manage subtitles. I should have realized. Should have known—he has a brain injury. I know that. He'll get better. He'll be okay. We'll be okay." I tried calling him. He wouldn't answer. Tried again. He'd turned off his phone.

I didn't hear from him for two days.

Then he called. As if nothing had happened. "Want to go to Pancho Villa and get something to eat?"

I tried to be calm. "What the fuck, man?"

"Look, sometimes I just get really angry...Sometimes I need my space."

"Well, can't you just tell me, instead of screaming at me and then refusing to talk to me?"

"Maybe. Next time I feel it coming on, I'll tell you 'Code Black' and you'll know to just give me some time."

I could sometimes see it coming. Usually it happened when he was drinking heavily...I started to get nervous every time he switched from beer to liquor. His expressive face would harden into an angry mask. Invariably, he said, "You don't understand," shutting me out. Sometimes I could still reach him, find a way to get past the wall and convince him to soften again. But more often than not, once Brian hit that point there was no turning back. He would be oblivious to my pain, indifferent to my tears, lost in his own rage and suffering, headed for a Code Black meltdown followed by days of isolation.

I HAD MY OWN Code Black moments.

When we were about to come home from Kuwait, I'd called my mom. She had power of attorney and my checkbook. "Can you make sure everything is okay?" I'd asked. "The water and electricity and everything at my house? We're about to come home." She'd assured me everything was fine.

The day after we got back, Zoe had just started a load of laundry when the water died. I didn't even have any of my files, so I called my mom. "What's going on?" I asked. "The water isn't working. Did you pay the bill?"

"No, that guy you let live there while you were gone took over the water bill," she said.

"Seriously, Mom? I just asked you about this. I told you we were coming home and this was really important to me."

"Well, I guess I fucked this up like I fuck everything else up!" she said, her voice rising and cracking. I was astonished to hear her curse, a habit she considered lazy. But I was also furious. We'd had lots of problems over the years, and I'd often felt like I had to be the adult, always the one to mend rifts in the relationship and apologize even when I didn't think I was wrong.

"No," I said. "No. You do not get to be crazy right now. It's *my turn* to be crazy. I just got back from a war. *It is my fucking turn to be crazy.* I don't have to put up with this shit."

I hung up on her and found the phone number for the water company.

We didn't speak for weeks.

She wasn't the only one I lost patience with. A friend of mine from college had struggled with drug addiction and depression for years. Now he wanted to talk about his problems, his feelings. It seemed ridiculous to me. He was like Bukowski or Burroughs (two authors he liked), who created their own problems and then whined about them.

I'd just gotten back from Iraq, where people lived under genuinely terrible conditions, were oppressed, threatened, killed by a dictatorial regime—then innocent women and children were getting caught in the crossfire of our war—these people had real problems. Our soldiers were getting blown up, injured, killed—they and their families had real problems. Watching Brian struggle—he had real problems. My friend? I couldn't see his problems as real. Couldn't bring myself to listen to him talk about his feelings. Couldn't read a description of how he'd lost his job and his apartment and couldn't make ends meet—not because he'd been injured, but because he was a drunk. I sent him a short, curt email. "I'm sorry, but I can't deal with your melodrama right now."

If you were bringing me down, you were out.

Code Black. Leave me the fuck alone.

I HELPED BRIAN pick out books for his daughter's birthday, wrap them, and ship them off. The day after Sonja's sixth birthday, his ex-wife emailed him some photos of the party and her opening presents. He smiled as he looked at them, but then his face hardened. "She didn't send any of Sonja opening the presents I sent."

"I'm sure she just forgot," I said. "It's no big deal."

"It's a big deal to me."

"Let it go," I advised. "It's not worth being pissed off about. My parents fought all the time after they were divorced—it sucked for me. You have to be a bigger man, don't sweat the small stuff."

"Fuck her," he said. "I'm gonna email her back and tell her she needs to lay off Sonja's birthday cake because she looks fat."

"Brian!" I cried, horrified. "You can't say that to your ex-wife! You have a daughter to raise together!"

"She should've sent me a photo of Sonja opening the presents I sent," he said doggedly.

I couldn't change his mind.

It wasn't just his ex-wife who was the target of inappropriate outbursts. We often ended up at Kickers, a big bar in Clarksville. They played country music downstairs, where people line danced. Upstairs they played different stuff, including industrial music I would dance to. There were "shot girls" who walked around with trays of shots. One of them had a phenomenal body, but when you saw her in better light, she was obviously no longer a shot "girl"—she was easily halfway through her forties. "You look amazing," I told her one night when she stopped in front of us with a tray of test tubes filled with blue liquid.

"Thanks," she said, sticking back her shoulders. "I just got new boobs!"

"You still look old as shit," Brian said, tossing back a shot.

"Brian!" I said. "What the fuck?!"

Her face tightened, but she shrugged and took his money. Then she smiled at me and raised her eyebrows as she walked away. I could almost hear what she was thinking: "Why are you with this asshole?"

He wasn't always an asshole.

Brian could be sweet, tender, and loving. He sent me flowers. Made me CDs with compilations of music he thought I'd like. And when we hung out with friends, though he was reserved at first, after a couple of drinks he was funny, outgoing, charismatic, charming. The life of the party, actually—sparking raucous laughter, drawing everyone into the conversation.

Then suddenly, out of nowhere, some nights a switch would flip—especially if he started doing shots instead of sticking to beer. It was like a shadow would pass over his face, the smile would disappear, replaced by a sneer. He would turn vicious, cruel. "You're fat," he told Zoe one night. "You're still ugly!" he shouted to a group of women he overheard talking about the face-lifts they'd gotten. He walked up to guys in bars and punched them with no warning or provocation. The bouncers would throw him out and I'd have to try to talk him down, get him into my car to go home.

That's if I was there. Some nights I wasn't.

The cell phone reception in my house was shitty. My phone didn't always ring, even when it was on. One morning when I woke up there were five or six messages on my voice mail from Brian. They started out innocuously enough: "Hey, we're about to leave the bar. You wanna hang out? We can come by your place and have a few beers." Then a little more frustrated. "You there? Pick up! Why haven't you called me back?" Then his mood clearly started to turn. "Why aren't you answering your phone? Are you with someone else?" Then the messages got ugly. "What are you doing, you fucking whore? Is some other guy's cock in your mouth right now, you dumb cunt? Is that why you aren't answering your phone? Well fuck you. You stupid bitch. I don't want you anyway. No one wants your nasty ass. Go fuck yourself."

I was too flabbergasted to even be angry at first. Had that really happened?

Before long, my phone rang. It was Brian. "Can you come pick me up?" he asked.

"What the fuck is up with those messages?"

"What are you talking about?" he asked.

"You left a bunch of nasty fucking messages on my voice mail. Seriously fucked up. What the hell?!"

"Oh yeah. You weren't answering your phone when I called, and I wanted to see you. I remember being pissed off. But that's all I remember; I was really drunk last night. In fact, I think I came home with the band—I woke up on the floor behind a drum set. Can you come get me?"

I sighed. Could I really be angry with Brian for something he didn't remember? There was a time in college when I was so wasted that I repeatedly told my boyfriend, "I want to go fuck Paul now"— that was not the boyfriend!—and was absolutely mortified once I sobered up. People can say dumb shit when they're drunk. "Sure. Where are you?"

"I don't know. And everyone is still asleep so I can't ask anyone."

"Well, can you find a piece of mail with an address on it? Or go outside and look at the street signs and tell me the intersection? I'll come pick you up."

I was willing to let it go.

Then it happened again: Brian leaving nasty, vicious messages on my voice mail after getting so drunk he didn't know where he was the next morning.

And again.

If any of my friends had told me a man was treating her like this, I would have told her to run, not walk, away. But I couldn't bring myself to leave him. What if he completely fell apart without me? I was helping him pay his bills, clean his house, eat real food. And I found excuses for his behavior, justifications. I hid the worst of it from my friends. He was alienating them by being an asshole, and I wouldn't have a good answer if they asked me why I stayed. I was ashamed of letting a man treat me this way, but also trying desperately to convince myself that it would get better—while wondering if I could do better anyway. My thoughts were jumbled, and it felt like I lived underwater.

Plus, every time things got so bad I thought I would walk away, they would flip and be wonderful. After his Code Black breakdowns, when he would shut me out entirely for days after shouting cruelties, suddenly the funny, tender, caring, charismatic Brian was back. And it was intoxicating for a man as tough as Brian to let me in, allow me to see his soft side, reveal his weaknesses and vulnerabilities—and make me comfortable enough to admit my own. Though at work and with my family I felt I had to keep up a front of being strong and fully in control, around Brian I could give in and admit to my anxieties, my fears and insecurities. He *understood*, never judging, just quietly offering support. I felt accepted, special, loved.

But then he'd flip again. And I'd be afraid—afraid he'd turn on me, afraid he'd get himself arrested, afraid he'd pick a fight with the wrong people and get killed.

———

HIS ANXIETY COULD BE overwhelming. Once we went to the Outback Steakhouse in Clarksville, a place Brian loved to go. We were getting ready to walk in and could tell it was pretty crowded;

Brian just stopped about five feet from the door. "What's wrong?" I asked him, not knowing if he was just pissed about something.

He muttered that he just couldn't do it, something about too many people. Brian turned and walked back to the car. We ended up going somewhere less crowded which was fine by me, I'm a vegetarian . . . what am I going to eat at a steakhouse anyway? A baked potato and a salad? Once we got to the Blackhorse, our favorite pub in town, and Brian was seated—back against the wall, one eye on the exit, as always—and he had a beer in hand, I asked him what was up.

"I just freaked out," he mumbled.

"Can you help me understand what it's like?" I asked. I knew he had anxiety attacks sometimes, but didn't know what that really meant.

He sighed heavily. "I'll try," he said, taking a deep draught of his Black and Tan and fixing his eyes on the wall across the room. "When I saw all those people in there, out of nowhere it felt like my entire body was revolting: my heart was beating fast enough to pop out of my chest, my head was spinning, I didn't feel like I could breathe even though I wasn't having a hard time breathing, I felt like I was going to throw up. My mind was telling me to run but my body seemed frozen by the fear." The fingers of his right hand were running through the exercises they had him do during neuropsych testing, fingers tapping thumb in complex patterns. The tapping seemed to start of its own accord while he was driving or nervous. I reached over and grabbed his hand, stilling the motion.

"I wish I could help."

He squeezed my fingers. "You do."

IN ADDITION TO THE cognitive deficits and mental health problems—post-traumatic stress disorder (PTSD), depression, anxiety attacks—crippling headaches left him prostrate in a dark-ened room for hours, immobile with agony. All this and more, and yet he was getting no rehabilitation, no real treatment. The Army acted as though he had no problem. He'd been sent back to his artil-lery battery, not a medical holding company,[1] and they had no idea what to do with him. The physician's assistant who was supposed to manage all his medical care knew nothing about TBI or PTSD, he was just the doc who acted as primary care provider for all the guys in Brian's artillery battery at the TMC (troop medical center) our brigade used.

Brian and I met at the bowling alley on post one day for lunch—they had great calzones—after one of his sporadic appointments. He was late and furious. "What happened?"

"This fucking corporal came up to me in the parking lot at the TMC and told me to put on my headgear. I know the fucking regu-lation! I know every NCO in the entire Army has a hard-on about wearing your headgear at every instant in time! But I can't wear a hat yet—the incision is still too fresh. I have a goddamned profile. I have to get my hair cut at the fucking hospital, since they're the only ones who know how to handle it. And this fucking corporal—who doesn't even have a fucking combat patch—has the fucking nerve to come up to me with this shit-eating grin on his face and say, 'Ser-geant, you forgot your headgear.' Little prick."

"What did you do?" I asked, worried. Would the military police show up any moment to arrest Brian?

"I threw my profile in his face and told him to mind his own business. He's lucky I didn't punch him in his stupid face."

We ate in silence for a few minutes.

---

1. The Warrior Transition Units of today, which provide support to wounded soldiers requiring at least six months of rehabilitative care and medical manage-ment, had yet to be created. http://wtc.army.mil/about_us/wtu.html.

"How was your appointment? Doc do anything to help?"

He pushed his tray away in disgust. "That fucking asshole doesn't do shit. You know what he said to me today? I was telling him how I can't keep track of my appointments, can't sleep, have these horrible headaches, freak out around crowds. And he had the nerve to say, 'It's all in your head.' You know what I told him? I said, 'Duh. You're goddamned right it's all in my head. There is shrapnel. In. My. Head. There are fucking pieces of fucking metal in my fucking brain.' He's an idiot. I'm never going to talk to him again. He can't do shit for me."

Meanwhile, doctors at Walter Reed and the hospital at Fort Campbell were cycling him through a huge variety of prescription medications: Neurontin at steadily increasing doses, Depakote, Topamax (all anti-seizure medicines, though he'd never had a seizure), Klonopin, Valium, a series of antidepressants, and more. None made him better, and many made him worse.

One made him feel like a zombie, he just sat and stared at the TV for hours, barely moving, not even interested in sex.

They refused to give him narcotics for his headaches, expressing worry about their addictive qualities and claiming that they could lead to rebound headaches. Besides, "headaches are not associated with open-skull brain injuries," medical providers insisted. So they prescribed Brian a whole series of worthless migraine medicines for his blast-induced headaches: Maxalt, propranolol, Elavil. They even tried a series of Botox injections.

He had no intensive psychotherapy, just occasional group therapy sessions. "I can't take this shit," he said after one. "This asshole has a tiny scar on his hand and he's in there whining about how no woman will ever love him because he's disfigured. It's like an inch long. You can't even see it. Look at me!" He pointed at the arrow-shaped scar pointing to his eye, the deep puckered scar on the back of his head where the shrapnel had entered and then the shunt had been.

"You don't hear me bitching about how I look. It's stupid. I can't listen to this shit. They have no idea what it's like. My life is fucking ruined—I can't do my job anymore, can't remember anything—I feel like an idiot. My future is totally up in the air. And they're in there complaining about their feelings and worrying about how a tiny little scar makes them look."

No wonder he was drinking so much whiskey. He was self-medicating.

WHILE BRIAN WAS FALLING apart, I struggled with my own transition back from the war. Many times I felt unable to handle everyday situations. Driving my little car sucked. After driving a Humvee in Iraq for a year, I assumed every car that cut me off in traffic was a threat and wanted to run them off the road. "This is why they make us leave our weapons locked up in the arms room," I laughed. "I'd shoot these assholes if I could." But I was only partly joking. We hadn't obeyed lights or stop signs in Iraq, and it was hard to do so now. Every piece of trash in the road loomed as a potential IED, and I would swerve wildly to avoid it. Hearing a gunshot on a back country road once sent me swerving off the road in a panic and left me sobbing into the steering wheel, wondering if I would ever feel normal again.

God forbid I overheard someone speaking Arabic—I'd draw closer and try to eavesdrop, listening for keywords I'd been alert for downrange. Suddenly it would dawn on me that I was acting crazy, and I'd have to forcibly turn away.

Shopping at Walmart was horrible: there was no way to see an exit from the vast interior, the fluorescent lights buzzed incessantly, oblivious shoppers constantly bumped into me. The shampoo aisle in particular set me off. After a year of only having one option, the number of choices was overwhelming, and made me worry I was picking the wrong thing. Silk proteins? Tea tree oil? Pro-vitamin B complex? What miraculous combination did my hair need to be shiny and perfect? Strangers would bump into me, invading my personal space, coming up behind me with no warning. More than once I walked away from an almost-full cart, shaking and hyperventilating.

I couldn't get past the contempt I felt for the spoiled and soft world I found myself stuck in. I vividly remembered the Yezidis on Sinjar Mountain asking for our empty cardboard boxes to use as flooring, and found the shallow pettiness of so many Americans incredibly off-putting. Me, I'd watched a man bleed to death, been shot at, heard mortars fall nearby, endured the fear and privation of a year at war, put up with sexual harassment and the isolation of being the only woman around for months on end. What did these selfish civilians with their insignificant concerns understand about that? I had nothing in common with them: how could I connect? I only felt normal when I was with others who had been in combat. When civilians asked ridiculous questions like "What was it really like over there?" I didn't even know how to respond. And what was the point? They'd never understand the incessant smell of burning shit, or what it felt like to point a weapon at a child, to be willing to kill. They'd never know what it meant to piss in front of dozens of men on the side of the road during a convoy break, or feel more naked without a weapon than without clothes, or joke about the prospect of death. They weren't like me. I was an alien in my own country.

WE WEREN'T ALONE IN our struggles. There had been a surge of problems after the division got back: drunk driving, bar fights, spousal abuse. Reintegration was hard. Behaviors that made sense when we were deployed—driving aggressively, constantly monitoring the environment for threats, being prepared to respond with immediate violence if necessary—were inappropriate in a civilian setting.

My roommate Matt had gotten a handgun. He slept with it under his pillow every night. After spending a year with a weapon, it was too weird to give up the habit—and though the Army wouldn't let him keep his M4, Walmart would sell him a pistol. I got it, don't get me wrong. The urge made total sense to me. But it also made me nervous, since we all drank so much. I was worried that one day I'd come home from the bar at 3 a.m. and he'd have a flashback or something and shoot me while I stumbled down the dark hallway.

WHEN I'D MET BRIAN'S family, it had made me keenly feel how disconnected I was from my own family compared to how deeply Brian's adored him. My mother wasn't speaking to me anymore after my freak-out when I told her it was my turn to be crazy. It reignited lingering feelings from childhood that if I weren't good enough, I wouldn't be loved. And now that I felt all fucked up from the war, how could anyone love me? Especially anyone who wasn't just as fucked up as I was . . .

Through his daughter Sonja, Brian already had a legacy, someone existed who would not without him—there was tangible proof of his future, in a way. I felt rootless, purposeless, alone, lonely. I cried easily when I was alone in the shower, wondering if it was post-deployment stress or something else. I missed Iraq, the sense of clarity that came with having a narrow focus and clear mission: stay alive, do your job. The broadening of coming home blurred everything.

Army culture made it all worse. The assumption that seeking help was a sign of weakness had been inculcated in both Brian and me. We had grown up as soldiers hearing catchphrases like "Pain is just weakness leaving the body" and "Suck it up and drive on."

I felt particularly loath as a woman to admit I was having trouble: there were still people who thought females didn't belong in the military at all, and I knew other women would also be judged if I couldn't hack it. In Iraq, I'd heard male troops who saw a woman break down say, "See—that's why none of you females should be here," even though men who cracked under the pressure were judged strictly as individuals. It was clear that many male troops were always watching us for signs of weakness, hints that we were unfit. I couldn't let the other women I served with down by proving the doubters correct.

I had to be tougher, stronger, harder.

But willing it to be true wasn't working.

Everything felt hopeless. To find meaning, I wanted to devote myself to saving the planet, helping humanity, making the world a better place. But watching the news made that endeavor seem foolish. Death was everywhere, people killing each other, starving—the future looked terribly bleak. What was the point of anything? Getting out of bed, eating, breathing—why do any of it?

Dostoyevsky wrote, "I have a longing for life, and I go on living in spite of logic. Though I may not believe in the order of the universe, yet I love the sticky little leaves as they open in spring... It's not a matter of intellect or logic, it's loving with one's inside, with one's stomach." It had resonated with me, this "thirst for life," since I first read *The Brothers Karamazov* a decade earlier. If I "lost faith in the order of things, were convinced, in fact, that everything is a disorderly, damnable, and perhaps devil-ridden chaos, if I were struck by every horror of man's disillusionment—still I should want to live and, having once tasted of the cup, I would not turn away from it till I had drained it!" And now, for the first time, I actually felt I understood the other line: "At thirty, though, I shall be sure to leave the cup, even if I've not emptied it." Fuck the sticky leaves and the blue sky—I was done with the cup of life, ready to throw it from me.

Brian was spiraling down, out of control. He was drinking heavily. I felt responsible for him—and not up to the responsibilities. Why wasn't the Army taking care of him? How had they let him go home without making sure he could take care of himself? Why didn't anyone come to make sure he could pay his bills? He'd gotten hit by an IED, had brain surgery in Baghdad, developed PTSD—how was it possible that the onus of caring for him was somehow falling on my shoulders? I felt overwhelmed. Angry. Scared. Exhausted.

MY PROBLEMS SEEMED PETTY next to Brian's. He'd been blown up, almost died. What excuse did I have? I was ashamed, embarrassed to be struggling so much. Convinced if I just pushed through, I'd feel better soon. It wasn't working, though, and Brian eventually pushed me to seek help. "There's no shame in talking to someone about how you're feeling," he said. "I do it. You should too. Maybe it will help." I argued that it didn't seem to be helping him and all he did was bitch about the sessions, but he pushed me to try anyway.

Since I was Military Intelligence, I had no expectation of privacy if I told an Army doctor about my problems—my medical records could be reviewed to ensure I still deserved to have a security clearance. Losing my clearance could hurt me not just now but for the rest of my life. And I was embarrassed to go during duty hours, admit to my chain of command—not to mention my subordinates—that I was struggling. So I called Army OneSource, a confidential service that got me a series of free appointments with a civilian psychologist in the community. I could go in civilian clothes where no one would recognize me.

Although I assumed my problems were related to the stress of war coupled with the enormous pressure of trying to help Brian alone, the civilian psychologist saw no connection between my symptoms and my combat deployment. She also told me that my penchant for orderliness (a trait that had won me accolades in the Army starting in basic training: "Everyone come and look at Williams' wall locker! This is the standard everyone should try to meet!") was probably obsessive-compulsive disorder and I should be medicated for it. She thought the depression I talked about was bipolar disorder and told me that going on antidepressants was the best way to figure it out, but since she couldn't prescribe them since she wasn't a doctor, she referred me to the division psychiatrist. *The* division psychiatrist— there was only one. For a division of 18,000 soldiers.

Nerves jangling, humiliated by the weakness that seeking mental health care implied in the Army, I listened to the troops working behind the counter make fun of some of the other patients. My face was burning. How had this happened? I'd done so well in Iraq, why was I here?

When I finally got into the psychiatrist's office, I burst into tears. Amid my litany of concerns, I admitted my fears that I would never adjust to civilian life. He laughed at me. "You'll definitely never make it in the civilian world if you start crying all the time," and sent me away with antidepressants.

The starter pack of pills made me unbearably thirsty; on the seven-mile runs our platoon did once a week I thought I would die of dehydration. I quit taking them, and the psychiatrist had humiliated me so much that I never went back.

5.

THERE'S ALWAYS
A WAY OUT

—— ★ ——

I was trying so hard to cling to my memory of the man Brian had been, the one I'd met all that time ago in the mountains of Iraq and gotten to know in that idyllic first month home. I was trying equally hard to get away from the desperate, lonely, overwhelmed Kayla I had become. What it required was an active state of denial. I knew this, but couldn't fight it. And so I increasingly retreated from my support network of family and friends.

If anyone asked why I put up with a man who treated me so badly, why I wanted a relationship with someone with so many problems, I had no logical answer. My default reply—that you never leave a fallen comrade on the battlefield—rang hollow even to me. Whenever Brian's friends, who loyally made sure he didn't drive drunk and pulled him out of bar fights, told me, "You deserve to be treated better than this," I simply didn't listen.

After all, logic and reason didn't figure into love. I took on faith that things would improve with time; somehow Brian would heal. I convinced myself that if I just loved him *enough*, he would get better. It was the type of magical thinking I had always mocked; kissing a frog won't make him a prince in the real world, and loving an asshole even harder won't suddenly make him a nice guy. "But this is *different*," I told myself. "It's not his fault. He's broken, but he can get better." I would make our relationship work through sheer force of will, loyalty, and perseverance.

Yet at the same time I was terrified that he was pulling me into the pit with him instead.

One night Brian and I had a few beers. We were outside my house, smoking, laughing, joking. Suddenly out of nowhere his face shut down, eyes turned cold, shoulders stiffened. He looked away, then looked back with clenched jaw. "You don't understand," he said. "You can never understand."

My chest tightened. *Not again.* The suddenness with which he turned was terrifying, and I never knew how bad the fights would be. If he would turn violent. I remembered him shredding a pillow while I cowered in the bed, afraid he would turn on me next. Could I take this, again and again? I was afraid, not just that he might hurt me but that it would never get better—that I was so damaged by the war no one else would ever love me, and that the man I loved was so broken, he was gone.

Helplessness and exhaustion washed over me, and my willpower snapped. I stood up wordlessly, walked inside, crept into Matt's bedroom, and reached under his pillow for what I knew was there— what he had kept there for comfort since we got back from Iraq. Then I slipped into my bathroom and locked the door.

The gun was heavy in my hand, cold, solid. I sat on the edge of my bathtub and stared at it. The door was shut and I was alone. I could hear my own breathing, uneven.

This I could control.

It felt like the only thing I could control. I couldn't control my anger, which flared up unexpectedly. I couldn't control the moments when Brian got lost in his rage and isolation. I couldn't control whether or not the Army would stop-loss me (hold me in past the time I was supposed to get out) or let me out and then call me back to Iraq before my contract was up—back to another year with no control over where I slept, what I ate, if rockets fell on me in the porta-john, if an IED blew off my limbs.

The toilet and sink faded to nothingness in my field of vision and my focus narrowed. My hands were pale next to the black of the handgun, and the cuticles I shredded under stress stood out on my white skin, red and raw. I took a deep breath to steady myself, still my sudden trembling. My ears strained but I heard nothing—I was alone with the moment. The edge of the bathtub felt hard. Solid.

I couldn't control the memories that suddenly, with no warning, invaded my consciousness: images of those men screaming, thrashing, bleeding on the ground. I couldn't control when the smell of diesel on the road or at the gas station made me feel like I was in Iraq again. I couldn't control flinching at sudden noises. Couldn't control my dreams, still couldn't even remember them, but knew they must be bad because I sometimes woke drenched in sweat, heart pounding.

But this, this I could control. This gun, this choice. It offered me a way out, and freedom from the fear that nothing would change. The thought of nothingness descending upon my consciousness seemed like it would be a relief—all the stress and fear and anger and confusion gone, replaced by blessed nothingness.

I couldn't imagine going to the chain of command in my unit and confessing this to my platoon sergeant, platoon leader, company commander, and on up, couldn't imagine being put on public, humiliating suicide watch, sleeping in the dayroom with no shoelaces or belt while people wandered in and out, staring with that mix of curiosity, pity, and disgust. I couldn't admit these feelings of weakness in front of my leaders or—worse—my soldiers. Couldn't own up to the shame of not knowing if I could do it anymore, keep going at all. Couldn't talk to my friends from before—couldn't even conceive of explaining the war to them: I was not who they used to know. I couldn't burden my family with this; they were dealing with enough. I couldn't let everyone down and face them afterward. Couldn't talk to Brian, he was too immersed in his own desolation to help me find the way out of mine.

I sat and stared at the gun. This was mine, my choice, my way out, my freedom, my escape from fear and hopelessness and desperation.

But what would they go through, Brian and Matt, dealing with blood and brains and death on the bathroom floor? What about my father? I was his only surviving child, and he'd lost his sister to suicide.

Suddenly Brian tapped on the bathroom door. "Kayla? What's going on in there?"

I startled back into the moment and hid the gun in the cupboard under the sink. "Nothing—I'll be right out."

I couldn't do this. Not now, not today. But the option was there. If it got worse. If nothing got better. I could control my ending, if nothing else.[1]

---

1. A version of this chapter appeared at www.huffingtonpost.com/Kayla-williams/army-suicides-my-experien_b_172651.html.

6.

ROLLERCOASTER

While my personal life felt like it was spinning out of control, my military duties continued. The 101st was in the middle of a massive restructuring from being a division-based to a brigade-based structure, and our Military Intelligence battalion was dissolved. Rather than being part of a separate battalion and then attached to 3rd Brigade when we went to war, our company would be part of a new Brigade Troops Battalion. We were temporarily attached to an infantry battalion as part of the reshuffling. I'd served with a lot of those guys in Iraq, and it was comforting to see them and be remembered.

On our first brigade run, seven miles at the brutal accordion-like sprint/jog combo of many hundreds of people trying to run in formation, I couldn't keep pace and slowly drifted back. The guys from D Co. 1/187, who I'd gone on combat foot patrols with in Baghdad, recognized me immediately. "You can do it, Williams!" some of them shouted. "Stay with us!" And suddenly, I could. I'd been with them on the ground in Iraq, I'd kept my shit together in front of them while a man bled to death in front of us. No way would I let them see me completely fall out of a stupid fucking run here in the States. So I stayed with them, astonished after all that time how much camaraderie and encouragement can provide the motivation to push through pain and exhaustion.

At the end, I made my way back to my own unit in time to hear our new brigade commander, Colonel (COL) Steele (the Captain Steele in *Black Hawk Down*) berating everyone for how many people had fallen out. Those who had given up were all being smoked while he screamed, "The next time you fall out of one of my brigade runs, you better take off your T-shirt so no one knows you're a Rakkasan!" I laughed at the image of the female soldiers wandering around in sports bras: "Well, COL Steele said we had to take off our T-shirts!" Clearly he wasn't tracking on the fact that there were now women serving as organic parts of the brigade. (Right after that run, he made everyone fight in pits without access to water, landing half a dozen troops in the ER with dehydration, dislocated shoulders, and other injuries.)[1] That wasn't the only semi-amusing reminder that the infantry still wasn't used to serving with women. The infantry battalion was always astonished when one of us showed up to pull staff duty,[2] and at a mandatory 100 percent urinalysis, there were no female latrines in the Battalion Headquarters.

When soldiers aren't fighting, they're training—and some mandatory training had piled up while we were busy fighting. There was a huge wait list to go to PLDC (Primary Leadership Development

---

1. COL Steele was not on board with counterinsurgency tactics, either. Before our unit headed to JRTC (Joint Readiness Training Center) for pre-deployment training, he reportedly said, "Everyone has to have at least one confirmed kill!" When I heard that, I immediately said, "There are going to be dead civilians in Iraq." Sure enough, there were reports of excessive force under his command when the unit went back: http://www.newyorker.com/reporting/2009/07/06/090706fa_fact_khatchadourian.
2. Pairs of troops take turns being on duty at the unit headquarters overnight to man the phones, clean, do security checks, and conduct other miscellaneous tasks.

Course, mandatory training for sergeants in the Army—since renamed the Warrior Leader Course as part of the Army's fixation on calling everyone a warrior), and they had to trim the length to push us through faster. When I finally got a slot, all but one of the thirty soldiers in my section had been to Iraq. Talking among ourselves when the instructors weren't in the room, *every single one of us* admitted to having at least a couple of problems with sleeping, nightmares, anger, irritability, jumpiness, heightened startle response, intrusive memories, numbness, or feeling disconnected from others. Realizing that I wasn't alone gave me a tremendous sense of relief. Though I still didn't feel comfortable talking about my struggles outside that safe environment, surrounded by people who had shared the experience of war but weren't above or below me in the chain of command, it had profoundly eased the sense of isolation and shame.

On a field training exercise that would involve "civilians on the battlefield"—Arabic speakers hired to provide a more realistic simulation of what we'd experience when the brigade went back to Iraq—I was sent out with the infantry guys to translate. I was amazed at how comfortable it was, how quickly I slipped into habits from the deployment, how fucking good it felt. I was good at my job and had skills and experience that were useful and important. I felt comfortable, happy, relaxed—then came back to the office and immediately felt my jaw tighten and stomach cramp up. In simulated combat, I felt more content than in "normal" life—going on a raid and getting in a firefight on the training exercise, I felt great, amped up, full of adrenaline, and able to direct it into action—it was such a contrast to getting a similar rush when a stranger would bump into me from behind at the grocery store, leaving me flinching and tense but with no appropriate response.

During some downtime on the exercise, I bumped into one of Brian's friends from his unit whom I hadn't seen since we were in

Iraq and we started catching up. His watch cap pulled down for warmth, smoking a cigarette, he casually dropped what for me at the time was a conversational bombshell: "Oh yeah, I totally have PTSD. I take meds for it, see a shrink. It's starting to help." I couldn't believe someone would be so open about it, right there in front of everyone else in his unit, and said as much. "Why the fuck not?" he asked. "We're all going through it. I bet you are too. And I know Brian is. We shouldn't all be hiding it, that's fucking stupid. I talk about it on purpose, so other guys know they can get help, too. It's not a big deal. I went through this after Afghanistan, too—but this time I'm not trying to 'suck it up and drive on' by myself. I got some help."

Until I had these conversations with outsiders, it hadn't occurred to me that all the problems we were experiencing might not be just because Brian got blown up, that my own issues might indeed be related to the deployment and not just personal weakness, that our reactions might be a common and relatively normal reaction to the horribly abnormal experience of war. Before we came home, our chaplain gave us a presentation about reintegration in which he told us not to beat our wives (I felt like saying, "Hey, 'Don't ask, don't tell!' sir!" but figured he wouldn't think it was funny for me to mock how poorly suited the stupid video was for an Army that was 15 percent female), but since we'd gotten back, no one had talked to us about the types of problems many of us were clearly facing. I'd even gone to see mental health professionals, and they hadn't chalked my problems up to war. Then again, I'm a woman—maybe they didn't realize that I'd been in combat, too, not behind some mythical "front line" that hasn't existed in decades.

Slowly, over six months or so, I started to feel better. My sleep normalized, and I stopped having unrecoverable nightmares and started having regular dreams I could actually remember. Cars back-firing stopped jolting me into a panic. Rage no longer threatened to consume me; I could talk to my mom without being overwhelmed with irritation. Life stateside started to feel normal. I was going to be okay.

———

BRIAN VACILLATED BETWEEN frustration, rage, and indifference. He couldn't balance his checkbook or pay his bills on time, and was angry and humiliated at having to accept my help. He would lash out, go into Code Black mode and ignore me for days, and then come back as if nothing had happened. The drinking was out of control; often, one of his friends would have to practically carry him inside after a night at the bars.

Desperate, I went to see his PA at the TMC. The lieutenant remembered me from Baghdad—we shared the same last name. "I understand that because of patient privacy rules, you can't discuss Brian's medical conditions with me. But I need to talk to you—I'm really concerned. He's not getting any better, and he seems to be getting worse. He can't remember things, can't pay his bills. His PTSD is really bad, and he's self-medicating with alcohol, drinking until he can't feel anything and just passes out. I'm scared, and I don't know what to do. Is there anything you can do?"

"You're right, I really can't talk to you—you're not even his wife, just his girlfriend. But I can tell you that he keeps refusing to come to appointments and skipping group therapy."

"No, you don't understand," I said. "He isn't refusing to go—he can't keep track of the times. He has a brain injury, and he mixes things up—ten o'clock, eleven o'clock, one o'clock—he goes at the wrong time and then calls me, frustrated."

"I don't think that's the case. He's fine, he's just trying to get out of doing his job."

Astonishment battled with fury inside me. "Thank you for your time," I said stiffly, and left. When Brian had told me his PA had told him, "It's all in your head," I honestly hadn't quite believed him. How could any medical professional be so ignorant and insensitive, when Brian quite literally had metal fragments in his brain and a hole in his skull? It seemed completely unreal that anyone could believe this wouldn't have any repercussions on his cognition or psychological health.

"Come on," I said to Brian the next day. "We're going to see the patient advocate at the hospital." I'd made an appointment to see the one person it seemed had a job title specifically devoted to making sure patients were getting the care they needed. We sat down with her together and explained what was going on: Brian didn't have a case manager or a social worker here, he was being shuttled back and forth from Walter Reed to Fort Campbell, no one seemed to be communicating—he was lost in the system, not getting proper care, and getting worse. She took down our information and promised to be in touch. We never heard from her.

As I devoted myself to improving Brian's situation, I was no perfect martyr—the more overwhelmed I felt, the tenser I got. When we first started dating, I was fun, relaxed, confident. Now I felt brittle, tightly wound, nervous. We turned on each other in fits of fury—but also turned to one another for solace and comfort. After every horrible fight, Brian and I ended up back together, clinging to one another in near desperation. I felt alone, struggling to meet his needs—caregiver, housekeeper, lover, and life manager rolled into one—but without any training or support, and without the access a wife would have had.

———

FORT CAMPBELL IS A small community; there aren't many places to go. During one of his Code Black incidents, I heard within days that he was seeing another woman, someone he had dated before

going to Iraq. It cut to the quick to be tossed over so easily, so casually, without an explanation or even a farewell. At first I refused to
accept it, even stopping by his house for lunch like I usually did. His
front door was open but his bedroom door was locked. Feeling like
a stalker after jiggling the doorknob, I guiltily crept back to my car.
What was happening to me? Staring at the other woman's car, I felt a
surge of anger. After all I'd done for him, he was fucking some other
girl? Without even the courtesy to tell me he wanted to break up?

"Fuck him. I don't need this shit," I muttered, driving back on
post to get fast food. "Let her deal with it. *She* can pay his bills. *She*
can take care of his drunk ass. He thinks *I* don't understand? She's a
fucking civilian. Let's see how well *she* understands."

So I tried to move on, as he clearly seemed to be. When another
guy, a handsome Puerto Rican from my old battalion, asked me out
on a date, I accepted.

Jorge picked me up, drove me to a nice restaurant in Nashville, held open doors, paid for dinner. A gentleman! He was funny,
charming, sweet, smart—what wasn't there to like? I enjoyed his
company but felt no spark. My thoughts returned over and over to
Brian: "I don't belong here . . ."

Back in Clarksville, we stopped at a bar for a drink. Small town.
Small world. Brian was there with his friends—and the new girl. We
ignored each other; he didn't even seem to notice me. It felt so imma-
ture, so ridiculous—I'd stayed friends with other ex-boyfriends,
why wouldn't he even talk to me? Refusing to let my shame and
anger show, I tried to act casual and relaxed, then left with Jorge
after one beer.

Back at my house, when he tried to kiss me, I turned my face
away. "I'm sorry, but I can't do this," I finally told him. "My heart
is somewhere else, this isn't fair to you."

As much as part of me wanted to be in a nice, normal relationship with a nice, normal guy, I couldn't let go.

A COUPLE WEEKS LATER, Brian returned. Out of nowhere, he called and said he wanted to stop by.

We sat on the front steps of my house.

"Why did you leave?" I asked, staring at the street. Eye contact could be difficult for Brian, and I didn't want to make it even harder for him to talk to me.

He took a slow drag off his cigarette, a swallow of beer. Looked down. "Kayla, I love you so much. You deserve better than me. I'm broken. I'm so fucked up. I don't want to ruin your life."

"Don't be ridiculous. We're both fucked up," I half laughed.

"I rubbed a cheeseburger in that other girl's face."

"What?!"

"After the bar one night, we went through a drive-through. I asked for a cheeseburger with no mustard. But it had mustard on it. So I rubbed it on her face. And she just took it."

"Well," I joked, "obviously she's not the right woman for you. I'd never put up with that shit. You need someone tougher than that."

"No, I'm serious," he said. "I have a brain injury. I have PTSD. I don't know if I'll ever get better. You should move on, find someone else, someone better. Be happy."

"Brian, *you* make me happy. I love you. I don't want to be with anyone else. I tried, and it sucked—you're all I can think about. Stop pushing me away and let me in. Let me love you."

He hesitated, struggling to express himself. "I don't want to burden you. You don't know what you're getting into."

I felt a surge of unexpected conviction: "I'm walking into this relationship with my eyes wide open. Let me worry about myself. I'm strong; I can take care of myself. I know exactly what I'm getting into, and I choose to be with you. I love you. We can make this work."

It was decided. It felt terribly momentous. I had committed myself completely to our future together. Why, exactly, wasn't clear, even to me. I could not spell out to family and friends, let alone myself, why I was willing to take a chance on a relationship that looked like such a losing bet. I just couldn't fight this love, and at times it seemed that the intensity of our fights only proved the depth of our passion.

Even after all this time, and the rollercoaster we had been on, I still had no idea what I was getting myself into. It was total self-delusion.

I STARTED REACHING OUT to Brian's mother, letting her know what was going on. While we were pushing medical providers and the patient advocate at Fort Campbell about how Brian seemed to be lost in the system and languishing without care, Peggy started calling people at Walter Reed. In late 2004, after ten months when Brian got no real care, we thought we'd finally succeeded: he was being transferred back to Walter Reed. Once there, we assumed, he would finally get the therapy and rehab he clearly still needed.

I helped him get his house ready to sell, bringing friends down to clean out years of accumulated junk. We filled the dumpster in his front yard a couple of times and finally had it hauled away, took carloads of stuff to the thrift store. Helping sort through his things, I tackled the dresser in his bedroom. There were no clothes in it.

Brian's method of handling laundry was to wash and dry a load, throw it all in the basket, pluck clean clothes out of the basket, discard dirty clothes on the floor, repeat when basket is empty. The exception was socks: these he virtually never washed. Dirty socks were chucked into his closet, which was a foot deep in clothes. He bought new socks in twelve-packs. Brian's mother reported that whenever he came to visit, he would claim he had forgotten socks and had to go buy some, which she believed was an excuse to be alone for a bit. Going through his house and fully seeing his system, I realized that was only partly true: he may want to get away from his family on vacations, but he probably also lacked clean socks.

Rather, the dresser drawers were stuffed full of mail. Unopened mail. I was horrified: Were there unpaid bills? Important legal notices? What might have been missed? I sat down heavily on the bed. How could the Army have believed he could handle himself and just send him off with no supervision, no help? Clearly it was worse than I had realized. He was so overwhelmed that he hadn't even *opened* his mail, much less tried to manage things.

We had the house professionally painted—the black walls in his room took extra coats of special primer to cover—and cleaned. The first people to look at it, a young couple with a baby on the way, bought it immediately. Their faces looked so shiny and young and full of hope; I felt jaded and old.

Brian moved into my house to wait for his orders to be finalized.

TALKING TO MY STEPMOTHER Chris one day, I told her that I was convinced we would spend our lives together, get married someday. I glossed over the worst of things, but admitted that Brian had PTSD and was having trouble. She paused before answering. Chris and my father had been patient with me since I got back from Iraq, never pushing me to talk about the war, welcoming me when I reached out, but never invading my privacy. They were the same way about my relationships, willing to listen and give advice when asked but never butting in uninvited.

When I was a child, I hadn't liked Chris. That was only to be expected: she was my stepmother; my mother, who had little pleasant to say about her, was raising me. And unlike my outgoing, emotional mother, Chris was reserved and quiet. It was easy to blow her off.

But over the years, my opinion had slowly changed. My mother had been divorced three times, my father twice. Their short emotional fuses could be exhausting to deal with; Chris's even temper was a steadying presence.

When she finally spoke, she sounded cautious, almost reluctant to speak. "Are you sure that's a good idea? All relationships are hard. Are you completely sure you want to get involved with someone who has so many problems? I mean, everyone has problems eventually. But to start out a relationship where they're already there . . . Without the time to build something solid first . . ." When my father had been having anger management issues, she had stuck by his side until he found ways to control them. I knew she wasn't speaking lightly.

"No, sure, we'll be fine," I said blithely. But what she was saying gave me pause. I loved Brian, but did I have her quiet strength, the patience that might be required to stand by him through it all? "Sometimes," I admitted, "I wonder if anyone else might think the same thing about me. You know, I'm no picnic myself. I'm not sure anyone else would put up with me, either."

"Oh, Kayla," she said, "don't say that."

THE LAST FEW WEEKS before he was scheduled to leave, Brian was drunker, more often than usual. His moods were black; he was withdrawn and sullen. "You're smothering me," he said. "I need space." He slept in the guest room. I was hurt and angry—but refused, for once, to take the bait. I had my own history of trying to push people away, and was convinced he was doing the same thing. If you believe strongly enough that everyone will leave you, eventually you find a way to force them to do it. This proves your point nicely—a self-fulfilling prophecy. Not this time, though. I wouldn't fall for the trap I'd so often set myself—so I was polite, friendly, and cheerful around him. Surely, I reasoned, he would come around. If I could just be good enough, patient enough, he would see that I loved him, only wanted the best for him. Every ridiculous trope of stupid teenage girl love: if you just adore that bad boy hard enough, he'll change and love you back!

One night, the sound of my door opening woke me. My body tensed, wondering if he had come in to start another fight. But he said nothing, just stumbled awkwardly into my bed. "Hey," I whispered, "what are you doing?"

"Coming to bed," he slurred. "What does it look like?"

I could smell the whiskey and beer on his breath, gag-inducingly strong. Brian flung his arm around me and I reached a hand up to hold it. Even though he was probably too wasted to know what he was doing, I felt vindicated. He did love me! He had come back to me after all! His breathing was steady, and I started to doze back off.

A sudden pain in my back woke me. "Ow!" I yelped. He had punched me in the back, hard. "What the fuck!" I yelled. "Why are you hitting me?"

Brian mumbled incoherently and rolled off the bed, crashing loudly to the floor. I sat up, pulling my knees up to my chest and hugging them tightly. What the hell was going on? My brain was sleep-fogged, it was dark and I was confused. Brian was crawling to the bathroom. When he got there, he hauled himself upright, pissed on the floor, then lurched back to collapse on the bed, where he promptly passed out.

In the morning, he remembered nothing. "Why am I in your bed?" he asked when he finally staggered into the living room near noon.

"You came in there to sleep last night," I answered. "And you punched me. And pissed on my bathroom floor."

"That sucks," he said. "Want to go to Waffle House for breakfast? I could really use some grease. You know. Best thing for a hangover."

OUR STATUS WAS UNCERTAIN when he left. We had no idea how long he would be there, and neither of us put much stock in long-distance relationships. We had no formal commitment—but we were clearly connected. We talked, emailed. Things were strained and awkward. He asked me to come spend New Year's Eve with him in D.C., then head up to his aunt's wedding in Philadelphia.

I went to visit a friend in New York first. My friend was horrified. "This guy breaks shit, starts fights in bars, he fucking punched you, and you're going to see him? What is wrong with you? Walk away. You don't need that shit. You deserve better than that."

I sighed. "It's not that easy. You can't be angry at someone for being sick. It's not his fault. He needs me."

My friend's continued protests fell on deaf ears. How could I explain it to a civilian, that commitment to never leave a fallen comrade? Was there any way to make someone else see? Outsiders wouldn't get it.

Brian picked me up from Union Station and took me back to his apartment in Silver Spring. There wasn't enough space at Walter Reed for all the patients, so they were putting people up in rental units in the community. It was a big complex; the halls full of the odd comingled smells of disparate people crammed together: curry, cigarette smoke, fried food, industrial cleansers.

We walked into his apartment, and when his roommate saw me he quickly shut the screen on his laptop. But not quite fast enough. Brian introduced us but we didn't linger. In Brian's room I said, "Dude, was your roommate watching porn in the living room?"

"Yeah," Brian said. "He does it all the time."

"Guys are weird," I said. Brian shrugged. I pointed at a hole in the wall, low down. "Temper?" I asked. It looked like someone had kicked the wall.

"Nope," he said. "It was like that when I moved in."

When I went into the kitchen to get something to drink, I opened every cupboard and the dishwasher looking for glasses. There were a couple of coffee cups, two bowls, three plates, and a handful of flatware.

"What the fuck, Brian?" I asked. "What kind of place are you living in here?"

"I don't know," he said. "The Army put me here."

"But..." I paused, didn't know what to say. "But...look at how you're living! There's no food, and nothing to cook it with if you had any. Hasn't anyone come to check up on you guys, make sure you can take care of yourselves?" He shook his head.

"You have to get out of here," I said. "This is not okay."

Our visit started out tense and weird, but by the end we were comfortable together, solid. Being away from each other had given us both the space to conclude we were better together than apart, let us think about how we felt and what we wanted with neither the pull of physical attraction nor the irritation of petty arguments. In previous relationships, I'd often decided on short trips away that I wanted to break up with someone—getting out of the rut let me see that I wasn't really that into them. This was the opposite: being together again after a separation of both time and space crystallized what I had felt all along. We talked for hours on the drive up to Philadelphia—it was always easier for Brian to talk to me when he wasn't expected to make eye contact and had something else to do.

I watched him tap his fingers to his thumb in complex patterns as he drove, the exercise he had to do during neuropsych testing that stayed with him. It made me smile—this little tic that was familiar to me after nearly a year together, one of those habits that a stranger might find odd but a lover finds comforting.

Being away from one another for a month had confirmed for both of us that we belonged together. Watching his aunt exchange vows, we started talking about rings. Though we abhorred long-distance relationships, we were certain ours could work.

A MONTH LATER, we decided to get married. There was no romantic proposal; we worked out the details on the phone. Many of the motivations to take care of it immediately instead of waiting were practical: I wasn't reenlisting, and would be out of the Army in a few more months—after which I would have no health insurance. Brian needed to get out of that horrible apartment, but as long as he was single, he'd be stuck there. If he were married, they'd let him get a place of his own. There would be somewhere to ship my household goods when my enlistment was up. I'd be allowed more access as a wife than a girlfriend to go with him to appointments at Walter Reed, take over his finances, and generally step up and help him. A life together was what we both wanted, and it made sense to do it right away.

Since I was working, it fell to Brian to set everything up. I mailed him my driver's license so he could get the necessary paperwork ready in advance. Then I'd fly out there for a long weekend and we'd do the deed.

When the date neared, he called, insisting my ID had never arrived.

"Yeah right," I said. "Look, if you don't want to marry me, that's fine. Just have the courage to say so!"

"Kayla, I'm serious! It never showed up. I want to marry you. Can't you send me another ID?"

"You're lying! Things don't get lost in the mail! Don't bullshit me!" I yelled, insecure and heartbroken.

But he finally convinced me, and I overnighted my passport to him days before flying out there.

He'd found a Presbyterian minister who was willing to make house calls, a kind African-American woman with short hair and perfect posture. She sat down with us on the couch of his sad, barren apartment. "Where are your families and friends?" she asked.

We explained all the logical reasons we had for getting married, then Brian continued, "My older sister just got engaged, and she's having a big wedding in June. Kayla and I have both been married before, but Shanna hasn't, and she's in her mid-thirties. Her wedding is so important to her, and we're worried if we announced we'd gotten married first it would take attention off her special day."

"Having a wedding is symbolically important, you know. I'm really not comfortable marrying you here, with no one else around."

"Don't worry!" I assured her. "We are going to have a wedding! I want my dad to walk me down the aisle, and I want Brian's daughter to see us publicly declare our love and commitment. We just aren't doing it yet. We're going to tell everyone we're engaged now, and have the wedding later."

It took a little more back-and-forth, but we finally convinced her that we were serious and she should take a chance on us. On February 18, 2005—just over a year after we started dating, and nearly two years since we had met—Brian and I exchanged vows in his living room. We told everyone the happy news about our "engagement" and started planning an August wedding.

GETTING READY TO LEAVE active duty, I started going through TAP, the transition assistance program—a series of classes to prepare you for the civilian world. Troops learn—or rather, are lectured about, whether or not they pay attention is totally variable—about Veterans Affairs benefits, how to write a résumé, how to act during job interviews, and more. The counselors are supposed to help you translate your military skills into résumés those in the civilian world can understand. You can find out how many college credits your military education can count for if you want to go back to school (well, for most kinds of training—some, like mine, are classified and the college credit equivalents not listed). A couple of friends from my unit were going through TAP at the same time; the counselors were not familiar with our Army Military Occupational Skills (MOS), basically military job descriptions, or what kind of civilian jobs we'd be applying for. "Keep your résumé to one page," they lectured. But in the intelligence community, more is often better.

"I have no idea what bullet points to put on my résumé," I confided to one of the other guys from my unit.

"Just take some off your NCOERs and awards," he said.

It was a great idea—my platoon sergeant and platoon leader had already spent lots of time figuring out how to best describe what I did for my non-commissioned officer evaluation report, and my awards might have useful stuff too. That night, I started digging through my Army paperwork for relevant blurbs.

Army awards are presented in green folders. When you open them, the award is under plastic on the right, and supporting paperwork is often tucked in on the left. I flipped through them. An Army Achievement Medal from a brigade exercise—nothing useful. Dozens of training certificates tucked into another folder. Worth listing—I wrote them all down. The Army Commendation Medal from my unit for Operation Iraqi Freedom, not in a folder. Maybe some good materials. I jotted down some phrases: "wrote the Standard Operating Procedures for the plan of attack for all Signals Intelligence collection". . . "established logging system that increased collection speed and reporting accuracy."

I opened the next folder and smiled. It was the Army Commendation Medal (ARCOM) the infantry company commander I'd translated for in Baghdad had put me in for. The only award that really meant anything to me, since this captain had no obligation at all to put me in for a medal; he did it because he genuinely thought I did a good job. My own commander hardly ever saw me but doubtless felt obligated to put everyone in for something. This guy, though— he really meant it. The language on the award itself was boilerplate:

> For extremely meritorious achievement while attached to Delta Company, 1st Battalion, 187th Infantry Regiment during combat and security operations in southern Baghdad from 14 April 2003 to 20 April 2003. Specialist Williams' courage, tireless efforts, professionalism, and dedication to duty reflect great credit upon herself, the Rakkasans, the 101st Airborne Division (Air Assault), and the United States Army.

Like most soldiers, I could recite that last part ("reflect great credit upon...") in my sleep, we'd all heard it so many times during award ceremonies.

I pulled out the recommendation and started skimming the achievements to see if they'd be useful on my CV.

> Achievement #1: SPC Kayla Williams performed above and beyond the scope of her duty position and the expectations of a soldier of her rank and experience while on combat patrols in the Daura area of Southern Baghdad with Delta Company, 1-187th Infantry. SPC Williams' ability to adapt from linguist to commander's interpreter during combat operations enabled this infantry company to succeed in its conduct of numerous QRF missions and combat security patrols by interacting with Iraqi civilians, police, and other Iraqi agents on the battlefield.

I paraphrased, "Served as commander's interpreter during combat operations, allowing infantry companies to succeed in conduct of numerous quick reaction force (QRF) missions and combat security patrols by interacting with Iraqi civilians and police during Operation Iraqi Freedom."

> Achievement #2: On 16 April 2003, SPC Williams assisted the D Company QRF reacting to a UXO explosion that resulted in the death of one Iraqi civilian and the wounding of three U.S. Soldiers and four Iraqi civilians. SPC Williams quickly realized that her linguist skills could be utilized best to help defuse the situation and determine the UXO status of the area and to help comfort the wounded Iraqis. Additionally, SPC Williams remained with the Iraqi wounded long after the accident in order to interpret for U.S. medical personnel who rendered aid.

Nothing useful for my resume. But the black-and-white words brought a host of memories into my mind. The heat, the palm trees. Men writhing on the ground calling out to God. Blood. A fly landing on a wound still bleeding. That poor man, screaming in pain...his wife. That woman! Oh god, that poor woman—and his children. What happened to them? Trembling, I set the paper down and sank to my haunches, breathing shallowly. He was dead, and it felt like his whole life had been reduced to a bullet point on an award recommendation. Of course his own family remembered him, but I knew that in those early days of the war we hadn't compensated families—we hadn't paid *diyyah*, the blood debt. I had no idea, and no way of knowing, how his family had coped with the loss of income. I would never forget those moments, but the memories had stopped pushing their way into my mind unexpectedly. It took something like this to bring them flooding back, but now here they were, demanding my attention, insisting on acknowledgment.

I grabbed the album of my photos from the war and flipped through them. It felt surreal to squat on the carpeted floor of my own

room in my own house, so far away from that reality. The chasm
between the two worlds felt immense, overwhelming. That world
still seemed so much more real. I was alive there, intensely so. My
fingers traced over pictures of me and my teammate Lauren, taking turns posing in front of artillery pieces in the haze. I squinted
at them, saw guys carrying artillery rounds, remembered that day.
They'd offered to let us pull the cord, actually fire a round, but the
timing hadn't worked out and we'd never gotten the chance.

They were killing people. The realization smacked me so hard that
I rocked back on my feet and landed heavily on my ass. I'd never
considered it before. In the moment, we'd just thought it was so cool
to see the guns being fired; it was a new experience for us, hence the
grinning poses. But it was war, and those were live-fire missions.
Those 105mm rounds were being deliberately fired toward (hopefully) enemy positions. I frowned. *How did I never think about that?*
Was it a conscious effort to bury the reality, to block out the horror
of what we were doing, of what war is? Or was I just such a fucking
dumbass that I really didn't realize it? The time and distance were
too great; I had no idea how to answer the question now. It seemed
impossible to reconcile the *me* from Iraq, willing to kill and die,
watching a man die, but oblivious to the death we were causing, as
the same exact *me* in the here and now, closing my album and shoving my awards back into a box and heading into the kitchen to grab
a beer and try to push the uncomfortable flashbacks out of my mind.

I sat on the front porch drinking the beer and smoking, wondering if the vivid memories would ever stop intruding unexpectedly into my mind. Sure, it happened less often now, but certain
smells (burning trash, diesel fuel) or sounds (fireworks, unexplained
booms) could still immediately throw my mind into Iraq, just like
reading about it had. Would that stick with me forever? Would
Brian and I ever feel normal again, calm and comfortable in crowds
of strangers? And did it matter; was it even a bad thing? Sure, it set

Brian and me apart from civilians—but it drew us closer to each other. Civilians seemed so shallow and selfish, oblivious to what was really important. Jung said, "There is no coming to conscious- ness without pain"... maybe this was just the price I had to pay for the greater awareness I had gained about what truly mattered. The jarring memories of Iraq, abrupt reminders of fear and death—they forced me to acknowledge how lucky I was to be alive and living comfortably in modern America.

7.

HUSBAND AND WIFE

While I was deployed, I'd written letters home—real, paper letters—to friends, family members, even strangers who sent care packages. I'd exchanged letters with one of my undergrad professors, Michael Staub, and when I got back he asked me if I'd ever thought about writing a book about my experiences. "It's a compelling story," he said, "and one that hasn't been told." He was right—everyone had some idea of what it was like for men at war, even if those images were pure Hollywood or terribly outdated. But the only military women that sprang to mind were Jessica Lynch and Lynddie England, the heroine and the villain, two cardboard cutouts of female soldiers plastered on the cover of every newsmagazine but not existing as real people.

I jumped at the chance to tell a richer, more nuanced story of what it was like to be a young, female soldier in the modern Army, and Michael and I had been working together for months. It was both cathartic and frustrating to relive the best and worst parts of my deployment with someone who had never served and to engage with a publisher and agent who lived in Manhattan, which seemed to be a whole different world from mine. (They were all astonished Bush was reelected, for example—living in Tennessee, I never expected otherwise.) Finally, as my enlistment was almost up, *Love My Rifle More Than You: Young and Female in the U.S. Army* was almost done.

Since I was MI, the Army had to clear my book for publication, confirm that I hadn't violated OPSEC and included anything the enemy could use against our troops.[1] Finding someone to do this was harder than I imagined it would be. I spent weeks asking, calling, making appointments. If it had been a scientific article—no problem. But this? Finally, someone convinced my former battalion commander, the highest-ranking MI officer in the division, to pick someone to do it. That person referred one chapter for further review. And without me knowing, this happened at a very inopportune time.

After the Abu Ghraib scandal broke, journalists sent Freedom of Information Act (FOIA) requests everywhere, trying to see if detainee abuses were more widespread. At the same time my chapter on having witnessed detainees being mistreated in Iraq was being reviewed, stories hit the press about detainee abuse in the 101st, and the lack of punishment of those involved. The investigation must have been fairly shoddy, since I never even knew it was going on—it appeared the initial investigators only interviewed the people actually involved. Shockingly, when the investigators asked, "Have you broken the law?" each of these people answered, "No sir." And then, end of story—there seemed to have been no follow up.

When my chapter popped up, they had new information, and opened a new investigation. I was wracked with guilt over not having done more to stop something I saw as morally wrong—had anyone simply asked if I wanted to assist in the investigation, tell what I

---

1. Amusingly, some critics complained later that I'd been so vague about my duties that you could read the entire book and never know what my actual job was—yet I got one letter from someone else with my MOS complaining I had clearly violated OPSEC and given too much away.

had seen, I'd have been happy to do so. But the legal system and the Army being what they are, that is not what happened.

They threatened to throw me in jail.

THEY THREATENED TO CHARGE me with dereliction of duty for not reporting what I saw. The Judge Advocate General (JAG) lawyer I talked to seemed unable or unwilling to help me, so I had to hire a civilian lawyer. I went with a retired JAG officer recommended by Zoe's mom.

It was frightening. My last day in the Army was so close that I'd already signed a contract to sell my house; all my household goods had already been picked up and were headed toward the apartment where Brian was waiting for me. I was just weeks away from signing out on terminal leave. They threatened to cancel my terminal leave and hold me on active duty as long as it took—I would be trapped in Fort Campbell with nothing to do for an indefinite period of time. The lawyer was able to figure out what was going on and what they wanted: a sworn statement about what I'd seen—which I gave after getting immunity.

Since I wanted the story told—hell, I'd written about it in my book and clearly wasn't trying to hide anything—I was happy to get the whole sordid incident off my chest to people who might do something about it. But the heavy-handed measures and the threats left a bitter taste in my mouth. Sure, the Army had sometimes pissed me off—but ultimately I loved the Army—and here, on my way out, it was trying to fuck me. I was angry.

At the same time, my publisher was repeatedly asking how long it would take the Army to clear the book for publication. "However long it takes," I would answer.

"Isn't there someone we can call, to speed up the process?"

I found this ludicrous, absolutely laughable. The Army was busy fighting two wars. Troops were dying. A publisher from Manhattan calling and asking them to please hurry along the process of reviewing a book by a junior NCO—one, by the way, that did not universally portray the Army in a positive light? That seemed as likely to make them slow the review process down as speed it up. "Nope, there's no one you can call."

"I'M COMING DOWN," Brian said. "I'll help you drive back." He'd moved into a new apartment near his aunt Padi and her husband Jim in Greenbelt, Maryland, not too far from Walter Reed. We talked and exchanged emails every day; he was doing relatively well—no Code Black incidents had occurred; he was going to group therapy sessions once a week. Brian seemed stable and even upbeat, looking forward to our future together.

"I might not even get to leave!" I protested. "Fuck the Army."

"It will all work out. Don't worry. I want to be with you, support you through this. I'm your husband; I should be there."

Even though I put forth some more desultory protests, I felt grateful and relieved. It would be nice to have my husband by my side as my fate was decided, as I faced the threats and the fear.

We slept on an air mattress on the floor of the kitchen. Empty of all my furniture, the house felt weird, wrong somehow. A small television propped up on a milk crate provided entertainment; we ate out, waited.

Through it all, my last days in, I still showed up and did PT. Brian teased me: "You're almost out, why keep doing this? Just tell them you're too busy clearing."

But I actually liked the PT, wanted to stay in the best shape of my life and look good in my wedding dress (hey, even tough Army women can be vain), plus the exercise helped me burn off nervous energy and keep it together. Hoping everything would work out, I checked items off the lengthy list that must be completed before you can sign out: turning in issued gear (not a speck of dust can sully a single item, requiring repeated washings), having bored workers confirm that you don't have any overdue library books or unpaid veterinary bills. There were buildings on Fort Campbell that I visited only during in-processing and out-processing.

Miraculously, everything came together. I got immunity, gave my statement. Not long after, the book was cleared. I cleared, signed out on terminal leave, signed the paperwork selling my house. We crammed every item we could into my car, leaving the tiny TV and a six-pack of beer for the new owner of the house, and drove away.

WHEN WE GOT TO Greenbelt, I was dismayed: Brian was sleeping on a twin-size pullout bed, eating off a single set of dishes. "Brian! This is no better than that shithole we wanted you moved out of!"

"Sure it is. I don't have a creepy roommate who watches porn in the living room, and there are no holes in the wall. Besides, our household goods will be delivered soon. Don't worry about it."

Our furniture arrived and we began to settle in, trying to figure out how to live together as—still secret, from most—husband and wife.

We had such great expectations. Marriage, Walter Reed: the road ahead looked clear. But neither made any difference in getting Brian officially retired with effective treatment and therapy. The system was layered with indifferent bureaucrats and lost paperwork. Finally, Brian thought he understood: "Kayla, they're trying to make me give up and go away. They think if they drag things out long enough, I'll be so frustrated that my time will just run out and they won't have to retire me, give me benefits. Maybe I should just give up—is it even worth it?"

When I complained to his PEBLO (physical evaluation board liaison officer, the man responsible for shepherding Brian through the byzantine system) that Brian seemed to be slipping through the cracks, he said, "Don't feel bad, this happens to everybody." I was horrified that Brian's struggles were considered the rule rather than the exception: didn't our wounded warriors deserve better? It would have been far better to hear, "His file *literally* slipped through a crack between my desk and the wall and got lost—it was a freak accident!" than "This happens to everybody."

He went from zero case managers at Fort Campbell to eight: psychiatry, neurology, neurosurgery, neuropsych, primary care, a social worker, the PEBLO, and an overall "case manager." Sounds promising, right? But none of these managers communicated with each other. Each time we went to an appointment, someone would suggest medication he'd already been on, then express bafflement when we said as much. "Oh, here it is, a couple pages back ... you sure have been on a lot of meds, haven't you?"

One of them (who can remember which?) actually asked Brian, "Why didn't you go to inpatient rehab?"—as if he, with TBI and PTSD, should have known what care he needed; as if he, an SSG and a patient, could have determined which facility would be best and then written military orders to send himself there. "Oh well," she shrugged cavalierly, "it's too late now. Any improvements would have come in the first eighteen months, and now you won't see any more."

"She's wrong," I insisted to him as we left her office. "She's just fucking wrong." I stalked angrily down the hall of the hospital. "How dare she?! You're going to prove her wrong. I know you will."

What were we going to do? Who could help us? There was no one for us to turn to for support. Ironically, I seemed more alone than Brian. At no point did any of his doctors, nurses, or case managers ask me how I was coping, and my Army habits kept me from asking for help and admitting that I couldn't manage on my own. If there were any formal support groups available, I'd never heard of them and was certainly not told about them.

Just as bad, I couldn't stand being treated as "just a wife" and not the veteran I was. Going from soldier to civilian and from sergeant to spouse was humiliating: I was embarrassed by my dependent ID card. Getting out had been the right decision: I needed to help Brian with his recovery and there was no way to do that if I was still on active duty. But I was ashamed that my troops were going back to Iraq without me and lonely for the camaraderie of being on active duty with people I'd been through combat with. I felt no connection to the other military spouses I saw around the hospital. Why should I? I had been a soldier, and they had not.

AFTER MONTHS DURING WHICH no one seemed to keep track of Brian, his chain of command suddenly started imposing new rules. "We have to go in for accountability formation every morning starting tomorrow," he told me one day.

"Why now?" I asked.

"They lost a few dozen soldiers."

"What do you mean 'lost'?"

"They were still on the books at Walter Reed, but no one knew where they were. And no one knew if they were supposed to be at Walter Reed or had been sent back to their units or what. So they're trying to get that whole situation under control, and everyone has to go in for accountability formation now."

"Well, it is the Army," I said, "It makes sense. I always thought it

was messed up that 320th didn't make you come in. What if something had happened? No one would've known."

Then he started participating in a program where patients at Walter Reed who were doing well could go and work in government
agencies, to help them transition back into civilian life and gain new
experiences. Brian was assigned as an intern at the VA, so he had to
go all the way into D.C. in a suit.

But—strangely—even though his place of duty was now that
office, he still had to go to accountability formation. It added well
over an hour to his commute, not to mention the frustration of driving on the Beltway and spending half an hour finding parking at the
crowded hospital for a fifteen-minute exercise. "Why can't they just
have the VA office manager call in?" he fumed. "This is ridiculous!"

One day when I went in with him, I was completely astonished
at what the formation looked like. Soldiers who had assignments
like Brian were there in suits. Others were in BDUs (battle dress
uniform—camouflage). Still others were wearing PTs (physical fitness uniforms). Many were on crutches and clearly struggling to
stand upright. Some were actually dragging IV stands with them.
"What the hell?" I said. "Isn't this excessive? Can't they just send the
squad leaders by their rooms or something?"

Brian just shook his head. "It's fucking ridiculous."

Another day, I went to accompany him to an appointment on a
day there was 100 percent urinalysis. I was shocked. Not at the piss
test per se—drug tests had been a standard part of my Army career.
But they were dragging people down from the inpatient substance
abuse treatment program—troops who were already getting more
frequent urinalyses—and from the inpatient psychiatric ward. They
literally brought troops who were locked in an inpatient psych ward,
wearing shoes with the shoelaces removed, down to stand in line
with everyone else rather than handling it on their own ward. I

shook my head in disgust. "Do you know how many people are going to piss hot anyway?" Brian said. "Half the people here are on prescription narcotics for pain. And yeah, people share drugs—but probably not the ones they test for. It's stupid."

The overlapping in accountability made it impossible for people recovering at Walter Reed to do anything except wait around for the next formation. Brian dropped out of the intern program and also stopped volunteering to help wounded soldiers get off the planes at Andrews Air Force Base. It was too frustrating for him to have to meet the demands of his chain of command at Walter Reed for in-person accountability given the traffic and distances involved.

SO MANY THINGS WERE out of my hands. Brian's anxiety made it hard to do anything—we had to get up and leave in the middle of a Bob Dylan concert at a local baseball stadium when he started having a panic attack. He quit going to group therapy again. "The guy leading the sessions—he's some major—asked us if we were mad at the Army about what happened to us. I said, 'Sure, sometimes.' And he started berating me, chastising me, telling me it's not the Army's fault I got hurt and I should have known what I signed up for. What the fuck is the point of going to counseling if you can't talk about how you feel?" And Brian still had crippling headaches once or twice a week—he'd have to lie silently in a dark silent room until they lessened to the point that he could engage again. He forgot what he was supposed to do, mixed up times, lost things. I couldn't count on him to do anything important.

Helplessly, automatically, I reverted to old habits and began to control absolutely everything that *was* in my power. The obsessive tendencies the Army had praised and the psychologist had questioned came out in full force: the apartment had to be organized *just so*. Canned goods were arranged by type of food, labels facing out, toiletries aligned precisely, towels trifolded with bottom edges perfectly symmetrical. The volume of the TV and radio had to be on an odd number, I silently counted my steps when I walked anywhere, laid out pieces of candy and ate them in color-coordinated groups of four. I wouldn't let Brian do laundry: "You're doing it wrong!" I'd insist. "I'll have to redo it. Just let me do it." He'd shake his head and walk away.

The apartment was pristine. Brian's vast collection of socks—the man had spent years buying more rather than washing and pairing the ones he had—were neatly mated and collected in an enormous storage tub. When his mother visited, she commented approvingly on the state of affairs: "This is the first time I've ever seen my son's closet clean! When I came to see him graduate from basic training and we toured the bay, I knew which wall locker was his from across the room—he's always been so messy!" I basked in the praise with pride, and then shook myself with surprise: always a strong feminist, here I was feeling proud of how neat I was able to keep my husband's clothes! What was happening to me? I ruthlessly suppressed the thought.

If I kept busy enough, I wouldn't even have time to think. I started scrapbooking, organizing photos into albums, planning our wedding. Surely there was more to do. I decorated a room for Brian's daughter. If I were just busy enough, I would not reflect, worry, fret, imagine... constant forward motion would substitute for contemplation.

HIS DAUGHTER SONJA came for a long summer visit, and her presence kept Brian from drinking too much. He was still on active duty and had to go to work every day. I threw myself into my new role as stepmother and wife-to-be, walking his daughter to camp every morning, working out, coming home and planning our upcoming wedding, keeping up the house, cooking, running errands. I planned family activities, trips to museums and sporting events, and get-togethers with Padi, Jim, and their son.

Spending time with Sonja was rewarding and fulfilling—and made me long to have my own child. That brought up frustrating and conflicting emotions—could I ever have kids? Brian would probably never be able to work full-time, so I would have to. But the very things that seemed likely to prevent him from full-time employment would probably preclude him from being a full-time dad. How could I in good conscience leave an infant in his care if he remained prone to bursts of rage, anxiety attacks, debilitating headaches? These concerns tinged the time we spent as a family with sadness, as I wondered if this was as close as I would come to being a mom.

Sadness, and also resentment. I had chosen to marry him knowing he had problems. But when I imagined our lives stretching out in front of us and envisioned no changes, no improvement...the vicious cruelties he spewed when angry, the drinking, the burden of having to take care of someone who seemed to not appreciate my sacrifice and struggle...it filled me with anger and bitterness. And then I'd feel overwhelmingly guilty. How could I be angry with him for the problems he had as a result of getting blown up? How could I possibly resent a hero? I was a terrible wife, a bad person. If I were better, I wouldn't feel this way; I'd be patient, gentle, understanding.

We tried going to marriage counseling together. After a particularly nasty argument, Brian reached out to Army OneSource and found a family therapist who would see us. She didn't know anything about combat trauma, and though we didn't click with her, we ended up bonding over our mutual dislike for her. We were alone again in our dysfunction, locked together, trapped.

AND THROUGH IT ALL, I held tiny pieces of myself back. I hated Brian's dishes, but he was insistent that we use them. I kept my own dishes in a box on the kitchen floor that we all tripped over. They came to take on a huge symbolic meaning in my mind: If we broke up, I still had my dishes. If this all fell apart, I could just take my dishes and leave. Start over somewhere new, but not from scratch. I would still have my dishes, my beautiful full set of twelve wonderful dishes, which had been my parents' when they were together and had been with me since I got my first apartment when I was seventeen. As long as I had them, I had a way out. Sure, I'd married him; yes, I was planning our big public wedding together, but I had an escape hatch. When we would fight, as quietly as possible so his daughter wouldn't hear, and occasionally the word "divorce" would get thrown out there, I fixated on the damned box of dishes, sitting there, waiting for me to pick them up and walk out.

In June, I flew out to Denver for Zoe's wedding, excited to see her start a new phase of her life. She was a beautiful bride, looking relaxed and happy despite having to lug the weight of a wedding dress in the unusual heat.

At the reception, I ended up chatting with her uncle Allan, a Vietnam veteran. He seemed tense, tightly wound, edgy. His voice had the gravelly burr of a longtime chain-smoker, and he laughed often but uncomfortably as we spoke. His eyes darted around, constantly scanning our surroundings. I could see them identify exits and linger on anything that might be unusual. "What are those?" he asked, pointing at black objects in tree branches above us. "Are people spying on us?"

"No, those are just microphones, so the videographer could get good audio while Zoe and Craig exchanged vows," I said calmly. "No big deal. They were for the wedding, not us."

"Oh, okay," he said, seeming mollified. He laughed again, grinding out one cigarette and immediately lighting another one. "You probably think I'm crazy!"

"Nope," I answered. And I meant it. I felt perfectly comfortable talking with Allan. His jumpy behavior and nervous tics didn't seem abnormal; his refusal to make eye contact reminded me of my husband.

When I went to refill my drink, one of Zoe's aunts approached me. "Is Allan...bothering you? I'm sorry. You know, he was in Vietnam, and then he got in this terrible car accident not long after he came home. So he has a brain injury and PTSD. He can be difficult. Do you want me to...do something?" She seemed genuinely concerned.

"No, we're fine," I said.

"Are you sure? I mean, I know he can be a little odd. If you need me to step in, I'd understand." An awkward laugh. I had the feeling she'd had this conversation before, with people who genuinely didn't know what to make of him, were nervous or uncomfortable. I wasn't.

"No, really. Um...My husband suffered a TBI in the war, and he has PTSD too. I'm happy to talk to Allan."

I rejoined him at the table. Over a couple of drinks, he started to open up and tell me stories about the war. Gradually, a few of his siblings drifted over and sat down nearby, listening. Later, one pulled me aside and said, "He told you more about his experiences in Vietnam today than he's ever told me. It was fascinating to see him open up to another veteran."

On my flight home, I thought about Allan. He'd struggled for decades with his TBI and PTSD, unable to hold down a steady job, enduring multiple brushes with the law, losing his license after driving drunk too many times—without his family's help, it seemed almost certain he would have spiraled even further down. Was this Brian's future? They had so many commonalities. It had been so easy for me to talk to him. What did that say about me? About Brian? I didn't know anything about TBI or PTSD, what Brian's prognosis was, whether or not he would ever get better. Blind faith wasn't enough anymore—I needed facts.

WHEN I WENT TO Walter Reed with Brian for appointments, I started looking for more information about TBIs. Not just a brochure with the bullet points, but real resources that would help me understand. One of the offices had several copies of a book from the VA called *Traumatic Brain Injury*.[2] "Mind if I take one of these?" I asked. "Sure, help yourself," the provider answered. Once I cracked it open and realized it was designed for clinicians, I wasn't sure it would help me, but decided to plow ahead and soon was immersed, making notes in the margins and highlighting lines that seemed important. Some of the tidbits left me feeling cold and heavy: "Individuals who have sustained moderate to severe TBI frequently never recover to pre-injury functional levels and may have behavioral difficulties" (p. 17). "There is an increased risk of Alzheimer's disease in those with a history of prior TBI" (p. 98).

But I was also struck by how powerfully lucky we are. Brain

2. *Traumatic Brain Injury*, Veterans Health Initiative/Department of Veterans Affairs Employee Education System, Independent Study Course released January 2004. Accessed at http://www.gesturetekhealth.com/pdf/research/neurological/ 4.4.2_USA_VA_TBI_Report.pdf October 2012. Updated 2010 version available at http://www.publichealth.va.gov/docs/vhi/traumatic-brain-injury-vhi.pdf.

injuries are categorized as mild (a.k.a. concussion), moderate, and severe. A penetrating TBI like Brian's is by definition severe—but he's doing remarkably well. My brother, a physician's assistant, always told me, "You never want to be an interesting patient"—my husband was definitely an interesting patient. He had told me that several times, doctors would bring other doctors into the room, show them his CT scans, and say, "Look! He's walking and talking!" Although our understanding of the brain is significantly greater than it used to be, there is still a tremendous amount that no one seems to know, such as why it is that while 80 percent of those who sustain a mild TBI (mTBI) have no long-term problems, 20 percent have persistent symptoms (p. 15). Since Brian inhabited some strange group—though he'd sustained a severe TBI, he was at the upper end of the functioning scale, more like someone who had sustained a mild brain injury—I read the whole book instead of skipping the parts about mTBI.

Looking at the list of post-concussive symptoms reported by patients following mTBI, I ticked off the ones Brian had—poor concentration, irritability, tired a lot more, depression, memory problems, headaches, anxiety, trouble thinking (p. 24). And he had all three of the common cognitive problems that affect those with moderate to severe brain injuries, at least to some degree: attention and concentration problems, new learning and memory deficits, and executive control dysfunction (p. 73). Learning more about the common symptoms of TBI paradoxically made me feel both better and worse. On the plus side, he wasn't just a lazy jackass. Of course I'd known he had a TBI, but it was so hard to untangle in my own mind what was likely a result of his injury and what might just be who he is, blamed on the injury. Seeing it here in writing made it clear: he wasn't making it up, these were real problems. At the same time, I was not at all reassured about our future—this book confirmed what we'd been told: most recovery happens early. On the other hand, he'd never been sent for intense rehab—maybe there would be some chance for further improvements, given the right interventions.

I started trying to tease apart what problems might be physical and which could be psychological. Cognitive deficits could cause emotional reactions (it's depressing to know that your brain doesn't work the way it used to), but that could work the other way, too: if you're too anxious to sleep all night, your brain doesn't work as well the next day. Apparently it's even hard for experts to know when "emotional symptoms are the direct result of neurological damage rather than psychological reactions secondary to having a brain injury, despite similar clinical appearance" (p. 75).

And when you throw PTSD into the mix? It's even harder to untangle.

Lining the symptoms of TBI up next to the common reactions to trauma, there's a remarkable amount of overlap:

TBI	COMMON REACTIONS AFTER TRAUMA
PHYSICAL	**PHYSICAL REACTIONS**
Headache	Stomach upset and trouble eating
Feeling dizzy	Trouble sleeping and feeling very tired
Being tired	Pounding heart, rapid breathing, feeling edgy
Trouble sleeping	Sweating
Vision problems	Severe headache if thinking of the event
Feeling bothered by noise and light	Failure to engage in exercise, diet, safe sex, regular health care
	Excess smoking, alcohol, drugs, food
	Having your ongoing medical problems get worse
EMOTIONAL (FEELINGS)	**EMOTIONAL TROUBLES**
Depression	Feeling nervous, helpless, fearful, sad
Anger outbursts and quick to anger	Feeling shocked, numb, and not able to feel love or joy

Anxiety (fear, worry, or feeling nervous)	Avoiding people, places, and things related to the event
Personality changes	Being irritable or having outbursts of anger
	Becoming easily upset or agitated
	Blaming yourself or having negative views of oneself or the world
	Distrust of others, getting into conflicts, being over-controlling
	Being withdrawn, feeling rejected or abandoned
	Loss of intimacy or feeling detached
COGNITIVE (MENTAL)	**REACTIONS TO TRAUMA**
Memory problems	Feeling hopeless about the future
Trouble staying focused	Feeling detached or unconcerned about others
Poor judgment and acting without thinking	Having trouble concentrating or making decisions
Being slowed down	Feeling jumpy and getting startled easily at sudden noises
Trouble putting thoughts into words	Feeling on guard and constantly alert
	Having disturbing dreams and memories or flashbacks
	Having work or school problems
http://www.ptsd.va.gov/public/pages/traumatic_brain_injury_and_ptsd.asp	
http://www.ptsd.va.gov/public/pages/common-reactions-after-trauma.asp	

How were we supposed to know what problem was caus-ing what symptoms? Did it matter? Should they be treated dif-ferently? I'd tried to practically force Brian out of his depression and hassled him for sleeping too long—now I learned that people recovering from TBIs actually need more sleep so their brains can heal. What if I'd been making it worse? Why had nobody told us something so basic? In ways, Brian had done so much better than expected—I was convinced that he could improve further with the right intervention. The book listed a number of specialists who could help TBI patients. One of them I'd never heard of before:

Physiatrist is the rehabilitation specialist who treats physical, cognitive, and behavioral sequelae and provides leadership for the rehabilitation therapies. The physiatrist coordinates treatment to maximize the level of function and is responsible for medical evaluations and plans of care most suitable for the individual and his/her family. Physiatrists are actively involved with rehabilitation therapists in planning the patient's rehabilitation program, including team meetings and family conferences.

This sounded perfect! That was exactly the kind of health care provider Brian needed to help us figure out what he needed to further heal and improve his functioning.

Triumphant and relieved that I'd figured out what was needed, we went back to Walter Reed and met with Brian's case manager. "He needs a physiatrist," I explained.

"A what?" she asked.

"A physiatrist," I repeated, and showed her the paragraph in the book.

"We don't have any of those here."

WE DID OUR BEST to hide our problems from the outside world, pressing forward with wedding plans and doing our best to be a happy family. Brian participated willingly in some aspects of the planning, like sampling food options, but acted uncaring about others. We were both relatively indifferent to the photographer and DJ, relieved that the venue had a list of preferred vendors to narrow the list of choices. Whenever he said, "Whatever you want, honey, I don't care," on another of the endless round of choices, I'd get extreme: "Okay, pink roses everywhere. On the invitations, the tables, Sonja's dress, in my bouquet, on everything." He would immediately protest, giving me the chance to say, "See, you do care. So get involved!" Part of my insistence was due to a genuine desire to have the ceremony and reception reflect who we both were, but it was also driven by a need for him to show that he was committed to the wedding, to the marriage, to me.

Our wedding was scheduled for a Sunday in August at a venue on the Chesapeake Bay. Family and friends had come in from around the country, including people we'd been to war with. Zoe was there to be one of my bridesmaids, along with Lauren, who had been on my team when we first crossed into Iraq. Seeing people we'd been to combat with for such a happy occasion relieved the frustrations of dealing with family.

Love My Rifle hit shelves at local bookstores two days before the ceremony. I gave copies to close friends and family members. My dad forced me to pose in front of a Barnes & Noble and again inside, holding the hardcover. Although he wasn't thrilled with all the details I'd included, he was beaming with pride. My mother was another story. She was furious at her portrayal in the book and in an interview that came out around the same time. But rather than just confront me with her hurt feelings, she distanced herself, refusing to help me get ready for the wedding. My bridesmaids, stepmother, and sister were there, but I could feel my mother's absence in the room like a tangible object. Adept by now at suppressing unpleasant emotions, I pushed the pain out of my mind and focused on the joys of the day.

We exchanged vows outside before our friends and family, the sun sparkling on the bay waters while a breeze blew away the worst of the heat. The same minister who had married us in Brian's living room six months before officiated. "I'm not going to ask you to *lie*," I had said, "since you're a woman of God. But could you . . . not mention that you already did this?" She agreed—perhaps simply relieved that we really had meant it when we assured her we were planning a big public ceremony.

My sister had gotten lost on her way there with my dress, but I hadn't worried. "What are they going to do? Start without me?"

The organizer responsible for ensuring the day went smoothly seemed bemused: "You are the calmest bride I've ever seen!"

I laughed. "Why shouldn't I be happy? No one is trying to kill me—the only thing people are shooting are photos. The decision to spend our lives together was private, this is just the public celebration of that decision—it's a party! What is there to be stressed about?"

She just shook her head. "Most brides are really tense."

THAT WAS JUST ONE example of how we didn't feel like normal Americans any more. Spending time with civilians could still be disconcerting. Regular people's concerns baffled us; everyone seemed selfish and shallow. We overheard people on their cell phones: "My latte took ten minutes at Starbucks! This is *the worst day of my life!*" Of course we understood that people were exaggerating—but they seemed wrapped up in the most meaningless, trivial crap. The news was full of coverage of celebrities, while what still mattered to me and Brian—stories about American troops getting killed in Iraq and Afghanistan—was relegated to the little ticker at the bottom of the screen. Everyone knew what movie star was pregnant or getting divorced, when many of our fellow citizens couldn't place Iraq on a map.

Brian and I were trying to make friends. Brian had connected with Jason online; they met on message boards frequented by people who liked hard-core music and ended up going to shows together. We got together with Jason and his girlfriend Nadean sometimes. He was a brash, outspoken Jew (he frequently called attention to his Jewishness, which I found mildly startling after my avowedly secular upbringing). Nadean was recently divorced from a sailor, and understood more of the military jargon and mind-set than many— plus two of her three kids were close to Sonja in age, so we could do family things together.

But it seemed almost impossible to get over that chasm that yawned between civilians and us. After living in the filth of Iraq, shitting in barrels, pissing on the side of the road, rarely bathing . . . civilian standards still seemed foreign even more than a year later. Jason was a germaphobe, and Nadean carried hand sanitizer at the ready in case he felt contaminated. We shrugged in bemusement. Our first double date night, they came back to our apartment. After Nadean used the bathroom, she swatted both of the men on their shoulders: "Who left the toilet seat up? Come on, guys! There are ladies present!"

I gaped at her. "Seriously?" People care what position the toilet seat is in, in real life? That isn't just a joke?

"Yeah! They should know better! My nine-year-old son knows better!"

I giggled. "You know, I'm still pretty excited about the toilet! After being in Iraq, having indoor plumbing still feels like a luxury—I don't really care about the seat being up or down."

Now it was her turn to gape at me. I relayed the story to Lauren later. "I just feel so distant from civilians."

"It takes a while!" she agreed. "When I first got back, the house was really full and there was only one bathroom. I went out and peed in the yard—it just seemed so normal after being deployed, where we peed anywhere." I burst out laughing. The chasm between civilians and combat veterans may loom large, but it was like we shared a secret code with each other.

No one was trying to kill us. We had electricity. When I paused to consider what we had, I felt lucky, blessed, grateful. I'd gained a degree of perspective from my deployment—a deeper understanding of what really matters, a more profound appreciation for how privileged we are. It enriched me, and I was glad for it.

NOT THAT I EXISTED in a constant state of grace. I still had my own little breakdowns.

One afternoon when I walked into the apartment after a day spent running errands, my heart sank. The apartment was a mess, empty beer bottles everywhere. Brian had promised to clean up while I was gone.

"Honey? I'm home!" I called, and headed into the kitchen. The counter was littered with more empties. Brian came in and greeted me warily. We halfheartedly hugged and brushed our lips together. We'd been arguing often since Sonja left, and both of us were trying to avoid another explosion.

"Did you eat lunch?" I asked.

He shrugged. "I forgot."

"How was your appointment?"

"I missed it. I thought it was at one-fifteen but it was at eleven-fifteen. The next available appointment is in two months."

I sighed. "Why don't they call to confirm?! They know you have a TBI. Shouldn't they double-check? Call the day before and the morning of?"

Brian just shrugged again, then pulled open the refrigerator door and stared inside. I stood there glaring at him, angry. At the same time, I felt guilty for the anger. Thoughts scurried through my head: "How can I be mad at him for forgetting things, mixing things up? It isn't his fault that he got blown up, or that his brain got damaged.

I should have gone with him, or at least made sure he left on time. But damn it, I'm tired of carrying the burden of caring for both of us, sick of putting on a happy face and pretending everything is fine. Nothing is fine. He's fucked up and I'm stuck with him. I'm trapped in this hell and I resent him for it, and *shit*, I'm a terrible person. How can I be pissed off at him, it's not his fault, none of it is his fault, but it is his fucking fault that he isn't trying to get better, he doesn't even try, *goddamnit*, I just don't know if I can take this anymore."

He was still standing there, refrigerator door wide open, cold air escaping into the room. I felt completely incapable of yelling at him for all the things I was actually angry about, how I felt forced to be responsible for every aspect of our lives while he got to blame his injury whenever he messed something up. Suddenly I couldn't control myself, and the rage at everything wrong in our lives boiled over and erupted. "Why do you hate the fucking environment?" I screamed, and started kicking him. "What the fuck is wrong with you? Shut the goddamned door! Why do you hate the environment?"

He stared at me in utter astonishment, looked down at my tennis shoe flailing away at his shin. "Ow," he said, "that kinda hurts."

I burst into tears and fled into the other room.

8.

BREAKING POINT

—— ⭑ ——

Not long after the wedding, I had to go on a book tour, and Brian was left alone, his routine disrupted. The first week I was gone, he completely fell apart. He called every night, drunk and enraged, over and over and over. "You're up there fucking other men, aren't you? You fucking whore. Couldn't wait to get away from me." My attempts to reassure him utterly failed, and Brian swirled deep into panicked, drunken misery. He promised to divorce me, threatened suicide. I tried to stay calm, talk him down—but eventually gave up. Around two in the morning, I turned off my phone and asked the front desk not to put any calls through so I could get a few hours of sleep in before the alarm sounded and I had to go do interviews.

My life seemed to be splitting: publicly, I calmly discussed the struggles of returning veterans; privately, I was in utter crisis. The gap between my polished public persona and the disaster at home felt jarring and surreal. Professional makeup artists ensured that I looked pretty on camera, but inside I was a jagged mess.

It took all my Army training to hold it together. "Suck it up and drive on"—"Right place, right time, right uniform"—"Pain is just weakness leaving the body"—"There's plenty of time to sleep when you're dead"—"False motivation is better than no motivation"—all the ridiculous phrases from my time in the Army echoed around in my mind while I told myself over and over, "You can do this. If you could manage a year in Iraq, you can handle this. The camera doesn't shoot bullets, just images—no reason to fear it."

The innocent, brutal casualness with which journalists asked searing personal questions was jarring. "What's it like to watch someone bleed to death?" asked a perky early morning host at one local TV station. Over and over, I had to expose raw, tender bits of myself. I'd written crappy poetry in high school, and somehow in the back of my mind that was what writing the book had come to symbolize for me, too: a cathartic way of working through my emotions. My publisher had asked, "Are you willing to do media?" and I'd blithely answered, "Sure"—not knowing what that meant at all. I was completely unprepared for the whirlwind of print, television, and radio interviews, the bruising pace, the shocking intimacy. "Tell me about aiming your gun at a child." "Let's talk about torture. Tell me about what you saw." It took all my willpower to stay calm and focused, to answer as smoothly as possible.

Regular people who came to readings and book signings often asked, "Have you ever killed anyone?" I stumbled through explanations of how grateful I was that I'd never been forced to fire my weapon in combat, how it stayed with people who had, while wanting to scream, "It's not a fucking video game!" But it wasn't all bad. I enjoyed giving civilians a window into what it was like to be a woman in the military, helping them get a sense of the war in Iraq from the perspective of a soldier rather than a journalist. And just as questions could elicit an emotional reaction in me, I found that what I had to say could do the same in others.

A woman came up to me after a signing and asked to speak to me privately. "I just wanted to thank you," she said, her eyes welling with tears. "I was in the first Gulf War, and when I came home, no one knew what it was like. I've felt crazy all these years—but then I read your book, and I realized I'm not alone. So much of what you wrote about, I experienced. I gave your book to my mom so she could finally understand what I went through." The tears spilled over. "Thank you so much," she choked out, clearly trying to maintain control. I awkwardly patted her shoulder, smiling uncertainly. Years in the Army had left me feeling completely incapable of responding to emotional vulnerability in strangers. It happened again and again, mainly women but men too, telling me how isolated they had felt, how reassuring it was to know someone else had felt what they had felt. Knowing I eased their burden helped lighten my own.

I came home for the weekend and tried to calm Brian down. My presence, the routine of our time together, soothed him. The second week away was better. Nadean had seen how badly he was coping—he'd posted online about suicide and divorce—and she called him repeatedly, insisting he come over to her house for dinner every night. Being around her and the kids seemed to stabilize him, and getting out of the house kept him from spiraling into an alcohol-induced tailspin. The third week, he came with me to Seattle to spend time with his daughter. We'd pulled through another crisis, barely.

Throughout, I had vacillated between empathizing with Brian's struggles and believing he was a selfish prick, just trying to take me down a notch and keep me from enjoying my success, unable to hold it together to support me when I'd had a tough day, always putting his own needs first. I wanted him to revel in my joys with me, but instead I felt I had to hide them to protect his ego. What should have been one of the happiest, proudest times of my life was tainted, bitter.

Sometimes I had dreamed of not going home at all.

LOVE MY RIFLE was coming out in Dutch, Spanish, and in the UK, and the European publishers wanted me to come over to do publicity. Brian and I decided to take advantage of the chance to travel overseas while only having to pay for his airfare and spend a couple more weeks in Europe after my official duties were done—it would be our honeymoon. There had been no movement on Brian's retirement, and his request for leave to travel abroad was approved and signed off on by his chain of command. We hoped that a honeymoon—a real vacation from all the stress and ugliness and pressure—would give us a fresh start on our foundering marriage, and decided to travel from Amsterdam through Spain, Italy, Switzerland, and France before ending up in London. Our only goal was to have fun and enjoy our time together exploring new places.

When we stopped in Pisa, tiny plaques on the damaged but still impressive frescoes and sculptures noted that the damage was caused by bombing in WWI and WWII. Brian and I pointed them out to each other and paused, noting the pockmarks in the art caused by shrapnel or bullets. Here, we could see the scars of war etched into more ancient historical artifacts—the reminder present, vivid, for everyone to notice. War, for the people who lived here, wasn't something that happened to other people in far away lands: it remained an intimate part of their landscape.

In Paris, we ended up spending hours at a special WWII exhibit at the Army Museum. It was tremendously emotionally moving to see the vast scale of WWII and the deep impact it had on Europe, both the land and the people. Overall, the signs explained, worldwide there were 50 million dead. An unimaginable number! I stared at the military gear in the display cases. "Look, Brian," I said, "their helmets and canteens are shaped exactly like ours—just made out of different materials. The canteen cups look identical." He nodded, lost in his own thoughts.

As we wandered through the exhibit I was struck over and over by the similarities between those troops and the ones I served with, their experiences and ours, their equipment and mine. I'd never been a history buff, and though I'd vaguely known that many of the names of roads (Market Garden Road, Bastogne Avenue) at Fort Campbell were from battles the 101st had fought in, I'd never known what they were—but here were descriptions of them. "Do you think they'll name streets after battles from our wars, too?" I wondered aloud.

Suddenly it struck me: "I'm a veteran." Brian looked at me, puzzled: "Yeah. And?" I tried to explain. "All this time, I've just felt like . . . some chick who happened to go to war. But seeing all of this—their gear, just like ours—I have something in common with them. All of them. We are veterans, and we have something in common with all veterans who have come before us." I paused. "I can't believe it took this for me to feel that, to realize it—that it finally clicked in Europe, in Paris of all places."

"I get it," he agreed. "They understand war more here. There are reminders of it everywhere. Even people who haven't gone to war know how much it sucks, they can see the scars of it in their cities."

"Exactly! Their parents or grandparents remember what it was like to have bombs falling in their cities. It isn't so remote for them, like it is in America. So even though some of the European journalists have asked me much tougher questions about what I did, the regular people, they have seemed much more sensitive and understanding about what it means to have been to war. They get it; they know war is hell. And for the first time I actually feel connected instead of isolated and alienated. I have a community—I share something with everyone who has been to war, some kind of fucked-up bond, but it's real. I am a veteran. We both are."

Toward the end of our trip, Brian and I were in London on Veterans Day—Remembrance Day there—and absolutely everyone was wearing a red poppy paper pin, exchanged for donations to the Royal British Legion to raise money for veterans. The entire city seemed to recognize the service and sacrifice of their veterans for days—while back home there were mattress sales. We felt accepted and welcomed as veterans, more so in a foreign country than our own homeland.

WHEN WE CHECKED OUR email and voice mail once on the trip, Brian had found a series of increasingly frantic messages from his platoon sergeant at Walter Reed. "Your retirement has come through, and you need to come in to out-process. Where are you? You need to be here *tomorrow*."

Brian called him back, irate: "I'm in Italy. On my honeymoon. There's no way I can be in tomorrow to out-process."

"Well who approved that?!"

"You did. And so did the company commander and a lieutenant colonel. I followed the proper procedures and everyone signed off on my leave."

"Well, you need to get back here right away." The voice through the phone sounded strained and tense.

"With all due respect, Sergeant, no," Brian said firmly. "My leave was approved. I'm in Europe on my honeymoon with my wife. We aren't changing our plane tickets back. I'll be back in when my leave is up."

The platoon sergeant spluttered and blustered, but what could he do? And what could we? We didn't have the money—or the desire—to cut our trip short and change our tickets home. I had appointments in London. We were having a great time. And Brian had a leave form signed by everyone who needed to approve it. Still, despite knowing that we were right and he had the authorization to be there, the incident had thrown a pall over our trip. Would they find a way to fuck him? Would there be some kind of repercussion, blowback, punishment? Was it risky to stick with the plan?

When we got home, Brian's chain of command wanted him to finalize his retirement as swiftly as possible, so he was rushed through the out-processing steps that had taken me weeks at Fort Campbell in just a few days. Despite his brain injury, no one took extra time to ensure he understood his benefits, what services were available to him, or where to turn for additional help. He wasn't at all clear on what resources were out there for him, what services he qualified for. I tentatively asked him about one I'd seen signs for at Walter Reed, the Army Wounded Warrior program. "From what I can tell, they make brochures," he answered bitterly. Representatives from a few programs just shoved brochures into his hands and sent him on his way.

To our astonishment, he wasn't allowed to take terminal leave—use the remaining vacation days he had saved up, basically. (This is important because while you are on leave, you still draw housing and food allowances [Basic Allowance for Housing (BAH) and Basic Allowance for Sustenance (BAS)], which add a significant amount to your paycheck [especially in the D.C. region, since BAH varies with local cost of living]. Many people save up a couple of months of terminal leave, and those final paychecks provide a cushion while you transition to civilian life.) Instead, they "bought back" Brian's leave, giving him a lump-sum final paycheck without BAH or BAS for the final two months of leave he had saved up. Unexpectedly, we had thousands of dollars less coming in than we expected.

Brian's final rating also shocked us: the Physical Evaluation Board (PEB) had rated him at only 30 percent disabled and put him on the Temporary Disability Retired List (TDRL) rather than the Permanent Disability Retired List since his "condition has not stabilized to the point that a permanent degree of severity can be determined." While on the TDRL, he would get 50 percent of his basic pay (the average of the highest thirty-six months of his pay). It was all terribly confusing to both of us, and I hadn't had a brain injury and had my own military experience—how, we wondered, did others navigate the process? The math made no sense to us—there was no single, easy-to-understand rating for traumatic brain injury, so he got a 10 percent rating for cognitive disorder secondary to the TBI, 10 percent for posttraumatic headaches caused by the TBI, 10 percent for PTSD, and 10 percent for loss of parts of skull—and somehow, $10 + 10 + 10 + 10 = 30$ in that system. While on the TDRL, he would be scheduled for periodic reexaminations and reevaluations . . . leaving us filled with dread that at some point in the future, they might suddenly decide to drop him below that crucial 30 percent total rating, leaving us without health insurance although he would clearly have what any other insurer would consider a pre-existing condition. Bafflingly, the PEB had also determined Brian was "competent to manage legal, financial, and medical affairs"—having lived with and helped care for him for over a year now, I knew this was simply not the case.

It was a smack in the face, after nearly losing his life serving his country, suffering what we had been told was irreparable harm to his brain, memory, emotional control, cognition, and functioning, having activities he enjoyed closed forever since the open hole in his skull made them too dangerous, facing the probability of early-onset dementia, not knowing if he would ever be able to have a successful career in the civilian world, told he was unfit to continue serving in the Army, now he was told that all of this only added up to a 30 percent disability rating. This is in part because the Army *only* rates people on "those medical conditions that result in the Soldier being determined unfit for continued military service"—not for lowered quality of life, pain, suffering, appearance, or anything else—just those things that keep them from doing their jobs in the Army.[1]

---

1. http://www.pdhealth.mil/downloads/Army_Physical_Disability_Evaluation_System_(APDES).pdf

Another big part of the problem was that the disability rating schedule did not have a good way to evaluate TBI. He contemplated
appealing the determination, but was exhausted, frustrated, fed up,
angry—and simply done. He signed the papers and retired from the
Army on November 29, 2005. Just four days after he turned thirty,
Brian was out of a job—out of a career—with a marriage barely
holding together, cognitive and mental health problems, an uncertain future, and no idea what to do next.

To suddenly go from getting Brian's full salary plus BAH and
BAS to suddenly getting less than half of his salary was a heavy
financial blow. The final paycheck would help, but not for long—the
rent for our two-bedroom apartment in Maryland was twice what
my mortgage had been for a three-bedroom house in Tennessee.
Brian immediately filed a disability claim with the VA, but we had
no idea how long it would take for it to be processed. I'd gotten a
job offer to do translation as a contractor for a government agency,
but couldn't start until my security clearance was adjudicated by the
new agency and transferred over from DoD, and we had no idea
how long that would take, either.

Options exhausted, we both had to go on unemployment.

The shame we both felt was profound. We were both too embarrassed to tell our families. The honeymoon was definitely over.

I BECAME INCREASINGLY tightly wound, feeling the burden
of managing all the responsibilities for both our lives. Sleep was
increasingly elusive; I tossed and turned all night, the insomnia
that had periodically plagued me for years becoming unbearable.
Though exhausted, I was unable to shut off the constant whir of
thoughts in my mind—I could almost picture a hamster frantically
running around in a little wheel in my brain: "What am I sacrificing

because of this marriage? How can I have children with a man who can barely care for himself? I can't have a family with someone so erratic. Maybe I should leave him. I can't; he might become homeless or even die. He seems completely incapable of surviving on his own. What am I going to do? I can't live like this. Fuck. Fuck!" I'd end up punching the pillow in frustration.

When Brian couldn't sleep, he just drank—but drinking that much made me feel like shit the next day; I hated being nonfunctional. Desperate, I got a prescription for sleeping pills. The first night on Ambien, I passed out immediately. The next morning I awoke feeling rested and relieved. That night, sleep eluding me again, I got up to pee and walked right into a wall. The third night, it did nothing. It seemed I'd have to resign myself to hours of watching the red numbers on my alarm clock slowly change or hoping marathons of *Law & Order* would lull me to sleep on the couch.

Periods of normalcy, the times Brian and I hewed together for solace or for joy, seemed shorter and shorter. Our bond as combat veterans didn't seem as strong. As I looked forward to starting a new job, Brian was stuck in the past. He didn't seem to be seriously looking for a job. He appeared to be lost in his own head, spiraling deeper into depression. He knew his brain injury had reduced his functioning, and feared he would never be able to succeed—and almost seemed too afraid to try, worried his worst fears would be realized and he would be proven a broken failure.

As he sat at home dwelling on his problems, his PTSD worsened—and the lack of sleep exacerbated his cognitive problems, making it harder for him to focus or remember things, offering further evidence of what he couldn't do. This depressed him, which he tried to alleviate with alcohol, which made him lose control, which made us fight, which threatened the future of our marriage, which made him feel like more of a failure... It was a self-perpetuating cycle, where the problems of TBI, PTSD, depression, and alcohol abuse were so profoundly intertwined that picking apart the causes or symptoms would have been impossible. As it was, we were too deeply immersed in the misery to see anything beyond the immediacy of each moment.

Whenever we had one of our screaming, bitter fights, I fantasized about leaving.

Then the worst night came.

IT WAS DECEMBER 6, 2005. We'd just watched a movie and were having a couple of beers. Brian and I were talking about how nervous I felt about applying to grad school and taking the entrance exam, the GRE—I'd joined the Army partly to get money for grad school, and was intent on accomplishing that goal. I was applying to international relations programs, and joked, "I want to make a difference in our foreign policy *without* carrying a gun."

All of a sudden his face closed like shutters slammed shut. "You don't understand. You can never understand," he snarled, lips curled, nostrils flared.

Code Black. Out of nowhere. Always the same phrase, the clue that it would be horrible: "You don't understand."

"Okay," I said, "I'm sorry. But I don't want to fight, and this is how our fights always start. I'm going to bed." I headed toward the bedroom.

He followed me, grabbed my arm, spun me around. "Don't you fucking walk away from me. Listen to me."

"Okay, okay. What?"

He breathed heavily, his eyes staring into mine. "You. Do. Not. Understand." Each word was punctuated by a finger jabbing me in the chest.

"You're right. I can't understand what it was like to get blown up.

I don't truly know. But I can try to support you and stand by you and love you." I tried to stay calm and bring him down from the sudden rage. Sometimes, sometimes I could talk him down.

"You don't love me. You don't even know me. I don't know you."

My anger surged. There would be no staying calm and talking him down this time. He knew all my buttons, and seemed to revel in pushing them, triggering an emotional reaction. "Oh for fuck's sake, Brian, not this again. I can't fucking do this. You know I love you. Haven't I proven that to you by now?"

He lit a cigarette. "Why can't you fucking do this? You've *done* enough people. The Queen of Sinjar Mountain. Morale booster of the desert." He often called me a slut when he was enraged. As much as I'd grown accustomed to it, it never stopped hurting.

I covered my face with my hands, took a deep breath. "Seriously, back to this? We're married. I can't control what did or didn't happen in the past, but we're together now. You slept with other people before we were married, too. Don't call me a whore."

Brian smirked, "I didn't."

Rolling my eyes, I sighed. "Semantics. You know what I mean."

He threw his arms out wide. "Don't fucking tell me what to do. You're not the boss of me."

I raised my hands. "Fine. Whatever. I'm done." I turned, walked away into the bedroom, shut the door.

Pacing the room, I was jittery and anxious. What should I, what could I do? Was this rage of his going to get uncontrollable? This time felt different somehow. Suddenly nervous, I locked the door, afraid he'd hurt me. At moments like this it was hard to remember there were good times when our love seemed clear and pure. Now there was only this fear and anger.

He started jiggling the knob. "You better unlock that fucking door. I'm not done talking to you." I stared at the handle and backed up. Which was going to be worse, opening the door or leaving it locked? Suddenly the door shook—he was throwing himself at it, trying to break it down. "Let me the fuck in. We're not done."

My nose filled with snot and out of nowhere I was crying, feeling overwhelmingly helpless and horrified. Was this really my life? Hiding from my husband in our bedroom, terrified of what was going to happen if I opened the door or didn't? I imagined our future stretching out before us, an endless cycle of fights and making up and PTSD and him drunk . . . and suddenly anything at all seemed better. Even death would have to be better than this living hell. Love wasn't enough anymore.

I jerked open the door and stared at Brian.

"Kill me," I shouted. I didn't have it in me to kill myself, but here was a new way to escape. If he was this miserable with me, I'd make him fucking deal with it, make him end it. Let his rage take him, wash over him and drown us both.

"What?"

"Kill me. I can't live like this. Just fucking kill me, put us both out of our misery."

He stalked to the closet and grabbed his gun from the top shelf. I went into the living room and sank onto the couch. My heart was pounding as I heard him walking into the room. I felt the soft fabric of the couch under my fingers. Was this the end?

I looked up, stood up, stared at him. Our eyes locked, and he lifted the gun and put the barrel on my forehead. I breathed shallowly, giddy, frightened, but also relieved. After feeling trapped for so long, the prospect of escape by any means seemed sweet. The metal was cold on my forehead. I refocused my eyes down to his hand, watched his finger on the trigger.

"Is this what you want?" he asked.

"Yes," I whispered, my voice catching in my throat.

"Is this what you fucking want?" he yelled.

"Yes," I said, more firmly, thinking, "Please, just let it all end.

Lift this burden. I can't live like this, and there's no fucking escape that won't be worse than this shit, other than death. Just make it stop, make it all fucking stop."

When his finger started to tighten, I closed my eyes in anticipation. I didn't exactly want to die, but the thought of this hell finally being over brought me some measure of serenity.

Click.

Nothing.

He'd pulled the trigger, but there was no bullet in the chamber.

Brian dropped the gun, pushed me into the wall, kicked over the coffee table.

"What the fuck is wrong with you?!" he yelled. "You crazy fucking bitch!"

Adrenaline coursed through me, and I started shaking. Not even sure what I was doing, I picked up my cell phone and took a picture of the coffee table, then walked out the door, shut it behind me, and headed to my car.

"911, what is your emergency?"

"My husband, I'm worried about him. I'm afraid he's going to hurt himself. He's a combat vet and has PTSD. Can you send someone to check on him? I'm leaving. I don't feel safe."

The operator asked for our address. Soon a police car pulled up. I tried to explain that Brian was a good man but had flashbacks from the wars. I asked them not to hurt him, just to check on him.

Then I left.

Threw my car into reverse, turned the wheel, and drove off as the cops walked down the sidewalk toward our apartment building. I went to a hotel.

Curled in a strange bed with crisp white sheets, I cried until I felt completely drained, spent, emptied. Then I rolled onto my back and stared at the ceiling as the tears dried and salt crusted on my face, wondering if I'd ever go home.

9.

THE TURN

When I woke up the next morning, my face was gritty with salt, my eyes sore and red. Going home right away was not an option—I felt open and raw, completely unable to engage with Brian. After briefly contemplating staying curled up in a ball all day long in the hotel room refusing to move, I decided it would be better to get out and see other people. Luckily, I already had plans.

Brian and I had been going indoor rock climbing at a local gym. It was more interesting and challenging than standard weight lifting, involving the brain as well as the body. And it was an athletic activity where his size and strength didn't give him an automatic advantage over me. We'd taken a class together, and the instructor had immediately noticed that Brian had balance issues. The injury had damaged Brian's inner ear, making plane rides unbearable—every minor pitch and yaw felt like the plane was wobbling wildly out of control. Most people would never be able to tell, but this guy, an expert climber trained in watching how other people move, could tell right away that something was off.[1]

---

1. Brian's jaw muscle had also been damaged, and his speech was very slightly impaired for several years. People who had known him before noticed it, but

During the class, he had us attempt one climb blindfolded—and I'd done significantly better that way. It fascinated me to get concrete evidence of how my own brain could undermine me: looking at a challenging section, my mind would say, "There's no way you can do that," and I couldn't. When the visual clues were taken away and I was forced to rely simply on the evidence my body gave me, my capabilities were almost miraculously enhanced. I loved the combination of mental and physical challenge.

Carrie, a woman I'd served with in Iraq, had recently moved to the area. She'd been on my team during the drive from Mosul to Kuwait; we shared indelible memories of our experiences together. Carrie and I had plans to go to the rock climbing gym together so she could try it, too. Spending time with her might settle my mind, I thought, and would let me put off dealing with Brian. Besides, I didn't even know if he'd remember last night. Not to mention that I didn't know if I wanted to go home. "Maybe," I said to myself, "I'll finally walk away."

Putting on my game face, I smiled brightly when I saw her. "Let's do this!"

"How's Brian?" she asked.

I shook my head and rolled my eyes. "I don't want to talk about it. Let's just say I really need this!"

Carrie rented gear and I worked the safety rope as she climbed. When she came back down, she was flushed and sweaty but smiling. I grinned back, knowing how she felt: in Iraq, we regularly got into situations when adrenaline coursed through our bodies. It became so normal that being back in America where everything was safe actually felt abnormal, and we ended up unconsciously seeking out the rush. Troops freshly back from the war would often drive fast,

---

strangers did not. The exception was non-native speakers of English, who had a noticeably difficult time understanding him.

buy motorcycles—the recklessness actually led to higher death rates at home, in many cases, than on deployment—certainly higher than before the unit deployed.[2] An awesome aspect of rock climbing was being able to do something that felt dangerous and delivered that adrenaline fix but was actually relatively safe.

Since she wasn't certified, Carrie couldn't belay me, feeding out rope or taking up the slack so if I lost my footing I wouldn't tumble down the wall. I decided to try bouldering, where you free-climb lower to the ground. It was a different challenge than climbing the vertical wall, and when I reached a point where I couldn't go any farther, I let go and fell to the mat. I was positioned poorly above it, and my foot turned under me as I landed. There was a sickening *crunch* and stabbing pain.

"Dude, are you okay?" Carrie asked.

Our time together in the Army kicked in, and I gritted out a smile: "I think so." I tried to get up and promptly fell on my ass. "Maybe not. I think I'm done for the day."

She helped me up. I hobbled toward the door but had to stop and sit down every few steps as my field of vision narrowed and I literally saw stars. "Maybe I should go to the hospital. It could just be a sprain, but I should get an X-ray. Can you drive me?"

"Of course!" she said.

We never thought to ask for help—we were Army vets. Tough girls. The staff were horrified that we'd kept silent about the fall and insisted I sign a liability waiver.

In the car, I tried to breathe slowly and steadily, control the pain,

---

2. http://maketheconnection.net/symptoms/reckless-behavior, http://www.msnbc.msn.com/id/43780686/ns/us_news-life/t/coaster-death-shows-risks-vets-thrill-seeking/#.UN2w2aWE-fQ, http://www.nytimes.com/2010/10/17/us/17bcvets.html?pagewanted=all

hold it together. Carrie had been one of my soldiers; I couldn't look weak in front of her.

Fuck.

My military ID, I suddenly remembered, was at home—it was my insurance card.

I had to call Brian. Thank god Carrie was still active duty, so we could at least get through the gate and get to the hospital.

Brian didn't pick up immediately, so I called again. And again. And again. Finally he answered, sounding groggy. "Why are you calling this early?"

"I need you to bring my ID and meet me at the hospital."

"What?!"

"I fell rock climbing and might have broken my ankle. Carrie is driving me to the ER at Andrews Air Force Base, but I don't have my ID. You have to bring it, Brian."

"Is this a joke, Kayla?"

"No, why?"

"You sound completely calm."

"It's not a joke, Brian. Please meet me at the ER."

"I'll be right there."

"Don't forget my ID!"

Carrie tried to make small talk, and I made a pretense of participating through clenched teeth. When we finally pulled up in front of the ER, Brian was there waiting to help me into the waiting room. As soon as Carrie was gone, I stopped holding back and started crying—I'd never experienced excruciating pain like this. I suffered through the wait, the exam, and the X-rays for five and a half hours, tears trickling slowly down my face the entire time, until they finally gave me morphine. Brian was a champ, only leaving my side to get coffee and snacks, trying to distract me, comforting me. We didn't talk about the night before. I didn't know if he could even remember what had happened—was he simply repressing his rage, waiting until we got home to erupt? Or was he totally unaware of what had happened, oblivious to the awkwardness of me leaning on him for comfort and support after what happened less than twenty-four hours before?

It was a bad break, and I narrowly escaped getting pins put in the bone. After putting the cast on my right leg, the doctor laid out the instructions: keep it elevated, take pain meds, no driving, no getting it wet. For six weeks. The morphine was kicking in, and none of this fully registered with me. I just wanted to go home.

Once we got back to the apartment, Brian helped me settle on the couch and brought pillows to prop up my leg. He made dinner and brought it into the living room. Gingerly, I asked, "Do you remember last night?"

"No," he said, "but it must have been fucked up. I had a brutal hangover when you called, and the coffee table was knocked over. What happened?"

I swallowed hard. No point in putting it off. "We had a pretty bad fight. I called the cops and spent the night in a hotel room. I wasn't sure I'd come back today."

My husband stared at me. "You called the cops on me? Did I get arrested?"

"No. I was afraid you were going to hurt yourself. They just checked on you. I'm sorry, Brian, but it was so scary, I didn't know what else to do. You put a gun to my head."

He was uncharacteristically solicitous. "It's okay. We'll get through this."

Later, he moved all the pillows back to the bed and helped me into the bedroom. I drifted easily into a narcotic-induced sleep and knew nothing until he was shaking me awake. My face was wet with tears; my leg had slid off the pillows. "You were moaning in your sleep. Are you okay?"

The pain was brutal. "My pain pills! I need a painkiller! Oh my god, it hurts so much!" Brian jumped up and came back with my prescription and a glass of water, then stroked my hair comfortingly until the drugs kicked in and I dozed back off.

The next morning, he helped me into the living room and settled me back on the couch. "What do you want for breakfast?" he asked.

"Um...Can you make me some eggs?" I asked reluctantly. I was so used to being the one to do everything; it made me uncomfortable requesting what felt like a favor.

"Sure. How do you want them?" I had been afraid I'd be trying to balance on crutches while cooking or carrying hot coffee, but Brian stepped up to care for me without complaint.

The next evening, he squeezed into our tiny bathroom with me, a drawstring plastic bag tied above my cast. "This is so embarrassing!" I protested as he lowered me into the bathtub. "I hate it!"

"Why? You're my wife. I've seen you naked before."

"But...I *hate* being so needy!"

He grimaced. "How do you think I've felt the past year and a half? You know, it's kinda nice to get to take care of you for once, see that you're human."

"What does *that* mean?!"

"Kayla, guys like to be needed. *I* like to be needed."

"Wouldn't you rather I just love you instead of *needing* you?"

"Can't it be both?" he asked.

I frowned and pondered this as he left me to soak in the tub. What *had* it been like for him, so many pieces of his identity stripped away, forced to rely on me, let me take over his bills and so many other aspects of his life because he couldn't manage them anymore? He'd forgotten to make payments on his dirt bike for so long that it had gone to collections; I'd had to pay it off for him before we were married to save his credit rating. Had that made him feel like less of a man?

How threatening was it to his sense of self to go from being needed to needy? It had only been a couple days and I was already chafing at the embarrassment of needing someone to take care of me. And I knew that as a woman it was more acceptable for me to be helpless than it was for men—it had to be even worse for Brian. Had my fixation on getting shit done overwhelmed the empathy I should have felt for him? Was it somehow going to be good for our relationship that I was being forced now to let him become my knight in shining armor, able to rescue me?

The days bled into weeks, and I did not accept the new situation gracefully. I was a cranky, crotchety patient. Unable to run, I tried the hand bike at the gym to get some exercise but abandoned it in frustration after one uncomfortable session. I hated it and couldn't dig up the motivation to force myself to keep it up. But my eating habits didn't change, and I could tell I was gaining weight—though not from the fit of my clothes; I'd worn nothing but sweatpants for weeks.

The enforced immobility and lack of purpose began to take their toll on all aspects of my motivation, and I stopped answering emails—or doing anything at all, really. I spent hours lying on the couch watching *Judging Amy* reruns. Brian ran errands, went shopping, even took in a couple of hard-core music shows. He seemed to be thriving as I stagnated; he even stood up straighter and looked more confident, self-assured—more like the man I fell in love with. Ever since that night, he hadn't gotten drunk. Brian still had a couple of beers every couple of days, but nothing like the binge drinking he had been doing.

"Need anything before I go out, kiddo?" he asked one day before going to a football game with his uncle, ruffling my hair.

"Don't patronize me!" I responded testily.

Brian didn't take the bait and snap back at me as he once might have. I was needy and a little lonely—a storm had rendered me afraid to navigate the icy sidewalks on crutches, and I hadn't been outside for days. There was a glass of water on the table; it was just beyond my fingertips. I looked at my husband imploringly. He looked at my hand, the glass, my body reclining on the couch. Raised an eyebrow. "Really?" he asked, "Are you kidding?" He shook his head, pushed it toward me, and left me there, petulant and pouting.

I called Zoe to whine. "What's up?!" she asked cheerfully. I told her how I'd been spending my days, watching TV, refusing to exercise, feeling sorry for myself. "Huh, sounds like Brian when we were still at the 101st," she commented.

I was floored. She was right. Not only had Brian and I reversed roles as giver and accepter of care, but in virtually every other way. Laid up and in pain, I had slid into exactly the pattern he had lived in Kentucky—depressed, sedentary, letting debility in one area bleed into all other areas of life. Only when my own relatively minor injury stopped me from taking care of us both had Brian shaken off his torpor. Now I was filling the empty spot he had left on the couch, and I hated it.

"I've got to get a fucking job," I said, "something to get me off my ass and out of the damned house!"

$$\sim$$

WE WERE BOTH ON unemployment and had to prove that we were searching for jobs. Since I had a job offer already and was just waiting for my security clearance to transfer over—a bureaucratic issue over which I had no control—I found this frustrating. With my leg in a cast, I was also hindered in my ability to go to job fairs and nervous it would hurt my chances of actually getting hired somewhere if I showed up for an interview on crutches. Nonetheless, I kept emailing out my résumé, filling out online applications, taking Arabic tests at home when potential employers expressed interest. Not only was this a requirement of being on unemployment, but I had no idea when or if the paperwork would clear and I'd be able to start the job I'd been offered. Brian assured me he was hunting for a job, too.

I also buckled down and started studying for the GRE. Getting money for graduate school had been one of the main reasons I'd joined the Army—it was time to press forward with the long-term plan. But my last scores were expired; it had been well over five years since I'd last taken the test. Math had never been my strong suit, and since I hadn't taken a math class in a decade, it seemed likely my score on that section would decline from the painfully mediocre one I'd earned the first time. I bought a remedial math book and literally started over again with basic arithmetic. Having goals to focus on helped drag me out of the depression that was gnawing at me: the mere act of working toward a long-term goal forced me to acknowledge that I had a future.

Brian seemed to be coming to that realization, too. When we'd been dating, he had mentioned a few times that he doubted he would live to see thirty. It wasn't clear to me whether this was the result of three combat tours and the fatalism that can bring, the sense of a foreshortened future that is a symptom of PTSD, or simply the posturing of a young man, but it had come up whenever I pressured him to make decisions about the future. Questions that to me seemed simple, like "Are you saving for retirement?" or even "Where do you want to go for Christmas next year, my parents' or yours?" seemed to baffle him. He'd shrug them off, unwilling or unable to think that far into the future. But this year he had turned thirty, and was obviously still alive. We'd bought plane tickets to spend Christmas in Colorado with his daughter well in advance.

And we kept those plans, even though I was still on crutches and we were unemployed when the dates rolled around. The tickets were nonrefundable; I was convinced my job would start before too long. And how long could it take for Brian's VA disability rating to be processed, anyway? Surely that would come through soon. I wanted desperately for us to be a normal family, a good family, a nice middle-class family going on a ski vacation over the holidays. My brother and sister were both going to be at Breckenridge with their kids; Brian and I both had family in the Denver area—this was what normal people did, right? Spent time with their families on the holidays? Went skiing?

"You look like a mountain man," I said as we waited for Sonja to get off her flight, running my fingers through Brian's hair. The day after he'd retired from the Army, Brian had stopped shaving and cutting his hair. "I spent over a decade following AR670-1," he said, "I'm fucking done." The rules on appearance laid out in the Army regulation are precise: men's sideburns may not extend "below the bottom of the ear opening," beards are forbidden, hair must be short and "tapered"; women's hair may not extend below the bottom edge of the collar, fingernails may not be "fire engine red," makeup must not be "trendy." By the time we got to Colorado, Brian had a full beard and head of hair.

"I don't care!" he said.

"I'm not complaining!" I replied. "It's just . . . different."

When Sonja walked into the waiting area with a flight attendant, she eyed him suspiciously. "Daddy?" she said uncertainly, hanging back.

"Yeah, honey, it's me," he said.

Once she heard his voice, she ran into his arms. I breathed a sigh of relief—for a moment, I'd feared the airline employees would whisk her away from this strange, shaggy man she didn't even recognize.

We linked up with my sister and headed to the car rental counter—and a major problem. With my right leg in a cast, they wouldn't let me pick up the car I'd reserved. And Brian's driver's license had expired. "How could you let that happen?" I hissed under my breath.

"I have a brain injury!" he shot back.

Biting my lip angrily, I sorted through options. My sister ended up renting the car, and would drive us out to our cousin's place to borrow their van. Brian had been able to renew his license by phone while we worked it all out, so if he got pulled over it would show up properly in the computer; he wasn't breaking the law by driving—but it hadn't been enough for the car rental company. Everything seemed more complicated than it needed to be. I briefly wondered whether all the little tasks of daily life, like remembering when to renew Brian's driver's license, were now my responsibility.

ONCE WE WERE HOME and the credit card bills started showing up, I wanted us to get our shit together. I made Brian return a pair of diamond earrings he'd gotten me for Christmas. "Honey, they're beautiful—but we just can't afford them right now." The pressure was mounting for at least one of us to get a job fast—the unemployment checks barely covered our rent, and didn't leave enough for any other bills. We were putting groceries on the credit card. Embarrassed, I called a contact at the government agency that had to adjudicate my clearance. "Is there anything you can do? Anyone you can call to speed up the process?" Whether or not my friend had been able to pull some strings, within days of me reaching out I got a phone call to schedule a time for me to come in and take the counterintelligence polygraph.

I took the GRE, improving my score on the math section. The logic section—on which I'd done exceptionally well years before—was gone, replaced by a writing portion. I got an average score on that, which seemed directly related to my time in the military: Army writing is focused on being clear and comprehensible at about the eighth-grade level, and there are strict rules prohibiting the passive voice and restricting the use of semicolons. Still, I'd done well enough to feel confident applying to graduate school, and I worked through the lengthy application packets for the international relations programs at Georgetown and American.

I passed the counterintelligence polygraph test and soon got a start date for my new job. My anxiety over our finances started to ease. We could get off unemployment; I could support us.

Excited and relieved, I started going through the closet. "What the hell am I going to wear?" I asked Brian. I'd spent the past five years either in a uniform or in jeans. Right before the book came out, I'd bought a couple of professional outfits, but they weren't enough for five days a week. And I felt terribly insecure about picking the right clothes. "What do women even wear to work in an office?"

"How the fuck should I know?" he asked.

I enlisted his aunt's help in a shopping trip. Everything seemed wrong—too tight, too short, no cargo pockets...And expensive. My starting salary was twice what I'd made in the Army and put us solidly in an upper-middle-class tax bracket, but I couldn't shake the *feeling* of being poor. "Twenty dollars for a shirt? That's ridiculous," I said. Growing up, the local thrift store had sales when you could fill a paper bag with clothes for two dollars—as much as you could cram in, the price stayed the same. Ten times that for one item? Absurd.

"Um, that's fairly standard," his aunt gently explained. "And it looks good on you. It goes with the suit you picked out. Get it."

I sighed. Being a civilian woman still felt awkward. "I'm not good at this," I moaned.

At my new job, about half the contractors were prior military and half were native speakers of various target languages. I'd even been in the same unit as one of the guys there. It was comforting to see a familiar face and be around lots of other veterans. We spoke the same language, had similar attitudes, carried ourselves the same way. Jumped at the same unexpected loud noises. "I can do this," I told Brian.

"Of course you can," he said.

"Well, you know," I said, pausing in embarrassment, "I wasn't sure I'd be able to fit in with a bunch of civilians. But since half my coworkers are prior service, it doesn't feel weird at all. I feel comfortable."

——

NOT LONG AFTER I started working, Brian got his disability rating from the VA. Their rating system was profoundly different from the Army's. VA rated him completely disabled for PTSD alone, with additional service-connected ratings for the skull defect and brain loss, pain and limited movement in his jaw, macular hole/bruise resulting in vision changes, and tinnitus, all from the IED—so 100 percent plus special compensation since the total rating would be well above that. It was a relief to see his suffering and debilities validated after the Army's infuriating decision. At the same time, reading the VA's reasoning, laid out in coldly clinical language, was depressing:

> VA examination dated January 3, 2006 diagnosed you with post traumatic stress disorder with a global assessment of functioning of 51. You are unable to be employed at this time due to the results of this current condition, according to the examining doctor. PTSD symptoms are currently interfering with job searches. Lack of motivation keeps you from submitting applications. You are afraid about your ability to do a job. You have trouble with authority, interacting with others, and significant anger-management problems.
>
> Some of your symptoms are nightmares, flashbacks, disrupted sleep, excessive drinking, intrusive thoughts, avoidance

of stimuli, hypervigilance, exaggerated startle response, anxiety attacks, depression, lack of motivation, feelings of worthlessness and hopelessness, low esteem, decreased concentration, memory loss, decreased libido and appetite.

You have no close friends, are prone to verbal and physical confrontations.

Based on the evidence above, we have granted service connection for post traumatic stress disorder at the 100 percent evaluation effective November 30, 2005, the day after you were discharged from the service.

Most of the symptoms were familiar to me from living with him. I zeroed in on one in particular. "What does that mean," I asked, "the part about job searches that says 'lack of motivation keeps you from submitting applications'? Haven't you been applying for jobs?"

He shook his head.

"But how are you getting unemployment checks?" I asked. Actively searching for a job was a condition of being on unemployment.

"I dunno," he answered.

I sighed in frustration but let it go. No point in arguing about it now—he could get off unemployment now that he was going to start getting disability payments and I had a job. It was a tremendous relief to see our financial crisis coming to an end—we'd had no idea how long the decision would take, and waiting was nerve-wracking. But we were also both shaken by reading the VA decision language. Like the Army, VA did not consider this a permanent evaluation— psychological problems can improve. He might get better. But what if he was truly doomed to a life of being only 51 percent functional? The money would save us from disaster, but where was the plan for recovery? Rather than just delivering cash benefits, shouldn't the VA be working to help him get better? Or were we on our own?

NOT LONG AFTER THAT, Brian was able to get a job at REI, a sporting goods store. "It's just retail," he said, "but it's something, right?" I agreed readily. Sitting around doing nothing was psychologically terrible for both of us—we need external purpose, direction, and motivation. He started shaving again and cut his hair.

"How do you like your job?" I asked after a few days.

"It's a job." His fingers started tapping out patterns. "I can't believe I'm working retail, you know? I'm thirty years old, working with a bunch of college kids. But we need the money. So..." he shrugged.

"Do you lose your disability?" I asked.

"No," he said. "I mean, we don't even know if I can keep the job! VA will reevaluate me in a year or something, and we'll see what they say then."

It was a weird feeling, to both hope and fear the results of that reexamination—to pray he would magically be completely cured, while simultaneously worrying what it would mean for us financially if he lost the rating. Besides, what if he got worse again? Just in the past year, I'd seen him do great for weeks, and then spiral out of control. What if he did better for a couple of years and they evaluated him as all better on the PTSD front, and then he lost it again, couldn't keep his job, stopped getting off the couch, started drinking heavily, got violent?

"What happened to the gun?" I asked suddenly.

"Huh?" he asked.

"The gun. What happened to the gun?"

"I got rid of it," Brian said.

I cocked my head quizzically.

He sighed. "I took it apart and took the pieces to the park and threw them into different places. Firing pin in one place. Body in the lake. Spring somewhere else. No one can put it back together. It's gone."

I nodded. That was for the best. We shouldn't have a gun in the house.

VAN NUYS LIBRARY

6250 Sylmar Ave.
Van Nuys, CA 91401
(818) 756-8453
www.lapl.org

Hours of Operation:

Monday & Wednesday	**10 am – 8 pm**
Tuesday & Thursday	**12 noon – 8 pm**
Friday & Saturday	**9:30 am – 5:30 pm**
Sunday & Holidays	**Closed**

10.

FRESH START

———— ★ ————

Our lease was up. We had to move, which was just as well: my commute was stressing me out within two weeks of starting my job. After sitting on the Beltway for hours every day, I ended up pounding on my dashboard screaming, "This is why they don't let us keep our weapons when we get back from Iraq, you assholes—I would fucking shoot you!" We wanted to be somewhere with a better commute, where we'd be closer to friends, and have more room for Brian's daughter Sonja when she came to visit. Brian got one more move paid for by the Army now that he was retired.

After searching for a couple of weeks we found a single-family home in Arlington that seemed perfect. The rent was twice what we were paying for our apartment, but it was more than twice the space and seemed to meet all our needs. There was a nice yard, a deck and a patio, a finished basement—"a man cave," Brian called it—a master bedroom for us, a bright pink bedroom for Sonja, and another room I could use as an office.

As we boxed up our possessions, I eyed my box of dishes on the kitchen floor. It seemed wrong to bring them to our new house. We were starting over, it wasn't fair to bring them with me—to lug around a box full of doubt. Committing completely to this marriage, to our future, required me to let go of this weighty symbol that I could start over without my husband at any moment. "Let's take these to the thrift store," I said to Brian. "Is there anything else you want to get rid of?"

I lugged them upstairs and hauled them out of the car at the Goodwill store. The box felt heavier than it should. I couldn't help but open it up to look at the dishes one more time. I adored them, the tiny speckling on the top, the rich brown on the bottom. Brian's dishes made an awful screeching noise when you cut food on them, there was an awkward transition between glazes. And that was only a set of eight. This was a full set of twelve! I loved them so much. They were one of the few symbols I had that my parents had ever been happily married other than my own existence. It seemed so unfair to get rid of them just to prove that I was committed to my own husband. But it was the right thing to do. Brian was indifferent to so many things about what we owned, how things were decorated. He wanted his dishes. I wanted him.

Firmly, resolutely, I closed the box and handed it over. Fresh start. No turning back.

"LET'S GET A DOG," Brian had said out of nowhere not long before getting his job. "I've read they can help calm people down. Maybe it would help me with my anxiety attacks. This group used to bring them into Walter Reed so patients could pet them. And we'd have to walk it—I wouldn't be able to just sit around the house, there would be a reason to get out of bed even if I felt depressed."

"Sure," I agreed. "But...I don't want to sound like a bitch, but...I can't be the only one to take care of the dog. If we get a dog, you have to do half the work."

"Of course," he assured me. "No problem! This will be my dog."

We found a woman online who had rescued three German shepherd dogs from a high-kill shelter in North Carolina and was fostering all of them until she could find homes for them. We went out to meet them and one came to me immediately, a calmer female who was a few years old. I liked her immediately.

Brian was drawn to another, younger female who seemed shy but full of energy.

"Which one should we get?" he asked.

"You choose," I said, "Since this is going to be your dog, your comfort animal."

He picked the younger one. She cowered between my legs in the car on our way back to the apartment as we discussed names. "Princess," the name she'd come with, was out of the question. "What about Thisbe?" I suggested. "It's from a Greek myth, the one *Romeo and Juliet* is based on. I love it."

"No way," Brian retorted.

We tossed around ideas. Finally I threw out, "How about Kelby? It means 'my dog' in Arabic, but Americans won't know that—and it sounds pretty."

He agreed. I scratched her ears. "Do you like that name? Kelby. Good girl."

They say dogs are just like their owners. It seems fitting, then, that our dog went crazy.

It took Kelby time to adjust to her new situation. The day we'd brought her home, she'd been terrified to even walk down the stairs to our basement apartment. When we tried to encourage her to sit and cuddle with us, she'd lain on the doggy bed we'd gotten her instead, eyeing us suspiciously. The dog had gone into a crate when we were going to leave the old apartment willingly enough at first; she responded immediately to hand signals we gave accidentally, sitting promptly at the sign of a raised hand and lying down when it was lowered. "I wonder what kind of situation she came from," Brian and I mused regularly.

She warmed up to us slowly. But once Kelby finally decided that she trusted us, she was all in—the poor animal loved us too much. She developed terrible separation anxiety. Left alone, Kelby began to destroy things. On walks, she was aggressive toward other dogs, seeming convinced that all other dogs posed a grave threat to my life. No amount of explanation or reassurance could convince her that I was perfectly capable of protecting myself from five-pound poodles.

We took her to doggy obedience training. It helped—a little. They urged us to crate-train her at home, but when we put her back in the crate, she shredded the dog bed we left in it. Then Kelby started gnawing on the wires of the crate until her gums bled.

We tried just shutting her in the basement instead. One day a stranger called me. "Hi, I have your dog here—your number is on her dog tags—I found her and she came right up to me, but I thought you might want her." I immediately went to retrieve her, then called Brian at work. "Did Kelby get away from you?"

"No," he answered. "Why do you ask?"

"Someone found her outside."

Once we got home, I went to the basement. From what I could piece together from the wreckage, she had jumped up onto a counter in the mini-kitchen area, shattering Brian's collection of shot glasses, trying to get at the garden window on that wall. When she couldn't dislodge it, she had climbed a wall (no, I am not kidding) in another part of the basement and knocked out a window.

At a routine veterinary appointment, she tested positive for heartworm. "But they said she'd just gotten treated for it!" I protested. Either the treatment hadn't worked, or they hadn't been honest about it—but she needed hundreds of dollars of medical care and then a period of enforced inactivity.

"Well," I said, "we committed to caring for her."

One day not long after she had recovered, Brian called me at work. "You won't believe what this fucking dog did," he said. "She flooded the basement."

"What?!"

"Kelby managed to lock herself in the bathroom in the basement. Then she panicked and chewed through the hose that connects the toilet to the wall. I came home and there was four inches of water on the floor; I could hear the water running in the bathroom. I had to pick the lock before I could turn it off."

"Are you joking?" I asked.

"Nope. That's not all. She also bit my laptop screen and cracked it."

I surveyed the damage when I got home. In addition to the hose, Kelby had gnawed off pieces of the shower stall and scratched deep gouges in the door. The entire laptop had to be replaced. There were thousands of dollars' worth of damage.

"I have to tell you," Brian said, "I'm starting to wonder if this is worth it."

"Brian!" I protested. "We can't get rid of her just because she has problems! That's awful!"

"Well, she's really expensive," he said.

"With as much as we've invested in her, now we *have* to keep her," I argued. We were in a classic sunk-costs dilemma. Brian was willing to jettison the whole Kelby project due to the money we'd already lost, while I was banking on the uncertain long-term returns of love and affection we might get.

We tried leaving her in the yard instead, and the neighbors complained that she barked incessantly from the moment we left the house in the morning until we got home in the afternoon. We gave her free run of the house, and she chewed through the curtains to get a clear view of the outside world.

One of the quirks of the house we were renting was that the kitchen was terribly designed. The neighborhood was from the

1950s, and the homes did not meet modern accepted standards in many ways—there was no electrical outlet in the bathroom, for example. The kitchen was tiny, and when it had been remodeled, they hadn't included any pantry space. (Or drawers, for that matter. Who doesn't include drawers in a kitchen?) We were using a small bookshelf as an open pantry area. Kelby would retrieve foodstuffs and chew them open, leaving a trail of breadcrumbs in her wake. Well, a couple of times it was breadcrumbs. Other times it was grated Parmesan cheese. Flour. Bits of potato. Half-chewed onions. She chewed open a bottle of vegetable oil on the futon, forcing us to buy a new mattress. Kelby gnawed the top off a bottle of A.1. sauce on the guest bed, giving us a moment of panic that she'd had horrible diarrhea until the vinegar smell drove a search that turned up the mangled bottle. She seemed to have a special affinity for large sizes freshly purchased at Costco.

The dog howled at sirens.

We lived two blocks from a hospital.

"Seriously, Kayla, we need to think about getting rid of this dog."

"Who is going to take a dog with mental health problems, Brian? We have to keep her. It's not her fault that she's crazy."

Nadean told us we should go on *The Dog Whisperer.* "I'm telling you," she said, "it would be a great episode. A combat-wounded veteran gets a dog to help with his anxiety but the dog causes even more problems. Cesar Millan can come and solve everything!"

I looked it up online—they didn't do house calls in Virginia.

In May 2006, my sister invited me to her son's high school graduation in North Carolina. We took Kelby with us and left her in an industrial-strength crate in our hotel room. When we stopped by to check on her after the ceremony, the hotel door was wide open. "Oh my god, have we been robbed?" I asked.

Brian pushed me behind him protectively. "Let me check it out."

He went in to check the room, then called me in to join him. "It's Kelby," he said. "She's gone."

"What?"

She had managed to break the crate—rated for a dog twice her weight. Then she tore down the window curtain, and was finally able to jostle the flapper-style handle and open the door. Kelby had escaped.

We called the police and animal control, then headed to my nephew's party. "Surely she'll turn up," we assured each other.

The next day, we learned that she'd probably been sighted a couple of miles away. A car had clipped a dog matching her description running across a busy road, but the driver had been unable to catch her. Employees of a Waffle House had spotted her nearby, favoring a leg. We spent hours walking through the woods behind the restaurant in the drizzling rain calling for her. Back in the hotel room, I cried in Brian's arms while we tried to figure out what to do.

"I have to go back to work," I said. "But what if we leave and they find her? We'll just have to turn right around and come back."

"Listen, if we stay here they'll never find her. That's just how things go—'A watched pot never boils.' We should go home. When they find her, we'll figure it out from there."

So we left. At home, I got photos of her together and started working on a flyer to send my nephew. Then the deputy sheriff who had been helping us called.

"Your dog has been found. Kelby went into a ditch near a car dealership to get some water and couldn't get back out; the owner spotted her and called animal control. She's at the vet now, you can call them to find out how she's doing."

The vet sounded grim. "The leg is very badly injured. I don't know if it can be saved. Do you want me to amputate or do you want to take her to your vet?"

We decided to bring her home. My nephew picked her up and met us halfway. When we got her from the backseat of his car, she looked terrible—too high on painkillers and malnourished from three days hiding in the woods to do more than feebly lift her head and thump her tail twice in recognition.

Back in Virginia, our vet referred us immediately to an emergency clinic. After they evaluated her, they sat us down. "The rear right leg has suffered a de-gloving injury: all the skin was ripped off, and the tendons have been detached. An infection has set in; the smell was terrible as soon as we removed the bandage. We have her on IV fluids, antibiotics, and painkillers. You have to decide whether to amputate or try to keep the leg. Dogs usually recover well from amputations. If you try to salvage the limb, it would require multiple skin grafts, external stabilization, and repeated surgeries over a period of months." He explained the options in detail—several thousand dollars to amputate, tens of thousands of dollars to attempt limb salvage—and left us alone to think.

"Do you think it's worth—" Brian said gently.

"Yes!" I retorted sharply. "She's young, otherwise healthy—of course. We can't put her to sleep. If she had internal injuries, was in tremendous pain, might die, it would be a different conversation. But this is just a leg."

"Okay, okay."

Staring at Brian, I was amazed that he didn't seem to be making the connection I was between their experiences. We had committed to this animal, just as I had committed to him—we couldn't abandon her because she was difficult or injured. She was part of our family now. You don't discard a loved one in a time of need. Just as I'd stood by him during the worse stages of his recovery, now the two of us had to stand by Kelby.

We agreed to amputate. "How much is a doggy prosthesis?" I joked.

"About thirty to forty thousand dollars," the vet replied seriously.

We burst out laughing. "She can be a tripod."

A few days later, we brought her home.

The vet warned us that we'd have to support her hindquarters with a towel while she urinated and defecated until she learned to balance. Then the vet tech brought her out. "Not this one," she said brightly. "She already figured it out! Kelby is a trooper. I've never seen such a fast recovery."

Kelby whined and wagged her tail, leaning against us one at a time.

To keep her from trying to follow me up and down the stairs like she would if we stayed upstairs, all of us stayed in the basement until she was better recovered—there was a TV, bathroom, and bed down there. Although we'd never let her get on the bed before, in the wake of her trauma we relaxed the rules, snuggling her between us as we slept.

For the first three nights, she had nightmares, yelping and kicking violently in her sleep until we woke and soothed her.

"Does our fucking *dog* have PTSD?" I asked. "Are you kidding me?"

"Figures," Brian said. "It just fucking figures."

<hr />

THAT FALL, I STARTED graduate school at the American University in D.C., studying international relations with a focus on the Middle East. When I applied for my education benefits from the VA, I was also in for a rude surprise: although my enlistment paperwork clearly said "Montgomery GI Bill + $50,000 Army College Fund," my actual entitlement was the Montgomery GI Bill plus the Army College Fund for a total of $50,000—a difference of tens of thousands of dollars. When I pressed for more information, I learned that I could appeal based on the misleading documentation—but the appeals board decided that unless my recruiter was willing to admit that he promised the higher amount, I was screwed. Frustrated, I gave up—no way would a recruiter admit to something like that, if I could even find him after all these years. "BOHICA," I said to Brian. Bend over, here it comes again—a common saying in the Army, almost up there with SNAFU (situation normal—all fucked up). So although my main motivation for joining the Army had been finding a way to pay for grad school so I wouldn't have to work full-time while I went to school full-time, my decision to attend a pricey private school in an expensive city, coupled with this bureaucratic letdown, shattered that dream.

"Well," I told myself, "if I could handle a year in Iraq, I can handle this." It would take ruthless discipline, but we would manage. Monday through Friday, I worked 6:30 a.m. to 3 p.m. Then two days a week I headed to campus straight from the office, hit the gym for a brief workout, and then sat in class for hours. I tried to appreciate the beautiful campus—designed by Frederick Law Olmsted (the same guy who designed Central Park)—and enjoy the intellectual opportunities opening up before me. But I was immediately overwhelmed by the effort required to simply stay afloat.

My first day of class, the professor threw out, "Surely you are all familiar with the formation of the state." I glanced around. Some of my fellow students were nodding. Others had the same deer-in-the-headlights expression that must have graced my own face. None were speaking up. I raised my hand. "Actually, sir, I'm not. I was a lit major in undergrad, so this is all new to me." A few others murmured in agreement, looking relieved. He posted a list of foundational materials for us to get familiar with.

Over the next few weeks, it became clear that there was a mix of grad students in the School of International Service: those who came straight from undergrad and others like me who had worked for a few years and were now coming back to further our educations. I felt nothing in common with those who had continued without a break. They—and the undergrads in some of the cross-listed courses—were often from privileged backgrounds and seemed to understand nothing about the world as it actually functioned, as opposed to how it might operate theoretically. They looked painfully young. And college students seemed to have changed significantly in the near-decade since I'd been an undergrad. Back then, I'd dutifully called my parents once a week and had lunch with my father once a month when he came to town. No one had a cell phone, and the only people I saw with pagers were doctors and drug dealers. Now everyone had a mobile phone, and kids called their parents constantly. "Hi, Mom! We just took a test. I think it went well..." I overheard often. It astonished me. Weren't they happy to get away from home, to get to figure out who they were independently? As a combat veteran, married, with a job and responsibilities, I felt completely disconnected from them.

I felt more comfortable around the other students who, like me, had been out of the ivory tower. American University's School of International Service has a somewhat more practical than theoretical focus, compared to the other IR programs in the D.C. area, and this was reflected both in the student body—many of whom had already served abroad with NGOs—and the professors, many of whom were adjuncts with experience at the State Department or elsewhere. Only one of my fellow students was also a combat veteran the first year, a male Marine who was still serving. I was almost embarrassed at how much more comfortable I felt around him. And one of my professors had spent years in Iraq, primarily Kurdistan. When I talked to her about where I had been, the people I had met, she knew exactly what I was talking about—and was able to put it into context, to help me understand the history and politics. "Why didn't we know this when we invaded?" I fumed to Brian. "Maybe everything wouldn't have gone to shit if we'd actually known who the fuck we were dealing with."

I struggled with much of the course materials the first semester. Some of the writing was so obtuse that I had to dissect it sentence by sentence, removing all the clauses to grasp the main point and then adding them back in one at a time to get the full meaning. Most of my papers came back with the annotation "Very clear"—leaving me to wonder if that was an insult or a compliment. Was I supposed to be obfuscating my ideas behind jargon and overcomplicated grammar, just to prove I could?

The theory professor who had terrified me that first day was firm: "If you cannot explain what you mean to your grandmother, you are doing a terrible job! Don't hide behind your words," he exhorted us. I clung to this reassurance and pushed on. And as I learned the language of international relations and the conventions of graduate-level writing, it became easier. After I got my grades for the first semester and they were all decent, I was convinced that the coursework was manageable—if the rest of my life was.

That wasn't so certain.

BEFORE I'D STARTED CLASSES, Brian and I had discussed the sacrifices it would entail for me to go to grad school. "You understand I'll be gone a lot," I'd said, "right? And when I'm home, I'll have a lot of schoolwork to do. I can't do all the housework anymore. I can't do most of the cooking. You have to step up, shoulder more of the household chores. This is an investment in our future—I'll be able to earn more once I have a master's—but I can't do it on my own. I need your help."

"Absolutely," he had sworn. "No problem."

He didn't clean any more than before I started school. When

I called him on it, he threw out what I considered to be bullshit excuses: "I'm too tall to see how dirty the floors are"... "Well, you're the one who wants the house to be clean—you should clean it"... "You're trying to change me—you knew I was like this when we got married." Furious about his inability or unwillingness to step up and fulfill his promise, I lapsed into nagging and snippy comments. He'd lashed out in return. After a few screaming fights, I gave up and hired a cleaning service.

"It's cheaper than a divorce," I told myself. And my friends. "I just don't get it, Zoe! He promised! I'm trying to understand where he's coming from. He probably feels neglected, since I spend so much time in class and on schoolwork—we hardly ever hang out anymore. But it's temporary! If I can just power through, it will only take me two years. Maybe he's feeling insecure that I'm furthering my education. Do you think he's worried that I'll have a master's and he doesn't even have his bachelor's? He says he doesn't care, but maybe he does. And I want to be supportive of his feelings, but I'm just pissed off. He promised! He fucking promised he would help. And he's not doing shit. I don't even know if it matters why. I'm so pissed."

Every few weeks I'd call her from the parking lot to vent. She was home with two babies, struggling to find balance in her own young marriage. "Craig doesn't do any housework either. I'm going to school full-time, and my GI Bill is bringing in just as much as his salary. But he expects me to do all the housework, do all the work raising the kids. Yesterday I put the trash bag in front of the door so he'd remember to take it out when he left for work, and he stepped over it."

"I put the laundry basket at the foot of the stairs and Brian does the same thing! And he told me he's *too tall* to see dirt on the floor."

"That's a total bullshit excuse!"

"But wait," I said. "Are you saying we're arguing about the same things with our husbands? I've been blaming a lot of this on Brian's TBI and PTSD—but maybe that isn't it. Maybe this is just normal marriage stuff. How do I tell the difference anymore?"

BRIAN WAS DOING MUCH better in many ways. Contrary to what his case manager had said about how improvements would only come in the first eighteen months, we were seeing new cognitive gains now that he was working. Brian's job wasn't glamorous. But it was a return to the normal world, and he began to relearn how to live in it. After a few months of stocking shelves, he applied for the Inventory Specialist position that opened up. "I probably won't get it," he said, quick to downplay his own expectations. But he did—and excelled. Then they made him a primary contact for all the civilian personnel who came in with vouchers to be outfitted for deployments to Iraq or Afghanistan—his experience gave him expertise that was respected and valued.

It was a relatively low-pressure environment, and the company clearly valued its employees. Each success showed him—slowly— that he could still function, contribute, survive. Although he'd been nervous about fitting in outside the military, he made friends. They met up a few times a month to play poker, eat lasagna, and drink beer. The job gave him a purpose and a paycheck he knew he earned. Brian felt he was contributing to our finances, and that helped us maintain the more equalized realignment of power in our marriage.

Time had taught us that sporadic therapy and new medications didn't do much good, and that sudden changes were tremendously destabilizing. Now we discovered that stable routines and increased integration back into society had a steadying effect. Having a set schedule prevented Brian from staying in bed or watching TV all day. Working and making friends helped him feel less hopeless. He was slowly climbing out of the deep hole of depression.

That didn't mean, though, that there weren't setbacks: forgotten appointments, personal conflicts, impulse purchases that caused checks to bounce—and though these were minor in light of how far he had come, Brian's tendency to "catastrophize" made each a major blow. A regular person who forgot to set the alarm clock would simply say, "Shit, I'm going to be fifteen minutes late to work." But when Brian forgot, it led to a panicked, "Shit, they're going to fire me when I show up fifteen minutes late to work today, how are we going to be able to pay our bills when I don't have a job?"

When his coworkers showed up late, *they* weren't fired. But Brian was unable to check his negative worldview against any rational perspective. His constant focus on possible downsides could suck the joy out of life. Me: "Isn't going to the beach going to be fun?" Him: "If it doesn't rain the whole time."

The clash between my attempts to jolly him into a better mood and his chronic state of moderate depression wore on me, as I'm sure it did on him—he called me a "hyper Chihuahua" when I bounced around in the morning trying to get him out of bed.

But the worst times by far were always when he was drinking. After avoiding drunkenness for a few months following the night of the gun, he'd slipped back into old habits. It was unclear to me whether he was actually addicted to alcohol or whether he simply thought he could control his drinking. If he stuck with a couple of beers things were usually fine, but I knew it would be bad when Brian progressed to shots of hard liquor. His ability to hold it together evaporated under the influence of alcohol, and he would shut down and lash out. If we were at home, sometimes I simply walked away and waited until he had slept it off. Other times, we would have screaming fights.

If we were out, though, I had much less ability to manage the situation. One night when we were out with Jason, Nadean, and other friends, I tried again to discourage hard liquor. "Just stick with beer!" I urged.

"You never want to have any fun!" Brian slurred.

I pursed my lips, nervous and tense. It was a fine line—if I managed the situation *just right*, sometimes I could gently ease him back from the brink. Sometimes I could lure him home with the promise of sex. Other times, nothing worked—he would be too deep into the euphoria of drinking that came right before the turn. One night after he almost started a fight that would have embroiled all our friends and a whole group of other people, Jason and the other guys were forced to practically drag him from the bar. On the way back to the car, Brian crashed through bushes, sustaining cuts and scrapes everywhere, then staggered down the middle of the road screaming profanities at the cars that honked while they swerved to avoid him. We finally all piled into Nadean's minivan, dragging Brian with us—Nadean hardly drank, so was always the designated driver—and headed back to Jason's apartment.

Once we were there, I got a beer and went out on the balcony to smoke and collect myself. I was mortified and scared about what might happen when we got home later. Would there be another screaming fight?

Nadean slipped out to join me. "Are you okay?" she asked.

I grimaced. "Embarrassed. Sorry you have to see him like this."

She squeezed my arm. "It's okay. I understand. And I'm used to it."

"Really?"

"Yeah." Nadean smiled at me sympathetically. "We hung out with Brian a lot before you got here. I've seen him do this before. One time after he started talking shit to some people in a bar, I almost ended up in a fistfight with some girl!"

I hid my face behind my hand, flushing with embarrassment. "Sorry."

"Don't be! I get it. I . . . had a personal tragedy when I was young. I've struggled with PTSD too. The first time I met Brian, I could see it in his eyes. You could just tell he was in so much pain. When I found out he was getting married, I wondered about the woman who was going to marry him, if she knew what she was in for. Then I met you, Kayla, and realized you were really tough and you'd be able to hold your own—to take care of both of you. We all know that Brian's a good guy who is just fighting some serious demons— and that he gets bad when he drinks."

We hugged. It was a relief to talk to someone who understood.

OVERALL, I KNEW OBJECTIVELY that we were doing better. Our finances were in order. Brian was holding down a job, seemed to be improving. Our fights were less frequent. But there were still moments when I fantasized about leaving. It could get so draining, always worrying something would go terribly wrong, fearing a crisis.

And the worst part for me was actually not the vicious arguments—a warped little part of me saw the extreme emotion as proof of the depth of his love and passion—but the coldness. The PTSD intersected with alcohol and Brian's notion of manliness to prevent him from showing softness—what he construed to be weakness. So if I broke down crying from a particularly vicious remark or from fear that things would never really be better, he never apologized, never knelt down to hold me, never reassured me. Even though I tried to tell myself that desiring those things was stupid, irrational, weak, it didn't matter. My logical mind knew no one could truly promise that everything would be okay, but a childlike part of me longed to hear my life partner say it. And though the strong woman and tough feminist in me knew I could stand on my own, there was a vulnerable part of me that longed for my husband to sweep me up, nestle me close, and comfort me with his strength.

But on the good days, we were fighting back against that coldness and anger, turning to research on the overlap of TBI, PTSD, and major depression. Finding out that those recovering from TBI needed extra sleep, I stopped trying to get him out of bed early. He learned to carry his anxiety and pain meds the way he once did his rifle, never out of reach. Rather than suffering in silence, he spoke up to our friends when we were out, asking to sit with his back to the wall where he felt secure and could monitor the exits. We reached a sort of equilibrium where our problems seemed manageable, merely the mundane issues between any normal couple. Our explosive arguments decreased from weekly to monthly to every now and then.

This was enormous progress. Still, I often wondered if this was as good as it would get. Brian was bonding with his coworkers, but I was having a hard time connecting with civilian women, with whom I felt terribly awkward and out of place. Other than Nadean, I just seemed to have so little in common with them. One of Brian's coworkers was getting married and had invited us to the wedding. His fiancée very kindly invited me to the bachelorette party. While I was there, I went out on the balcony to smoke with some of the other guests. One of them rested her hand on a shelf next to a bird's nest. A startled bird flew off, and the woman freaked out. After shrieking, she said, "That's the scariest thing that's ever happened to me in my life!" I laughed. "No, I am serious!" she said. "That is literally the most frightening thing that has happened to me in my entire life."

I blinked at her in astonishment. Despite having my own mild bird phobia, I found this reaction completely disproportionate. What did we possibly have to talk about after that admission? I'd been to war, taken direct and indirect fire, watched a man bleed to death, pointed a loaded weapon at people, peered at trash in the road fearing IEDs . . . and the scariest thing she'd ever experienced was being startled by a tiny bird? Standing there smoking, I'd rarely felt so completely out of place. It made me wonder if I would ever fit into the civilian world again, ever be able to make friends with normal women.

And I still doubted we would ever be able to have children: there was too much volatility in our relationship. Brian could tell I wasn't fully satisfied, and if I complained about something—even a tiny matter like him putting too much sugar in my coffee—he would half-jokingly say, "I bet your next husband will get it right."

"Why don't you try going to VA?" I suggested. "You're doing so much better, but maybe they can help you go even farther. Go to counseling or get some rehab. Remember how that case manager asked why you never went to rehab? Maybe you can get some at VA, and do even better."

He came back from an appointment at the D.C. VA Medical Center visibly shaken. "It was awful. Traffic sucked, so I was already stressed out by the time I got there. Then when I first walked in, there were veterans who are obviously homeless, and crazy guys sitting there rocking back and forth and drooling on themselves in the lobby. Is that my future?"

"No, honey, no." I reached out, rubbed his shoulder. Brian flinched and started the finger tapping. "How was the medical side of things?" I asked, trying to gently shift his focus.

He shook his head. "It was totally fucked up. I went to where I was told to go, the green clinic. They said I was in the wrong place and sent me to the silver clinic. Then *they* said I should be in the red clinic. I have no idea what they were talking about. And I didn't know where anything was, but no one would help me figure it out, so I just wandered around lost. When I finally saw a doctor, he told me I should be happy to be alive given the severity of my injuries and that he didn't think they could do anything for me. Fuck it—forget it—I'm not going back."

⁓

ONE EVENING A STORY about the journalist Bob Woodruff came on the news, and we watched attentively. Woodruff had also sustained a TBI in Iraq, and his recovery got lots of media coverage. It was a mixed blessing to see how well he was doing: his progress was inspirational, providing hope about how far Brian might be able to go—but it also triggered insecurity about why Brian wasn't doing better faster, along with frustration that Woodruff had clearly gotten a much higher standard of care.

As his wife Lee spoke, she referred to herself as a "caregiver," and my mind swirled; the room seemed to tilt and sway around me.

I had never thought of myself that way, never realized that there were others like me, that the pressures and stresses I felt might be normal. For years I had been plowing ahead on my own, never putting what we were going through into any context. Her words forced me to think instead of simply reacting.

Should I be getting therapy? Join a support group? Was there anything out there to help me deal with the pressure of managing all our household responsibilities, the strain of trying to help Brian recover without becoming his mother instead of his wife, the mixed emotions—anger at what I was going through and guilt that I was angry at a hero, grief at what might never be, fear that things might get worse? I didn't even know where to start.

Within a few weeks, I got a phone call from VA. As the caller went through a standard script, asking if I'd suffered a blow to the head during my deployment, ever lost consciousness or seen stars, I realized it was a TBI screen—they were trying to find people who had suffered mild TBIs and not been diagnosed. "I didn't sustain a TBI," I told her, "but my husband did. A severe, penetrating one. And things are really difficult. Can you help us? Is there anything to help me? I'm not sure I can keep doing this alone."

"I'm sorry," she said, "but that's not what I'm calling about."

"Figures," I said. Just as the Army had let us down before, I felt that we couldn't count on the VA now. The government that was responsible for sending Brian off to war wasn't going to take care of us—we had to take care of ourselves.

Hearing Lee Woodruff, a stranger, talk about experiences we had in common had also made me realize exactly how isolated Brian and I still were. We had no network other than a handful of supportive friends and family members. It was clear we had to change that—but we didn't know where to begin.

11.

INTO THE LIGHT

I t was a guy I'd served with in Iraq who inadvertently came to the
rescue. I had translated for Brandon when he'd been a platoon
leader in Baghdad; he had been right there when the man bled to
death in front of me. After he got out of the Army, he'd published
his own memoir, *The War I Always Wanted: The Illusion of Glory
and the Reality of War* about his experiences in Afghanistan and Iraq
(like Brian, he had been in Operation Anaconda). In 2007, he was
working for an organization called VoteVets.org that was dedicated
to getting veterans of Iraq and Afghanistan engaged in politics and
elected to public office. When he got in touch out of the blue and
asked if I'd be interested in getting involved, I figured why not: it
was a good cause. And we were feeling so isolated.

Unable to buy a house where we'd been renting one in Arlington, we'd moved out to the suburbs that spring. My office was only
twenty minutes away, but the sporting goods store Brian worked at
was far away—after a few weeks of an hour-long commute, Brian
had quit. Now he was home all the time again, alone and bored.
Because we had a big yard, he wouldn't even walk Kelby, and without a purpose forcing him out of bed, I could see him starting to

sink back into depression. Brian and I agreed to attend a VoteVets event and see what it was like.

And so one day we found ourselves sitting in a room packed with other combat vets from the Iraq and Afghanistan wars. We didn't know anyone, yet talk flowed immediately and easily, faster and more freely than it did with civilians we'd known for months. When construction noise outside made everyone flinch, someone yelled out, "Can we get a warning? There are combat vets in here!" The room erupted in laughter. At last we were with people who understood what we had been through and joked about reactions civilians thought were weird.

That room was a revelation. Those vets meant a rediscovery of community. We had finally come home. We both got involved with VoteVets—but especially Brian. With full-time work and full-time school, I didn't have the time or energy to devote to a new cause, but he threw himself into volunteering. His first role was helping Peter, one of the organization's employees, organize the next event they had in D.C. Brian enjoyed having something to do again, a reason to get out of bed in the morning.

It didn't take long to realize that our new service to our country, our new purpose, could be using our own experiences to advocate for veterans. As we learned more, Brian and I came to understand that our problems were not due to personal failings but were normal reactions to abnormal events—and that we hadn't just "slipped through the cracks," we had fallen through gaping holes in the safety net that should have been there to ease our readjustment and reintegration. We were meeting other veterans facing serious challenges as they came home from war. Even those who hadn't suffered physical or psychological wounds were often having a hard time readjusting to a civilian society that didn't seem to understand what they had been through—or even remember we were a nation at war. Those

who had sustained wounds, visible or invisible, were often struggling
to navigate confusing and outdated systems of care.

And the research suggested that the anecdotes we were hearing
were, in fact, representative of far larger problems. Studies showed
that close to 30 percent of Operation Iraqi Freedom/Operation
Enduring Freedom (OIF/OEF) veterans meet the criteria for PTSD,
major depression, or TBI—and the three conditions often co-occur.[1]
But only around half of those who met the criteria for PTSD or
depression were getting care for their mental health problems, and
of those, only around half were getting even minimally adequate
care.[2] Lack of recovery coordinators allowed wounded warriors to
slip through the cracks, the disability compensation system was confusing, and family members lacked adequate support and training.[3]
Rather than simply hope things would get better, VoteVets sought
to get veterans of Iraq and Afghanistan involved in politics, either
by lobbying on veterans issues or actually running for office.

RATHER THAN CONTINUING TO hide the worst of our struggles in shame, we began to speak about them openly, using our
examples to push for systematic change so the vast cohort of vets
struggling to readjust would not have to go through what we had.
While Brian worked through VoteVets, I used the platform my
book had given me to begin making my own voice heard. I started

1. See, for example, Terri Tanielian and Lisa Jaycox, eds., *Invisible Wounds of War:
Psychological and Cognitive Injuries, Their Consequences, and Services to Assist Recovery*
(Santa Monica, Calif.: RAND Corporation, 2007), p. 96.

2. Ibid, pp. xxi–xxii.

3. See, for example, the President's Commission on Care for America's
Returning Wounded Warriors (a.k.a. Dole-Shalala) report, available at http://
militarymedicine.com/node/77.

getting requests to speak at universities, and found that I enjoyed speaking to audiences of students, helping them understand what today's military was like.

Many of them simply had no idea, and shared common assumptions that troops were the dregs of society, who enlisted because they had no other options. Many asked me why I joined the Army, seeming to think that only dumb people and criminals enlisted. I got to challenge these assumptions with facts: today, 75 percent of young Americans don't even qualify for the military.[4] Most are too overweight, don't have high school diplomas, or have criminal backgrounds. College recruiters and military recruiters are by and large targeting the same cohort—98 percent of troops have high school diplomas, compared to only 85 percent of the civilian population.

In addition to universities, I started speaking on panels at conferences and other events. As it became obvious that large numbers of veterans were struggling to readjust to civilian society after combat, nonprofits, state governments, and community groups were starting to come together to seek solutions to the challenges they faced. When event organizers put together panels of veterans to speak about their own experiences, too often they were all men—with perhaps one token woman. I got used to being that token. Though everyone knew women veterans were out there in growing numbers, we seemed harder to find, less likely to be engaged, or both. Rather than portray my experiences as *the* female soldier story, I hoped that by putting myself out there I could encourage other women to come forward and tell their own stories.

Even at larger veterans' events, it was usually just like my time in the Army: I was in the minority, usually by a lot. Women are only 15 percent of the military, and perhaps since we are less likely

---

4. http://www.missionreadiness.org

to self-identify as veterans,[5] are also less present in veterans' organizations and activities. There were plenty of veterans' events at
which I was the only woman—and though being around other vets
was comforting compared to being around civilians, being the sole
female brought back feelings of the pressure I felt in the Army. The
traditional veterans service organizations (VSOs) didn't feel like a
good fit for me at all—they appeared to be dominated by old white
men wearing crazy hats and drinking in dreary smoke-filled bars.
After hearing stories from a couple of women who went in to join
and were handed applications to the "ladies' auxiliary," I'd never
even tried.[6]

Older male vets often assumed I was just at events to support
my husband. Several times, one would come up to Brian and say,
"Thank you for your service." Brian would pointedly say, "My wife
was in the Army, too." They'd smile and nod, then keep talking to
him, asking if he'd been to Iraq or Afghanistan. Brian would try
again: "Both, actually. My wife was in Iraq, too." It didn't seem to
click. Many from those earlier generations seemed to assume that
even if I had been deployed, I couldn't have been in combat. They
seemed to think front lines still existed.

Even some vets from the current conflict assumed I'd been a
"Fobbit"—had never left the wire and spent my entire deployment
on a cushy, well-provisioned base. There was always a subtle under-
current of feeling I still had something to prove: it wasn't taken for
granted that if I'd been to Iraq, I had actually been to war; I had to
specifically talk about being outside the wire to earn respect. While
I was incredibly glad Brian was thriving as a part of VoteVets, I still

---

5. http://www.dol.gov/wb/trauma/traumaguide.htm#1

6. See also http://www.blogs.va.gov/VAntage/5387/veteran-redefining-the-
word/.

hadn't found a larger support network or organization where I felt truly connected.

IN THE FALL OF 2007, Brian decided to go back to school. "If I want a good job, it would be good to have a degree," he said. "And I think I'm ready." He reached out to the VA to sign up. After a seminar, he was linked up with a vocational rehabilitation counselor. He came back frustrated from his first meeting with her. "She gave me these dumb tests to assess my interests and strengths. Then I had to pick a career field. I said I wanted to do information technology [IT], but she couldn't find it in her book. The closest thing was 'computer operator'—what, is this book from 1975?! But I can't get benefits without picking a job code, so I went with that one."

Nonetheless, Brian was given a new computer and they paid for him to take classes at the local community college. "It should be fine," I reassured him. "There are lots of non-traditional students at community colleges." But Brian's classes, all during the day, were full of seventeen- and eighteen-year-olds.

"I don't fit in at all," he told me. "They're just kids—I'm the oldest student. Actually, I think I may be older than one of my teachers." Although he enjoyed his history and English classes—especially English, where the teacher assigned Tim O'Brien's *The Things They Carried*, a renowned book about the Vietnam War—he hated the IT classes, which did not bode well for his planned major.

There was no support system in place, and Brian was embarrassed to ask for additional assistance. "Don't give up," I encouraged him. "Just push through. They have to help you if you need it. Can your vocational rehabilitation counselor help you?"

He shook his head. "She seems totally overloaded, I think she has way too many clients." But despite his reservations, he kept going.

THAT SUMMER, THE COMPANY I worked for lost the government contract I was on. Within months, I would be out of a
job—unless I switched to one of the companies that had won the re-
compete, in which case I would sit at the same desk doing the exact
same work but getting pay stubs with a different corporate name
on them. It felt like an omen. The pay was good, and I appreciated
that the flexible hours were facilitating my graduate studies—but
the work was boring and unfulfilling. There's no real career path
as an Arabic translator working in national security, and translating
documents just wasn't that interesting.

My job was also getting more stressful. I'd been placed into a
quality assurance role, and was finding that native speakers of Arabic who were twice my age—especially the men—were not terribly
receptive to being corrected by a young American woman. It didn't
help that my communication style—already more direct than most
women's—had been made even more so by the Army. Arabs, by
contrast, have a much more indirect communication style, and my
approach regularly raised hackles. I often arrived home flustered and
frustrated. One day I complained for what seemed the hundredth
time, "I don't understand this! We're all on the same team, working
for the same goal. No one benefits if I let bad work get through.
They can learn from this and improve. It doesn't have to be so con-
frontational! Why can't they just be rational?"

Brian gently laughed at me. "Honey, when are you going to figure out that people aren't logical?"

I'd been applying for analyst positions at all the major defense
contractors in the area, but wasn't getting anywhere. Once they
learned I spoke Arabic, linguist jobs were usually the only ones
available—and the few analyst jobs I was offered would have required
a 40 percent pay cut. No matter how many government jobs I applied

for, I didn't get a single call for an interview. "I don't know how to do these stupid KSAs!" I moaned about the knowledge, skills, and achievements portions of the online applications. It was starting to feel hopeless until one of my adjunct professors at American, who worked at the RAND Corporation, a nonpartisan think tank that does research and analysis, including a large portfolio of work on military and defense issues, encouraged me to apply. After a daylong interview, they extended an offer. Could I start the Monday after my current contract ended? The timing was perfect.

It was challenging for me to adjust to the new environment. Fewer of my colleagues were prior service than at my previous job, and almost everyone was more highly educated than I was. My administrative assistant had a master's degree—I was terribly reluctant to ask her to do secretarial tasks for me. Everyone assumed I had been an officer, and would introduce me as a "former Military Intelligence officer." This left me feeling awkward and uncomfortable—should I correct them to say I'd been enlisted, possibly in front of a client, or just let it go?

Officers enter the military primarily through the military service academies and ROTC; they have "commissions" from the president. Most of the rest of us—about 85 percent of the Army—simply enlist, showing up and signing a contract. After a few years, I'd become a non-commissioned officer or NCO, a group known as "the backbone of the Army" for its professionalism and leadership skills. I was proud of having been an NCO, had enjoyed training and leading soldiers at an intimate level, and regularly teased former officers about how all they did was make PowerPoint presentations. The typical joke among enlisted personnel was, "Don't call me sir/ma'am—I worked for a living." Were my new colleagues falsely assuming I'd been an officer because I was educated and articulate—thus obligating me to correct them, so they'd know better than to misjudge my fellow enlisted troops? Or were they just misspeaking?

When I talked about it at home, Brian just shook his head at me. "You're overthinking this! Just let it go. They probably don't even know the difference."

I sighed in frustration. It was true, though—I did overthink everything.

"You should have seen it at the last VoteVets event," he went on. "Everyone immediately reverted to the roles they had in the military. I swear to God. About fifteen of us went to Capitol Hill on the metro, and the former officers were in front—but they didn't know where they were going, so they got lost. One of them would come to a dead halt as soon as he got off the escalator, everyone piling up behind him. Two of the Joes[7] forgot their metro cards, so we had to buy them new ones. I stayed in the rear policing up stragglers. Completely fucking typical."

I laughed. "You know what I can't get used to? All the freedom. RAND strives to be non-hierarchical. It makes me crazy sometimes! All I want is task, condition, and standards. Don't just say, 'I want a chapter on this general topic sometime.' Tell me how long it should be, what citation style I should use, what the deadline is! If you can't give me a deadline, your project is last on my list of priorities. Do you know how inefficient it is to have everyone use different citation styles and then have to standardize them later? It's like people don't want to be in charge or make decisions. There's nothing wrong with hierarchy!"

I paused for a moment, startled at myself. My younger punk-rock self would have been completely astounded at what had just come out of my mouth.

Brian nodded. "I totally know what you're saying. It was hard to deal with that at the sporting goods store. All you get is the task, no

---

7. Army nickname for lower-enlisted soldiers.

conditions or standards! And there's no yelling . . . the expectations are totally different in the civilian world."

"You know, most people actually want some structure. And one of the great things about a hierarchy is that if you don't like it you can find ways to circumvent it. But if you don't even know who's in charge, there's no way to do that."

—————

NOT LONG AFTER STARTING the new job, I ended up on a project that would require me to go to Iraq for a few weeks. I sat down with Brian to discuss it. "Do you think you can handle it?" I asked.

"Sure," he said. "I have a good support network, I'm taking classes, I'm volunteering at VoteVets."

"Are you sure?" I asked. "I'll be gone for several weeks. Remember what happened when I went on my book tour?"

"Don't worry about it," he assured me. "I'll be busy. It will be fine." Calling on his experience from REI, he helped me pack, sorting through my military gear for stuff that would be useful—I still had my beloved woobie[8] and black fleece jacket, my boots and a stuff sack. Wondering if I was being paranoid, I decided to wear my web belt—to help someone pick me up if I got injured and needed to be carried—and a dog tag, so they'd know my blood type.

My parents thought I was crazy. "Why would you want to go back there?"

Despite Brian's assurances, I was worried about him. I called Brandon, Nadean, and Zoe, making them promise to call him while I was gone.

Everything was surreal about going back to Iraq as a civilian. It

———

8. The poncho liner is an Army blankie, basically. http://military-surplus.us/ Poncho-Liner.

felt all wrong to get on a C-130 in civilian clothes, without carrying a weapon. When the plane landed in Baghdad and the ramp opened, the blast of hot air pummeled me in the face.

"Smells like home," I murmured. And it did. Not like my house in the States, but like where I belonged. It was as if my brain clicked on again for the first time in years; I felt alert and energized. But everything that happened after that was filled with tiny disconnects that reinforced how different Iraq was and how I no longer belonged there. I didn't seem to fit in anywhere anymore. I didn't belong back in America, but I wasn't a soldier either.

The military complex was enormous—several camps linked together, serviced by buses. I stayed in a bizarre version of a hotel, a trailer filled with bunk beds administered by a National Guard unit. "What would that be like," I wondered to Brian on the phone, "to get orders for Iraq and find out your unit's mission would be to hand out keys to people passing through who need a place to sleep?" There were refrigerators filled with cold bottled water instead of just large wooden pallets stacked with warm dusty cases of the 1.5-liter bottles. Buildings were air-conditioned. There was a Burger King. Everyone had cell phones. "I'm not even sure it's better," I confided to my husband. "How can you focus on your mission? It isn't like they're at war at all."

Then the mortars fell, and I was reminded that it was, in fact, still a war zone. But I wasn't a soldier in it this time. As I stood outside the trailer in the dark, my fingers clenched spasmodically at where my weapon should be but wasn't. I hated not having a rifle, not knowing where there was a bunker, what the different sirens meant, where there was a combat lifesaver bag. What the fuck was I supposed to do if something terrible happened? I felt twitchy, useless.

Back home, Brian did an ad for VoteVets disagreeing with the way the Iraq war was being waged. Shortly thereafter, Rush Limbaugh

said that troops who disagree with the war are "phony soldiers."
Brian starred in a VoteVets ad in response, closing with, "Until you
have the guts to call me a 'phony soldier' to my face, stop telling lies
about my service." Limbaugh responded by going on his radio show
and saying, "You know, this is such a blatant use of a valiant combat
veteran, lying to him about what I said, then strapping those lies to
his belt, sending him out via the media in a TV ad to walk into as
many people as he can walk into."[9]

Brian told me bits and pieces about what was going on. He
seemed to be doing well, even thriving on the engagement and
activity, going on TV to talk about it. A blurb about the story even
made it into *Stars and Stripes*, the newspaper that deployed troops
get. I showed it to my RAND colleague: "That's my husband!" I
was full of pride that he was standing up to a bully like Limbaugh.

The next day my colleague and I walked past a group of Iraqis
on the other side of a fence on our way to a meeting. They were
talking loudly and excitedly. I could feel their eyes on me. And I
could feel my body respond: my heart started beating harder, my
stomach tightened in anticipation, my breath started coming faster.
"Holy shit," I thought to myself, taking a deep breath. "I'm freaking
out!" I forced myself to take stock of the situation, notice the armed
guards, acknowledge the reality—there was no threat. Slow, steady
breaths. I forced myself to calmness. "I can do this." Alongside the
immediate panic was a lower foreboding of dread: was I ever going
to get better, get back to normal? Or would an anxiety attack always
loom just below the surface, ready to slip out and overpower me?

WHILE I WAS TRYING to hold it together in Iraq, Brian had started falling apart at home.

After the flurry of attention from the Limbaugh incident faded, he was back to feeling isolated and lonely due to my absence. The anniversary of his injury was often a trigger for PTSD symptoms, and this year that was especially true. When it hit, Brian went into a complete tailspin. He quit going to classes. Stayed up all night drinking. Sent me cryptic emails full of song lyrics. Threatened suicide.

I vacillated between panic and rage, circling around and around inside my head. "Should I fly home? I can't. Can I? I haven't been at RAND long, it would ruin my reputation to bail on this type of assignment. But he's my husband. He is the most important thing in my life. Why couldn't he just hold it together? It's only a few weeks! Why wouldn't he just go to class, stick to his routine? What if he does kill himself? Who would find him? How would anyone know? Would the dog get so hungry she would start to eat him? Oh my god, I'm totally losing it if that's what I'm thinking about." I emailed Zoe, telling her everything and begging her to call him and check on him. I emailed Brandon and Nadean, who also understood PTSD.

Brian and I had a few tense, bitter conversations. He was furious that I wasn't putting him first; I was irate that he couldn't keep it together for a few short weeks. I finished out my time and came home—only to get back on another plane twelve hours later to head to a speaking engagement in Alaska, stopping in NYC for another before finally coming home. We barely communicated before I left again. By the time I got on the plane for the flight home, the smell of jet fuel almost made me vomit. The world seemed to shimmer and vibrate—in just a few days I'd gone from the deserts of Iraq to snowy Alaska, jumping between multiple time zones and ecosystems. Everything felt wrong. And I dreaded going home to more arguments.

When I got back, Brian and I were cautious around one another, barely touching. We argued often, about everything. Who would do what chores, how much Brian was drinking, what tone of voice I used to address him, how much money he was spending, where to go out to eat, what to watch on TV—the most innocuous subject could touch off a firestorm. I felt brittle, ready to shatter.

We stopped having sex. There had been dry spells before—some of the medications he'd cycled through decreased libido, and when I was going to grad school full-time and working full-time, we'd rarely been able to find the time. Whenever Brian and I had argued a lot, we had also had sex less: unlike other relationships I'd had in the past, where a fight could be cathartic, leading to new understanding and ending with passionate make-up sex, our disputes often hung on, with low-grade sniping that gradually trailed off after days or weeks rather than apologies and clear closure. But this felt different—not so much a lull as a break. We were both bitterly angry and unwilling or unable to move on.

Lonely and frustrated, I fantasized about dating another man. The colleague I had been working with in Iraq was young, handsome, brilliant, and incredibly fit. We'd talked quite a bit while I was over there, and I loved how he had challenged me to think more deeply. I knew better than to think we could be happy as a couple: his strident views on autonomy were incompatible with the interdependence that accompanies relationships. But, feeling trapped and miserable, it was somehow comforting to contemplate a different kind of unhappiness, one in which the problem wasn't being too deeply entangled but having no profound emotional connection.

I quit going to the gym. There were plenty of valid excuses: I had too much schoolwork to catch up on after missing a few weeks of classes while in Iraq, it was too hard with the commute, there wasn't time with the new job—but the truth was that I was just too miserable. Intellectually, I knew it was the worst thing for me;

exercise helped level my mood and improve my sleep. But emotionally, I simply didn't have the energy anymore. The weight I'd put on after breaking my ankle had never come off, and now I started to add more. Having to buy new clothes as I got too heavy for what I already owned just made me feel worse.

One night I found a half-packed backpack in the hallway. There was a woobie in it and a knife. "What the fuck is this?" I asked.

Brian shrugged. "I dunno. I think I'm going to go live in the woods."

I stared at him in total astonishment. It was cold out, nearly winter. This was too much. "What are you *thinking*?!" I asked.

"What the fuck do you care?" he shot back.

I was yelling now, too pissed to stay in control. "What the fuck is wrong with you?! You have a daughter. We own a house. We're married. You're an adult. You can't pull this crap. Grow the fuck up!"

"Don't fucking tell me what to do!" He started putting on the backpack.

Grabbing his arm, I tried to calm down, be rational. "What do you *want*?" I asked. "Sometimes I feel like you'd rather just live in some shitty one-bedroom apartment, living off your disability, drinking yourself to death."

"Yeah, well, sometimes I think that would be better than living here with you. Go back to Iraq—do whatever or whoever the fuck you want." He stormed off to the bar and came home hours later, roaring drunk.

I felt drained, defeated: all the progress we had made over the past couple of years was demolished. It was as if I were holding a cat's cradle, and if I dropped even one thread the entire thing would unravel and fall in a tangled mess at my feet. My worst fears were coming true. I couldn't leave Brian—he would fall apart. He needed those disability payments, because we would never know what trigger might set him off. He'd stopped going to classes while

I was in Iraq and since dropped out of school—how could he ever hold down a job?

I can handle almost any degree of stress, knowing it will end; I just think about the duration and break it into smaller chunks and plot out how to tackle them. Working full-time while going to grad school full-time? Shitty, but manageable: it's just two years. Four semesters plus a summer. A set number of classes. Just plow through. Whenever something really sucked, I could always tell myself, "If I could do a year in Iraq, I can do this." But my marriage—that was something else.

After this latest crisis, I was back to envisioning a fucked up codependent relationship stretching before me until one of us died: one crisis after another; a period of quiescence to lull me into complacency, then another breakdown; screaming fights and threats of divorce; me sobbing on the floor, Brian with flattened affect turning away coldly. There was just no escape—I was trapped. That suffocating, horrible, oppressive feeling was sufficient to push me toward the edge. I started looking at apartments online, wondering if we could sell our house, fantasizing about leaving. One day I called Nadean.

"I think I'm going to file for divorce. I just can't take it anymore." She had been there through so much of it—surely she, of all people, would understand. Nadean would support me in this, reassure me that it was the right decision.

"You can't do that," she said.

"What?!" I was astonished. Angry even. "Look, this is just too much to ask of any one person. I can't be his caregiver forever—I have to take care of myself, too. I deserve to be happy. I want a baby, and we can never bring a child into this fucked-up home." I was crying by now. "I want to be able to travel for my job. I wanted to work for the State Department—but Brian said he couldn't handle living overseas, so I shelved that dream. It's just not fair. I just... I don't want to do this anymore. I'm done."

"I'm sorry you feel that way, Kayla, but you can't leave him. You knew what you were getting into when you married him. This is what you signed up for. It's too late—you made a commitment to stand by him no matter what. You made a vow to him, and to his daughter, and you have to fulfill it."

When we hung up I sat in the bathroom with my back against the door, tears leaving hot trails down my cheeks. The feeling of isolation was overwhelming—I was alone in this. There was no one to support me, no one who understood what I felt like, no one to give me advice on how to cope with the meltdowns.

The next day I turned to the Internet.

Iraq and Afghanistan Veterans of America (IAVA) had an online forum called Community of Veterans; membership was only open to people who sent in copies of their DD214s to prove their service. Poking around some forums on PTSD and reintegration, I saw people posting things like "I haven't been able to sleep for days. What should I do?" A few responses were along the lines of "Try a fifth of Jack Daniel's! That helps me sleep." I sighed, despondent—from experience, I knew that would make things worse in the long run. Over time the community was supposed to come together to provide helpful responses that would drown out the negative coping mechanisms, but so far that wasn't true. And right now I felt overwhelmed by my husband's problems—I wasn't looking for a community of my fellow veterans at this moment, but one of other caregivers.

After a little more digging, I found some forums populated by wives and girlfriends of combat vets. I saw post after post with variations of "My husband just got back from Iraq. He hardly sleeps, and he keeps having these violent outbursts. I found him walking around in the yard with a handgun last night, and when I asked him what he was doing he said, 'Patrolling the perimeter.' When I got him inside he started screaming at me and punched a hole in the wall.

I'm scared he's going to hurt me or our baby. Is this PTSD? What do I do? Is there someone I can call?"

It was like driving past a car accident on the highway—I felt compelled to stare, my eyes riveted on the tragedy before me. Post after post of agony, confusion, fear. Before long I was trembling, feeling totally overwhelmed. How many of us were there? How many thousands of people were going through the same thing Brian and I were? I couldn't engage on this level, couldn't handle the horror stories and raw emotions. I barely felt capable of shouldering my own burden, there was no way I could add anyone else's—and each one I read made me ache with the desire to run to the writer, offer hugs and suggestions. Knowing about others' pain wasn't helping me—I felt worse rather than better. The feeling of isolation might be better than knowing the magnitude of suffering out there. I turned off the computer and walked away.

AFTER A COUPLE MORE weeks of walking on eggshells, Brian and I decided to try marriage counseling again. We found a therapist nearby who took our insurance and showed up. She practiced from a home office. There was a bird in a huge cage in the "waiting room." My bird phobia kicked in, focusing all my anxiety, and I spent the entire time we sat filling out paperwork cringing in horror. Over the next few sessions, we did some helpful exercises, like listing things we liked about one another. We didn't really click with her, and quit after a couple months. But she had helped us past the crisis. We were reminded of why we had fallen in love and decided to stick it out. And our mutual dislike of her had actually pulled us together.

After a few sessions, my trapped feeling eased, and I was glad I hadn't succumbed to the temptation of running away. Our marriage wasn't perfect. Brian's recovery wasn't complete. But we were surviving. We were slowly building a support network, a community of people who understood us. It wasn't always a pretty life we shared, but it was generally functional. And despite periodic setbacks, we could still tell that we were moving forward. It felt like crawling out of a pit towing a weight, sometimes slipping back, but still making progress toward the light.

12.

GOOD NEIGHBORS

———— ★ ————

After he volunteered for a few months, VoteVets offered Brian a job. It was an organization in which all the employees telecommuted, and they lived all over the country—Texas, Florida, New York. But they did a lot of events in D.C., and Brian's help organizing a couple had shown how helpful having a local person could be. Rather than hoping he would remain available as a volunteer, they brought him on board formally, and also charged him with helping do outreach to veterans. He enjoyed the freedom to work largely on his own schedule, being able to take breaks and lie down if he got one of his searing headaches. And slowly, over a period of months, his responsibilities began first to shift and then to grow.

Brian had enjoyed working with computers before his injury, and he'd been an early adopter of social media even after the TBI, active on message boards and MySpace before Facebook hit. His colleagues weren't as comfortable or proficient with IT, and frequently struggled to use the organization's outreach and organizing software effectively. Brian began playing around with the system, eventually teaching himself how to use it, and became the go-to guy for IT issues and social media. Succeeding at something that came relatively easily to him while others were baffled by it boosted his confidence—and teaching himself new software stretched his brain and spurred new cognitive improvements.

He wasn't just gaining new technical skills. When Brian was still a volunteer, he and Peter had walked to all 538 Senate and House offices on Capitol Hill to deliver invitations to a VoteVets event. (After coming home with bloodied feet, Brian had bought his first good pair of shoes.) Since he was local, Brian became the point person for all outreach to national-level politicians and legislative issues, like setting up meetings with congressmen or staffers for VoteVets members coming in from out of town. Although he had always hated meeting strangers, having a purpose he believed in gave him the strength to make cold calls and walk into offices where he knew no one. Over time, he learned how the Hill ran and formed relationships with the staffers who handled military and veterans' issues in many of the offices.

Over a period of months, Brian exhibited remarkable cognitive improvement. I was stunned to learn that he had memorized all of the senators and most of the representatives. He knew who was on key committees and how they voted on issues that mattered to veterans. Brian knew what legislation was pending and how likely it was to pass. "How do you know all this stuff?" I asked.

He shrugged. "I don't know. Just . . . doing it, I guess." It amazed me.

But it did come at a cost. He was excelling at his professional responsibilities, but at the expense of household tasks. Although he worked from home and I now had a forty-five-minute commute, he insisted that he couldn't manage to take the dog to the vet around the corner from our house. He didn't vacuum, neglected to open his mail, forgot to buy birthday presents. Multitasking was still impossible: if he was going to focus on his job, he had to do so exclusively, without family distractions. Grumbling, I continued to shoulder the majority of our household responsibilities.

Although having a job with a mission he believed in was giving him purpose and direction that kept him occupied and eased his symptoms of depression, he still struggled with symptoms of PTSD. There were times we had to leave crowded events abruptly because he started to have anxiety attacks. Fireworks on the Fourth of July still triggered panic. And bonding with other veterans was a double-edged sword in some ways: when he would go out for "a couple of beers" with a group of other vets, it often devolved into staying up all night getting profoundly drunk and sharing war stories. There were times when Brian was too hungover to be on morning confer-ence calls and Peter had to cover for him. Not having regular hours in an office had pros and cons: the flexibility was vital when Brian needed time or space to manage pain and anxiety, but also allowed him to hide the worst of his psychological symptoms. Although that let him keep his job when he might have gotten fired in a more formal situation, it also made it seem he was more functional than he actually was at times.

DURING THE 2008 ELECTION season, Brian and I found our-selves drawn into campaigning. While many people automatically assumed that we would support John McCain for president since he was a decorated war hero, his Senate record was actually not strong on veterans' issues.[1] He had never supported the Post-9/11 GI Bill, a bipartisan effort to increase college benefits for today's veterans, and wasn't a strong supporter of increased funding for the VA. Con-versely, Senator Obama's record was solid. Brian and I decided to support his election effort and spoke at a number of events, both together and separately.

At one campaign event, on a whim I talked about what it had

1. http://www.veteranreportcard.org/reportcard.pdf

been like when we first got out of the military. Shakily at first, I stared at the ground in shame as I admitted out loud to strangers for the first time that when we lost Brian's paycheck but his disability benefits weren't yet coming in and I was still searching for a job, we were both forced to go on unemployment. When I glanced around the room, though, I didn't encounter judgment or disgust on people's faces—what I saw was empathy and concern. My voice gaining strength, I turned to how we must elect officials who will fully fund the VA and fulfill their oversight role, closing with, "There are men and women fighting for us in Iraq and Afghanistan every day. It's our responsibility to fight for them here at home." I was astonished at the positive response.

That year, we were invited to the Democratic National Convention out in Denver, and stood on the stage with a group of other veterans of Iraq and Afghanistan as Congressman Patrick Murphy— one of us—spoke to the audience of thousands. My throat felt tight as they cheered for us. After years of feeling alienated from my own country, I finally felt as if we were coming home. When I came up to Brian after we left the stage, his face was full of emotion. "That was so powerful," he said, uncharacteristically gripping my hand. "It's hard to believe that just a few years ago I was in the hospital after getting blown up in Iraq. Can you believe how far I've come?"

The convention was a series of festive, high-energy days. Zoe, who lived in Denver, was there. So were Brandon and Peter, along with VoteVets volunteers we'd met before. Brian knew some of the other people working with Veterans for Obama. Zoe and I ran into a classmate of ours from the Defense Language Institute (DLI). Having often felt surrounded by conservatives in the military, almost nervous to discuss politics, it was invigorating to meet lots of young, liberal vets. Nights were raucous; when we got together with groups of vets and the beer started flowing we all opened up, slurring "So no shit, there I was . . ." war stories into the wee hours of the morning.

During the days we talked to the media about how the candidates' stances on issues mattered to us as veterans of the current conflicts. Our opinions on who should be the next commander in chief were sought after, respected.

The night Obama accepted the nomination, some of the highly coveted tickets for the seats close to the stage were set aside for Veterans for Obama. Brian, Zoe, and I, along with some of our friends, were in the third row as Senator Obama officially became the Democratic nominee for president. Being right there because of our status as veterans was gratifying—and looking up at tens of thousands of people in the stadium around us almost dizzying. All of us were caught up in the moment, grinning excitedly while enthusiastically waving tiny American flags. Usually a tiny bit embarrassed by overt displays of patriotism (having risked my life in combat for my nation, I feel absolutely no need to signify my love of America with flag lapel pins), I was bursting with pride in my country: despite our nasty history of slavery and racism, we had chosen a black man to run for the highest office in the land.

The moment Obama was done speaking, cannons boomed. We instinctively ducked, looking for cover. It took a moment for it to click: confetti. Red, white, and blue confetti rained down on us, balloons drifting after. Brian, Zoe, and I laughed with the other vets, clapping each other on the back. "Confetti! Fucking confetti!" The moment of panic had been a sharp reminder that the memories of war were never far from our minds, but hadn't been able to dampen our spirits that night.

WE BEGAN TO SPEND time with vets who had made more progress than we had, and with those who hadn't.

One of the VoteVets guys was among the latter. Apparently

flashing back to the threat of IEDs in Iraq, he would practically climb out of the car if they drove by garbage on the road, yelling "Trash! Trash! Trash!" and pounding on the dashboard. But he never talked about what he had experienced, never revealed the source of his PTSD. Telling me about it, Brian seemed vaguely pleased. "You know, sometimes I think I'm *so* fucked up. Then I see stuff like that and I realize I'm doing pretty well, you know? I mean, I may freak out sometimes, and I need to carry Valium around, but at least I can drive. But it also scares me—what if I take a turn for the worse? That might be me in the future . . ."

Some wounded warriors were tremendous role models. One day, Brian came home from a meeting on Capitol Hill. "So the legislative aide I met with today is a combat vet too."

"Mmm-hmm," I mumbled, chopping vegetables for dinner.

"He got shot in the head."

I put down the knife and looked up. "Really? How's he doing?"

"Amazing. You'd never know." Brian was shaking his head. "I mean, this guy's an LA. He runs the senator's entire legislative port-folio on veterans and military issues! He's doing so much. And he got shot in the head."

"That's awesome. Really makes you think about what you could do, doesn't it?"

He grimaced. "Kinda. It is inspiring—but it also makes me won-der what the fuck is wrong with me that I'm not doing more."

The rediscovery of purpose and the demands of his VoteVets job were acting as the rehab he'd never gotten from the Army or VA. What we'd been told years ago about a time limit on improvement had been completely wrong: when Brian was pushed to learn new things, his brain was able to reroute around the damaged areas.[2] And seeing people who were doing both better and worse than he

---

2. http://www.time.com/time/magazine/article/0,9171,1580438,00.html

was forced Brian to acknowledge that recovery could come on a spectrum—he wasn't permanently broken or completely fucked up. And maybe, as far as he had already come, he could go even farther.

OUT OF THE BLUE one day, Brian said, "I want to join the fire department."

"Huh?"

"I want to be more involved in the community. Joining the local volunteer fire and rescue department seems like a good way to do it. My uncle was a volunteer firefighter when I was a kid. It seemed cool. They're having an informational meeting on Thursday; I read about it on the Internet. Want to come?"

"Sure," I answered. It was so unusual and exciting for Brian to want to do something like this, I had to support it.

Sitting through the briefings on what the department did and how we could be involved was inspiring. I missed doing hands-on work, and could tell I was losing some of the skills that had given me the most pride when I left active duty: the certain ability to respond appropriately in a crisis, to be able to perform basic first aid if I saw someone injured. So when Brian signed up to become a firefighter, I volunteered to become an EMT. I had just finished graduate school, and had no idea what to do with all the free time that had suddenly opened up in my schedule. This would fill the gap. It was almost a relief—I harbored lingering fears of what would happen if I ever slowed down enough to think. Keeping constantly active seemed safest.

Early on, one of the officers in the department briefed us on stress. "You will see things that will fuck you up," he said. "That's okay. It's totally normal. Hell, you *should* feel fucked up if you see a dead kid! Just call CISM, Critical Incident Stress Management, and they'll help you out. It's completely normal to have a hard time after some really messed-up calls, and we have a system in place to help get you back to normal. Just don't hide it. Reach out. We're here to help." It was a revelation: there was an entirely different way to respond to trauma than the one we'd experienced in the military. Why hadn't it ever occurred to me before? Firefighters go through traumatic events on a regular basis—of course they've developed ways to address it, to help people cope. This approach seemed so much healthier and more balanced than the way the Army had handled traumatic experiences while I was active duty.

Of course that didn't mean it always worked that way at the fire department, or that there wasn't peer pressure to suck it up and drive on. But the message from the establishment from the very first day was unambiguous: post-traumatic stress is a normal reaction to abnormal events, and needing assistance coping with that is expected and acceptable.

"It's like a paramilitary organization," Brian joked. But he was right—virtually everything about the department had echoes of the military. There were uniforms, ceremonies, traditions, rituals. There was training, camaraderie, hazing. Everyone had volunteered to be there, and nonetheless bitched about the more unsavory or boring aspects. People were united in a spirit of sacrifice and motivated by lofty ideals—but also shared gallows humor and a tendency to let off steam by partying hard. Many of the volunteers were young males who did dumb shit and got publicly punished for it. There was structure, ranks of leadership, pettiness. It felt familiar. Comfortable.

Brian thrived in fire school. He studied evenings and weekends, going over the book again and again to understand how fire worked and learn about the emergency management system. He was getting A's on all the tests, scoring better than most of his classmates—and they didn't have brain injuries. I felt like I could *see* new connections being forged in his brain. Brian was training hard, losing weight, and getting stronger. He was visibly fitter within a matter of weeks; the softness that had been growing around his middle was fading away. He was sexier than I'd seen him in years, keeping his hair cut short and shaving daily.

I enjoyed EMT school, too. Many of the skills we covered were familiar to me from the Army—though there were major differences. Combat lifesaver (CLS) bags all have IV kits, and all combat lifesavers were trained on how to give them. Civilian EMT-Basics cannot give IVs—you have to be a paramedic. Pretty much all you can do as an EMT-B is give oxygen and transport to the hospital. Giving oxygen was something I'd never practiced before—there were no oxygen tanks on our Humvees. Too explosive in case an IED went off. When we practiced on fake patients, I was regularly complimented on my manner—that I seemed calmer and more confident than many of my classmates. It boosted my self-esteem to know that some of what I'd drilled on over and over had stuck, and to be reminded that I could stay cool in a crisis, be useful.

When fire school ended, Brian signed up for EMT school, and did just as well. For the first time since he got out of the military, he was doing physically challenging activities. He had bonded easily with some of the other guys, and hung out with them on weekends, so his social support system was building back up. The fire department, like the military, in many ways felt like family: you trusted people with your life even if you didn't necessarily like them.

At the fire department, though, there was less pressure. No one had known him before the injury, so they didn't have any expectations about who he "should" be, didn't wonder if he would ever get back to "normal." Many of the other volunteer firefighters were also veterans—or were still in the military, a couple on active duty stationed at the Pentagon and others in the National Guard or Reserves. They all got it, and could trade "So no shit, there I was" war stories. Even those who hadn't served in a war zone had experienced some

kind of trauma on duty: saw mangled bodies pulled from car acci-
dents with the Jaws of Life, defeated a fire too late to save everyone,
been unable to bring someone back from a cardiac event. They
shared the dark humor that develops in professions where death is
not so far removed from daily life. Those experiences provided a
bond that was as deep as blood ties. It was a relief to find a part of
our local community where we seemed to fit in.

Learning new things was mentally demanding for Brian, but
the environment kept the new challenges from overwhelming him.
Brian enjoyed the camaraderie and structure so much that he even
initiated a color guard[3] and volunteered for events on weekends. He
seemed destined for a leadership role in the department.

The gains all seemed to be feeding off one another: learning
new skills was spurring cognitive and physical improvements, which
improved his psychological health, which cut down on his drinking,
which reduced the number of fights we got into, which improved
our relationship, which reduced his stress level, which encouraged
him to try new things in his personal and professional spheres, which
spurred further improvements. Just as he had spiraled down when
things were headed in a bad direction, the same was happening in
reverse now.

"I read a book," he told me one day.

"What?" I asked in surprise.

"I read a book," he repeated. "For pleasure. From start to finish."

We smiled at each other. A minor thing, but a huge step. It was
the first time since his injury. Six years later—far longer than eighteen months—and he was still improving.

---

3. Color guards are very common in the military and are also used in some other
settings, such as fire or police departments. Participants carry flags during formal
ceremonies.

"ARE YOU GOING TO leave me?" Brian asked.

"What?!" I felt as if things had been going so well; this came out of nowhere. We were sitting on the deck drinking beers while dinner grilled.

His fingers started tapping out their familiar patterns. "Sometimes I feel like I'm a...project for you. Like you've been trying to fix me. And I worry that now that I'm better you're going to leave me."

I went and sat on his lap, pulling his head to my chest and holding him close. "No, I'm not going to leave you. Things are finally getting easier—why would I leave now? The only thing that kept me going through the worst times was the belief that this day would come—now it finally has. We can relax and actually enjoy it!"

"Can you?" he asked. "Are you sure?"

I bit back my immediately defensive retort. Brian was right—I was having a hard time adjusting to our new situation. Over the years, I'd gotten so used to controlling all aspects of our lives that I didn't know how to let go. I was so used to seeing him as someone with cognitive and psychological problems that I was having a hard time stepping back and seeing him clearly and openly as he was now. It was time for me to stop focusing so much on Brian and spend a little more time on self-reflection.

So I started going to a therapist on my own, Dr. Judith. Although she was a civilian, her son was in the Marines, and she understood military terminology and mind-sets. I felt comfortable with her. She used a cognitive behavior therapy approach, focusing on identifying maladaptive responses and modifying them. "Automatic thoughts lead to automatic feelings which cause automatic actions. You have to identify where you're interpreting things incorrectly and stop the cycle." Dr. Judith recognized right away that a touchy-feely, warm and fuzzy approach wouldn't work with me, and approached my issues intellectually. I described some of the negative experiences I'd had in therapy before, complaining about how the OneSource psychologist had told me I probably had OCD for behaviors the military rewarded. Dr. Judith said, "Well, are these habits harmful? Do they make your life worse? Because they're really only maladaptive if they cause problems for you."

That resonated with me. Years before, I'd had an employee who had been late to work almost every day because she would get halfway to the office and then turn around and drive home to make sure she had unplugged the coffeemaker out of a fear her house would burn down. That was maladaptive. Me taking pleasure in having a nicely organized spice rack wasn't making me late for work. "On the other hand," I admitted, "it has caused problems with every roommate I've ever had. And it drives my husband crazy that I want him to live by my systems."

So Dr. Judith gave me a homework assignment. When I got home, I told Brian, "You have to go into the pantry and turn around five cans so the labels face backward."

"Are you sure?" he asked, alarmed. "Can you handle it?"

"Do it!"

The next week she asked me how I had done. Had I left the cans alone? "Oh yes," I responded. "I'm very good at following instructions. I know exactly which cans are facing the wrong direction, but I haven't touched them. Is the assignment over, though? Because we really need to discuss this. It's out of control. Cans are migrating onto non-can shelves. It's really not acceptable."

She quirked her eyebrows at me.

I paused and took a deep breath. "I sound like a crazy person."

Dr. Judith smiled.

"Okay," I said. "Yeah. I need to let go a little."

It was painful to admit that after years of blaming Brian for all our problems and thinking of him as being fucked up while I was the one holding it all together, I had to take responsibility as well. He may have been the one with an official diagnosis, but he wasn't the only one with maladaptive coping mechanisms. If we were going to get better as a couple, we both had to work on getting better as individuals. And with Dr. Judith's help, I was finally making progress.

DR. JUDITH SUGGESTED I get away for a weekend—to be totally alone, ponder, think, prioritize, envision. So after months of drifting, feeling disconnected and scattered, I headed down to Key West on my first solo vacation since Brian and I married—or maybe even longer. I couldn't even remember how many years it had been since I went somewhere alone, with no plan or agenda, no responsibilities other than to my own self, no speaking engagements, friends, weddings, family—no duties or obligations. It was remarkably calming. I had imagined my nature would rebel against it, would wish for connectivity, would crave purpose. But I felt relaxed. Perhaps not content—though I wasn't even sure what that meant.

As I drove down from Miami, a realization struck me:

I loved my husband.

Perhaps that sounds ridiculous—I mean, I married him! Of course I must love him! But over the five years since we had begun our relationship, and even over the nearly four years of our marriage, I had been plagued by doubts and fears. Not just about him, but also myself. Would he ever get "better"? Was I suited for marriage? Were we together only because no one else would have us? Did we share enough values and interests to forge a life together? Would he be a good father? Would it be right to bring children into the world—or our fucked-up household—at all? Could I be a good mother? Was I too neurotic to be a good wife or parent or partner? Was I doomed to be a caregiver to a perpetual virtual child who outweighed me and possessed the capacity for inflicting devastating cruelty?

But as Brian had pointed out, it was clear now that he had grown—was growing—into the man we both glimpsed as possible five years before. It did not happen on my schedule or at my urging—it never could have happened that way, I suppose. But it had come. Working at VoteVets, helping others, proving his worth—these helped him immensely, stimulating his neurons to grow and find new pathways while helping to heal his soul and psyche. Now, volunteering as a firefighter, he was also striving to improve his health, eating better and working out, which were contributing to the virtuous cycle.

And somewhere in all this, I don't even know when, he had become a supportive and trusting partner and husband. Not in everything—he may never care about cleaning the house or our retirement plans—but at his core. He urged me to take care of myself and never begrudged me money I wanted to spend on myself, on clothes or at the spa or on this vacation. Part of me felt a twinge of guilt for how much I had hassled him about spending over the years, but the situation was different; I was often the only wage earner, trying to secure our future and fearful he would never have a career. That had all changed—he had a good job, got bonuses, had gotten a raise—and I could relax, let go of the burden.

He also trusted, me, finally—no more 3 a.m. phone calls, no doubts about my fidelity. We could finally be partners of the kind I had envisioned. There were still going to be fights, we still needed to improve our ability to communicate effectively, but I finally truly knew and believed that this marriage could and would last, that we would grow old together, that we could fully rely upon one another.

Driving down through the Florida Keys, as the sun set and the sky turned fiery orange, the ocean bright and shining, I was suffused with a deep love for my husband. And I also knew that I needed to release my anger, fear, and frustration at how hard it had been for us to reach this point. We knew going into our relationship that it would be hard—I may not have known how hard, and in some of our deepest valleys I may have begun to doubt our marriage would even survive, but here we were. We belonged together, I truly loved him, and we would continue to grow together.

WHILE BRIAN WAS THRIVING at work and at the fire department, I was slowly coming into my own as an advocate in the veterans' community, focusing on women. I had started serving on the board of directors of a new nonprofit dedicated to helping women veterans, Grace After Fire. And I was asked to testify about women veterans on Capitol Hill.

I was terribly nervous preparing to speak on a panel before the Senate Committee on Veterans Affairs at a hearing entitled "Women Veterans: Bridging the Gaps in Care." "No one is trying to kill me," I reminded myself. "The worst thing that can happen to me is that I'll humiliate myself. And that isn't deadly!" I hid my hands in my lap while the first panelist spoke, grateful that the tables had long white cloths so no one could see me disassembling and reassembling the puzzle ring I'd brought back from Iraq or tapping my foot anxiously.

Then it was my turn. I read the speech I'd worked on for hours, trying to balance critiques of gaps and shortcomings with praise for successes while interleaving data with compelling personal anecdotes, including one about friends having to change babies' diapers on bathroom floors.[4] After finishing, I stayed through the rest of the

---

4. http://veterans.senate.gov/hearings.cfm?action=release.display&release_id= efef9edf-ff53-474b-befb-62edc87ed9d9

speeches and a question-and-answer period, then left, feeling drained but relieved. I hadn't humiliated myself.

Just two days later, I testified before the House Committee on Veterans Affairs Subcommittee on Disability Assistance and Memorial Affairs at a hearing on "Eliminating the Gaps: Examining Women Veterans' Issues."[5] The second time on the Hill, I was much less nervous. After the hearing, a woman from the VA approached me and introduced herself. Since I hadn't had universally glowing things to say about my experiences at VA, I was immediately wary. To my surprise, she asked, "Ms. Williams, would you be interested in applying to serve on the VA Advisory Committee on Women Veterans? We're always looking for new members and you might be a great addition."

"Absolutely! What do I need to do?" She handed me her card and asked me to send her my résumé.

Later that summer, I spoke at a VA conference. A women veterans' coordinator from a VA hospital in Florida came up to me: "Ms. Williams? I just wanted to let you know that the director of the hospital I work at watched your Senate testimony live-streaming over the Internet. We'd been pushing for changing tables for months and he wouldn't listen. After hearing your speech, he ordered them installed. Thank you."

I called Zoe, who had told me about changing her sons' diapers on the floor of the Denver VA Medical Center, in exultation: "Because of something I said, there is a physical object where there didn't used to be one! I made a difference, I actually made a difference!"

"That is so awesome, Kayla! I am really proud of you."

Brian and I spend a lot of time talking about how to be effective

---

5. http://veterans.house.gov/witness-testimony/kayla-m-williams-ma

in pushing for change. It makes us crazy when advocates, pundits, and politicians talk about military and veteran suicide without using the evidence-based guidelines developed to minimize the contagion effect[6] or mentioning the Crisis Line (800-273-TALK, veterans press 1)—don't exacerbate a problem you claim to be trying to solve! And it's ineffective to always be on the attack without recognizing progress and positive efforts, which is why when I criticized the negative experiences Brian had at the D.C. VA or female veteran friends had at other VA medical centers, I always made a point of also recognizing the good experience I had at the Martinsburg VA. When I went there, I was immediately recognized as a veteran and compassionately asked about my combat experiences. The social worker even asked me what my plans were for handling the fireworks on the Fourth of July because she knew those triggered anxiety in many combat veterans—it was a small gesture that made me feel understood and validated.

Context helps, too: rather than simply complaining about the high backlog of disability claims at VA, it's also important to note that VA is processing new claims faster than ever before, but they're coming in at an even faster rate and are ever more complicated.[7] Constantly bashing the VA could be counterproductive: the VA actually provides higher-quality care on a number of measures than civilian systems.[8] If all vets ever hear are horror stories, they may never go at all, therefore either getting no care at all or getting suboptimal

---

6. You can find these at http://www.nimh.nih.gov/health/topics/suicide-prevention/recommendations-for-reporting-on-suicide.shtml.

7. For more, see http://www.armytimes.com/news/2012/07/military-veterans-affairs-promises-results-claim-process-fixes-071112w/—also includes the great suggestion that veterans with complicated claims work through a VSO to ensure a smoother process.

8. http://www.rand.org/pubs/research_briefs/RB9100/index1.html

care elsewhere. Fixating on problems without acknowledging successes also opens the door for more politicians to suggest moving away from the VA system.[9]

So I basked in that moment, genuinely amazed that my efforts had actually gotten something accomplished. It seemed to vindicate our approach and showed me I wasn't just tilting at windmills—I was making things better for other veterans. One changing table at a time.

---

9. See, for example, former Senator McCain's plan to move some vets to vouchers: http://www.military.com/cs/Satellite?c=maArticle&cid=1199420644504& pagename=News%2FnwsLayout. And while it is wonderful that community providers work through nonprofits like Give an Hour to help fill in gaps or provide confidential care for those worried about their careers, when troops and vets seek help outside the system, it also obscures the magnitude of mental health problems returning troops are facing.

13.

THE HONEYBADGER
BOOK CLUB

———— ★ ————

In my advocacy efforts, I'd started to meet others who were working on behalf of veterans. One tiny, adorable, hyper woman I met chirpily informed me, "You wrote about me!" I was baffled until Tia explained. In *Love My Rifle*, I wrote about women who were sexually assaulted at DLI and threatened with being charged for drinking. She was one of those women. Now, she worked for an established nonprofit out in San Francisco called Swords to Plowshares, and speaking out about military sexual trauma (MST) was a big component of her mission.[1] Her courage and openness astonished

---

1. Tia and I spoke at the Senate hearing together; her remarks are at http:// veterans.senate.gov/hearings.cfm?action=release.display&release_id=36f78b3c-95e7-4732-9f03-063ff694c2bf. According to the VA, "The definition of MST used by the VA is given by U.S. Code (1720D of Title 38). It is 'psychological trauma, which in the judgment of a VA mental health professional, resulted from a physical assault of a sexual nature, battery of a sexual nature, or sexual harassment which occurred while the Veteran was serving on active duty or active duty for training.' Sexual harassment is further defined as 'repeated, unsolicited verbal or physical contact of a sexual nature which is threatening in character.'" For more information, see http://www.ptsd.va.gov/public/pages/military-sexual-trauma-general.asp. Both men and women experience MST, and it is more strongly correlated with symptoms of PTSD than either combat trauma

me. I hated being asked about my worst experiences and discussed them reluctantly. Tia's willingness to share her own trauma in order to help others was inspirational.

When Tia got Swords to put on a show called *SHOUT! Art by Women Veterans*,[2] she asked me to come and speak at opening night. When I got to the event, it was amazing to be around so many other women veterans at one time. Please don't misunderstand me—I love my brothers-in-arms, too. Truly, we have shared experiences that civilians can never understand. But women in a combat zone face added pressures. We must deal with sexual harassment and be wary of sexual assault. Women have to keep their guard up not only around the enemy, but even among some of their fellow soldiers. We face pressure not to report sexual harassment just because we "can't take a joke." Being with a group of creative, strong women—and the friends and loved ones who support them—was moving.

And then something happened that truly shocked me.

An Army LTC was at the event in uniform. "I have to share this with you," he told a group of us. He explained that a local teacher asked her students to draw pictures of what the word "veteran" meant to them, and lots of students drew American flags or soldiers at war. So the teacher had asked him to come into her class to talk to the students about what it means to be a veteran. But among all the other drawings, there was one that stood out.

The LTC pulled it out and showed it to us.

It was a drawing of a pretty, smiling girl in an Army uniform.

Mind you, as an Army vet, I have been well trained in the

---

or civilian sexual assault; see, for example, http://www.ncbi.nlm.nih.gov/pmc/articles/PMC1513167/.

2. It's become an annual event: http://www.swords-to-plowshares.org/2012/03/09/shout-art-by-women-veterans-may-9-2012/.

philosophy of "suck it up and drive on." I can speak to hundreds of people calmly.

But when I saw that drawing, tears filled my eyes. I was so overcome with emotion that I had to turn around and pull myself together.

FOR A COUPLE OF weeks after the art show, I had pondered why I had such a strong emotional reaction to that drawing. It's funny how some things just hit you.

My twin nephews are really into the Army, and at first they didn't believe that I was really a soldier, because I'm a girl.

When I go places with groups of vets, I often have to explain that I'm not "just" a spouse or girlfriend. Being ignored when free beers were passed out when Zoe and I went to the bars with groups of guys fresh back from Iraq still stings all these years later.

Once when I was walking Kelby in the park, an old man walked up and asked, "IUD?"

I stared at him in total confusion. "Huh?"

He gestured at her stump. "Was it one of them IUDs that got her? In Iraq?"

"Oh. You mean IED. No, she isn't a retired military working dog. She got hit by a car." As Kelby and I walked away, it hit me: no one had *ever*, on sight alone, assumed I was a combat veteran. More people had now officially assumed that my *dog* was a combat vet than that I was.[3] When Brian had first gotten Purple Heart plates on his car, he'd gotten deeply offended when a few people had asked him

---

3. It happened again after that, too. Since Kelby was a German shepherd missing a leg, several people assumed she'd been a military working dog injured in combat.

if it was his dad's car—shoving in his face the realization that most people didn't truly realize we were a nation at war, with injured troops coming home. Little incidents like the one with Kelby regularly drove home to me that many Americans—if they were conscious of the wars at all—either didn't know women were serving or didn't understand the types of roles we were playing.

So by the time I spoke at the art show in San Francisco, I was used to speaking out about veterans' issues, and the special issues that women veterans face. Used to biting my tongue when asked if I was allowed to carry a gun in Iraq because I'm "just a girl." Used to explaining that, yes, women are actually in combat, they have died in combat, earned Silver Stars for their valor in combat in Iraq and Afghanistan. Used to being patient and calm and citing facts and figures and statistics to prove my points.

What I was not used to was having a little girl think first of someone like me when she thinks of what a veteran is. Not used to feeling so included, having our service recognized by an outsider without prompting, being . . . accepted. I blogged about the drawing by that little girl, thanking her for all the hope it symbolized for me.[4] And, thinking about how deeply moving being around a group of other women veterans had been, I decided to take action. Rather than just accepting the feelings of isolation and accepting my status as an oddity (a relatively rare woman in the veterans' community, an extremely rare veteran in groups of women), I needed to find—or make—a community of *my* peers, other women veterans.

Brian was more than supportive through all of this, urging me to develop a support network of my own like the one he had built up at the fire department. He was standing on his own now, and I wanted to as well. Neither of us thought it would be healthy to be

---

4. http://www.huffingtonpost.com/kayla-williams/being-a-woman-veteran_b_178894.html

immersed only in one another, and we were strong enough in ourselves now to support each other in cultivating individual interests. Having lives that were both separate and together reinvigorated our relationship, and I found myself slowly backing away from the obsession with control I once had. I let Brian take the lead in more areas but made sure he knew that I would be there to support him. Now I was finally ready to learn that our marriage would thrive if I was just his wife, not his mother or his caseworker.

WHEN I HEARD ABOUT an all-female-veteran Outward Bound trip not long after that, I knew I had to go. For a week in August 2009, I went kayaking in the Apostle Islands on Lake Superior. Through the generosity of Sierra Club donors, this women-veteran-only trip was completely free, even the travel. I was terrified to leave Brian alone after how badly my trip back to Iraq had gone a couple of years before, but he assured me that he would be fine and pushed me to go. "Do something for yourself. You deserve this. You need a break, Kayla."

The drive from the airport to the shore of Lake Superior was lushly beautiful. In the van, bonds were immediately formed—it is so easy and comfortable to be around other women vets, who speak the same language and think the same shit is funny. Right after we got to our first camping site, we repacked what we had brought into seaworthy gear, and packed away our mobile phones. It felt fantastic to turn mine off and put it away—both symbolically and actually cutting ties with the demanding regular world for a week.

We had Army, Navy, and Air Force, ranging in age from twenties to forties, some more fit than others, in all different stages of dealing with our deployment experiences and ability to share, with different strengths and weaknesses, traits and quirks. The first day, we got briefed on all the basics of how the next week would go. One of the guides was a nurse at an OB/GYN clinic. When she was giving us a briefing about what we should do if we had any medical problems on the trip, she mentioned that sitting in wet gear for hours could sometimes cause problems and we should come see her if we had any issues "down there."

It reminded me of the way every single time the question of women in combat comes up, someone will mention "the hygiene issue."[5] They never spell out what this means. It's just, "You know, the hygiene issue." At first I tried to be polite during those conversations, explaining that there wasn't a real area of concern. But eventually I started to smile sweetly and say, "I'm not sure what you're talking about, can you please explain it?"... Trying to force them to explain that they believe we will get infections *in our vaginas* if we lacked access to running water. Then I could point out that if women couldn't survive without indoor plumbing, the species wouldn't have survived long enough to develop it. For goodness' sake, half the world's population doesn't have indoor plumbing today.

So I said to the nurse, "You mean *in our vaginas*? You know, if you can't *say* 'vagina,' I'm not that likely to come talk to you about mine." Everyone laughed and she said, "Yes, your vaginas." And we all said it: "Vagina!" It felt goofy and ridiculous but also strangely comforting—I would not have said anything in a group that also included guys.

---

5. When I was in the Army, an astonishing number of guys actually believed that the Army was *required* to pull us out of the field every three days so we could shower. It's just not that big of a deal. The exception is that some women are uncomfortable urinating in front of men—perhaps understandably so, given the sexual assault rate—and so wouldn't drink enough water on deployments and got urinary tract infections. Luckily, there's a tool for that—http://www.backpacker. com/gear-zone-gear-review-female-urination-devices/gear/14173—and they're even available through the Army logistics chain these days.

We then learned how to handle ourselves on the water (basically), packed, and kayaked ten miles. We camped on Oak Island for two nights. There were wild thimbleberries (an exciting new food for me) and raspberries. We went hiking, and I learned a lot about useful local plants from one of our guides, including which is best for wiping your ass. The guides—clearly experienced at dealing with groups of people from challenging backgrounds—were able to tailor their approaches to each of us individually, and knew what we needed. Given my own obliviousness to subtleties of human interaction (as Brian had pointed out to me when I complained about troubles at the office), I was impressed.

The next morning we got up early, kayaked another ten miles to Stockton Island, set up camp again, and camped there for another two nights. There were wild blueberries and blackberries. Here, our luck with the weather broke, and life became damp and cold and sandy.

My OCD tendencies must have been clear when I was younger (a guy I dropped acid with once gave me a mop as a gift...), but this way of compensating for the unpredictability of life by controlling my immediate surroundings had become more extreme as I'd gotten older. The Army encouraged these behaviors, and I felt that embracing them was the only way to manage our lives after I married Brian and had to help him cope with his TBI and PTSD. I'd been working on them with my therapist—the damned canned goods exercise—but still tended to be hyper-controlling of my environment.

On this trip, there were different roles (e.g., cook, navigator, leader, kitchen cleanup) that rotated daily. The second day on Stockton, the group decided that my role was to do nothing: I was not allowed to help (meddle? fiddle? fuss?). This made me twitchy. Surely things would fall apart if I wasn't actively engaged in running them! That woman is doing a task wrong! That won't work!

But it was actually good for me. Nothing terrible happened, nothing blew up, nothing burned down. No one starved or got hurt. Everything was...fine. A few times I literally bit my knuckles to restrain myself from jumping in to help out—okay, to take over. Being forced to wait and watch problems get resolved without my intervention was humbling and strangely soothing.

The final morning out on the water, we got up at 3 a.m. and kayaked fourteen miles back to the mainland—battling high winds and waves as well as our own exhaustion and crankiness. We camped on the mainland and went rock climbing the next day.

I was nervous.

I hadn't been able to get back into climbing after breaking my ankle. We went back to the gym a couple of times, but whenever I got to a certain height, I would hear the sound my ankle made when it snapped echo through my memory and immediately come back down. Then we moved, and there was no indoor gym near us, so I had a good excuse to quit entirely.

At an indoor gym, you climb up and rappel down. Out on this cliff above Lake Superior, we rappelled down and then had to climb up. Once down, you *must* come up (like gravity is reversed! but it isn't...). So down I went. And up I tried to go. But I froze. I couldn't do it. Couldn't bring myself to move, to risk it, to try.

I stayed at the bottom of the cliff for what felt like an eternity before—with lots of encouragement from one of the instructors and another vet—finally dredging up the courage to scale the rock wall. And throughout the climb, I was believing my eyes, listening to the voice in my head telling me I couldn't, worrying about how long I was taking, freaking out.

At the top, I had a little emotional meltdown, and started crying. One of the other women took me aside. I'd known her from the 101st; we'd actually been co-located in Iraq for a couple of months. "What's going on?" she asked.

"I used to be good at this! I used to enjoy it! I used to listen to my body, trust myself, believe in my abilities on the wall, have fun—oh."

She laughed and hugged me.

Hmm. It was unmistakable that all of these things were as true symbolically as literally. I used to have fun at lots of things, believe in my abilities more broadly, be more loose and relaxed, not try to control everything, trust my instincts . . . That worked pretty well for me. And I was a lot more fun to be around. But now I had become tight, tense, controlling. Brittle.

We returned to the Outward Bound base, cleaned all the gear, got showers, sat in a sauna, slept on bunk beds, and graduated. The next morning, breakfast and back to the airport. I felt cleansed, simultaneously lighter and more grounded.

When I got home, my house was still standing, the dog was still alive, and Brian had managed to feed and clothe himself while I was gone. He admitted that he only ate sandwiches, but he ate. Nothing terrible happened, nothing blew up, nothing burned down. No one starved or got hurt. Everything was . . . fine.

This was a bit jarring. Did he not need me at all? What was my purpose? Could I genuinely let myself step back and unwind?

I was able to become much more relaxed, regain perspective, and try not to control things as much. Let a lot more little shit go. I had open, honest, and not-tense conversations with Brian about important things like money. We took the TV out of the living room to set up an exercise room. Brian said, "You know, you're much more pleasant to be around. Maybe you should go on an Outward Bound trip every year." And I started to listen to my instincts (intuition, the voices in my head, whatever) more. I felt good. For the first time in a long time, I felt genuinely *good*—about myself, my place in the world, the prospects for the future of the world, all of it.

BACK HOME, I BECAME part of a small and tight-knit group of women vets in my area. Our glue was not just our military experience: it was a book club that became both a psychological and an emotional outlet for us all. The book club was Carolyn's idea. We'd met at a VoteVets event—as usual, almost all the attendees were men. She came up to me right away, saying, "It's so nice to not be the only woman at one of these things!" As we chatted, we realized how much we had in common. Carolyn and I were close to the same age and had both enlisted to become linguists in the Army when we already had bachelor's degrees. She'd studied Russian and been in the National Guard; both of us had deployed to Iraq. Carolyn is tall for a woman, with red hair and a gentle smile. She was the organized one who always planned get-togethers, and after a few times when small groups of women vets Carolyn invited to her place hit it off, she suggested we formalize a regular session.

"What about a book club? We could meet once a month—switch between military books and fluff. A different person could host each time. It would be fun!" The rest of us readily agreed. Especially for those who were married with kids, it was too easy to bail on informal plans—but this might work. A regular get-together with a loose purpose to draw us together. We'd discuss the book of the month briefly, and quickly move to random topics, wine, and laughter. After the first session, we started calling it the Honeybadger Book Club, after a goofy YouTube spoof of nature videos in which the narrator says several times, "Honeybadger don't give a shit."[6]

One month, Rachel was hosting. I met Rachel through her husband, Jason. We had hit it off when we worked together at my first post-Army job, and I'd invited him to bring his family to a barbecue we hosted. Jason was a lower-leg amputee from a training accident at Fort Drum, an artillery misfire. The first time we all hung out, he

---

6. http://www.youtube.com/watch?v=4r7wHMg5Yjg

got drunk and ended up talking to our three-legged dog. Normally averse to strangers, she was curled up at his feet, and he slurred, "You and me, we're the same, Kelby!" He pointed at his prosthesis and her stump. "We're both missing our legs! We're the same, dog!" She thumped her tail and licked his hand.

Rachel and I chatted about what it was like to have husbands who had been severely wounded while serving. She and Jason had been dating but not yet married when he was injured, and their young relationship had been strained by the need to cope with intense trauma before they had a solid foundation yet. Though neither of them had deployed, we still felt kinship as couples. Their two kids, a boy and a girl both younger than Brian's daughter, were polite and bouncily active. Rachel is petite and blond, speaks half a dozen languages, and is visibly ambitious.

Rachel had put out an amazing spread of snacks and drinks, and we spent an hour eating and drinking wine and catching up before even turning to the book. It was military book month, and we had read Jane Blair's *Hesitation Kills: A Female Marine Officer's Combat Experience in Iraq*. "I thought I wouldn't like her based on her photo," I admitted, "She looked so blond and perfect! But I really did like her by the end."

"I didn't like her," Meg said bluntly. "She made it sound like she was the only woman in all of Kuwait, not just in her unit." The first time I met Meg was when we spoke on a panel together at a fund-raiser for a nonprofit devoted to raising awareness about women veterans that a mutual acquaintance was trying to get off the ground, American Women Veterans. In groups of women, I often felt too loud and brash, worrying that I dominated conversations and needed to consciously give space for others to talk—I get so excitable that I can just run right over demure people in conversations. This was never a concern of mine with Meg. Her curly brown hair is as uncontainable as her big, bold smile and infectious laugh. When we start talking, we immediately trample all over each other's sentences, happily clicking into a fast-paced conversation that leaves no one else a chance to join. She'd been a medic who had spent time at Fort Campbell while on active duty and was now in the Reserves. We eventually figured out that there was a fifty-fifty chance she was on the plane that flew Brian from Baghdad to Germany.

"The thing that did actually set me off at the beginning of the book," I admitted, "was that she seemed to think she wouldn't go to war as a female."

"I wanted to ask about that," Carolyn said, "That never crossed my mind, but I wasn't there at the beginning."

Meg and I spoke simultaneously: "It *never* crossed my mind." I had always known that if I enlisted in the Army, I could go to war—though when I signed up pre-9/11, it didn't seem terribly likely.

"And she seemed willing not to go," I added.

"Right, like if they said, 'You're a woman, you don't have to go,' she might have said, 'Oh, okay!'" Carolyn chimed in.

"You both went into the military older, so you had more life experience," Jen broke in. She was one of Meg's friends, a reservist married to a guy in her unit. Jen is a blonde with an undergraduate degree from American University, and her sweet smile makes her bitingly sarcastic humor come as a surprise. She received a Purple Heart during her deployment to Iraq after an IED peppered her face with shrapnel, but when the infantry brigade commander, a colonel known to his men as "the Dragon," presented her with the medal during an awards ceremony, the injury she chose to mention was getting "shocked in the buttocks."

"I was only seventeen when I enlisted in the Army," Jen continued. "If I could talk to my eighteen-year-old self, I would shake her! My recruiter said, 'You're Civil Affairs, you're a woman, you're a reservist, you won't go anywhere.' So even though this was right after 9/11—sorry, I got caught up in the patriotic fervor, I was seventeen—I really thought that as a reservist and Civil Affairs, I wouldn't be going anywhere!"

"Don't be sorry. A lot of people did. On that note, she really seemed to buy the official party line that we were going there to liberate the Iraqi people," I said.

"Do you think that's because she was still in? She's still a reservist," Carolyn offered.

"Maybe—I definitely didn't want my book to come out until I was out of the military," I said.

"Or because she was an officer," Rachel suggested.

"Well, I did wholeheartedly believe that both times I was there," Meg said. "That we were doing the right thing and needed to be there. I had in my head that we were doing the right thing."

"When I got to meet individual Iraqis," Jen said, "we could see how maybe my micro-grant helped them, I thought, 'Oh, this is a really good program.' But most of the time—and I was there during the surge—I felt like I was a placeholder to send X number of troops to Iraq, and anything I did wasn't really going to matter in the long run."

"The conclusion I tentatively came to was that maybe even though we had the wrong reasons we might have done the right thing..." I suggested.

"Me too," Meg cut in.

"... but we won't know for a generation, and maybe it's going to go to shit," I finished.

"My biggest issue was her definition of a combat mission and mine—they're very different. I was on a combat mission. She wasn't," Meg added.

"Yeah, she was a REMF [rear-echelon motherfucker] officer who got to look through a camera. If her drone gets shot down she's fine. I've still got shrapnel coming out of my chin," Jen said.

"I will say, though, there were some things I thought she captured really well—like the surreality of calling for fire. When Lauren and I watched artillery being fired, it didn't register with me at the time that people were getting killed. And being possessive about 'her boys'—that resonated with me," I threw out.

"She seemed kind of like a prude, though," Rachel said.

"Yeah, she was one of those women who wouldn't drink enough water so she wouldn't have to pee in front of anyone. Fuck that! You have to drink water! Just pee!" Jen added, her voice noticeably louder at the end.

"I did that sometimes," Carolyn said, "Because missions could be so long, and I didn't want to make everyone stop for me."

"But she did it because she was too modest to pee in front of people!" Rachel said.

"Oh no, I didn't care about that," Carolyn said. "You learn how to manage. One day I'm pulling security and this lieutenant colonel came up to me and said, 'How do you pee out here?' I said, 'I pee.'"

Meg interjected, "'I pull my pants down, squat...'"

"And he said, 'Because I had this genius idea from this other girl that you could put your poncho on!'" Carolyn continued. "And I said, 'But then you get pee on your poncho.' I'm like, uh, I'm not going to carry around a pee-covered poncho. I just tell guys not to look this way and then I drop trou."

"Even if they do look," Meg added, "if you haven't seen it by now..."

We laughed in mutual understanding and recognition.

To be honest, we didn't each always even read the book. The composition of women changed through time, and we couldn't all make it to each meeting—but the friendships were powerful. We supported one another through major life changes: celebrating weddings, births, and promotions, brainstorming about how to tackle troubles at work, venting about our partners. Though our military experiences had been different, we shared some core traits: all of us were strong women with low tolerance levels for bullshit and the ability—desire, even—to laugh about shitty experiences.

I'd talked to a documentary filmmaker who had filmed lots of veterans about whether she saw any differences between the men and women vets she'd worked with. She had immediately answered, "Yes. All of the men cry. It's clearly a very cathartic thing for them; many of them have never described the war trauma they experienced before opening up to me. But the women can laugh about it. They've obviously already discussed what they went through with each other and started to process their feelings." In the Honeybadger Book Club, we had formed a community of our peers, a safe space where we could share our secrets, admit our anger and fear, brag about our successes, brainstorm solutions to vexing problems, and laugh about it all. Still a tiny minority in the larger community of veterans, we had each other's backs.

14.

FULFILLMENT

⸺ ★ ⸺

It was obvious to us both that our lives were finally coming together. The only thing missing was children. After a contentious revisiting of their custody arrangement a few years before, Brian and his ex-wife had agreed to a regular schedule: his daughter spent six weeks with us every summer and every other major holiday. For much of the summer, our lives were busy shuttling her to day camp, heading to the pool with Nadean and her kids, going for bike rides and taking the dog to the park, family vacations and trips to see the grandparents. Every other Thanksgiving, Christmas, and spring break we had a little ball of energy around, forcing us to celebrate. On off years, we were as likely as not to skip the holidays entirely. It simply wasn't festive to decorate a tree or cook a turkey for two. When Sonja wasn't with us, Brian, Kelby, and I rattled around in our four-bedroom house (we'd paid for more space by moving to the suburbs, where the commute into the city was awful), never even entering some of the spaces.

After thinking for years that we might never be healthy enough to risk it, we finally decided it was safe to bring a baby into our home. I was close to getting my master's degree. We both had steady jobs. Our marriage was solid; though we still had occasional arguments, we'd learned to work through them and no longer threatened divorce in regular screaming matches. Brian was more stable over-all. Although he occasionally sank into depressions, they weren't as severe or as long-lasting as they had been before. He was also better at recognizing them when they started, and would see his physician for medication before they worsened. His PTSD symptoms were largely under control. Not only that, but Sonja actually served as a steadying force, her sheer presence forcing Brian to remember that the future was coming whether he believed in it or not. Perhaps, we thought, having a baby would do the same thing. We were ready.

I stopped taking birth control, excited to start a new stage of our lives.

And didn't get pregnant.

"It might take a few months," we assured each other.

A few months passed. We went from simply no longer trying to avoid pregnancy to actively trying to get pregnant, monitoring the calendar and scheduling sex. Still nothing.

The memory of my first OB-GYN appointment after I left the Army started flashing in my mind. Brian was still active duty, and we were both getting all our medical care at Walter Reed. Every time I showed up for myself, I was wracked with guilt: seeing ampu-tees, young troops with severe burns, and uniformed personnel who were newly blind and just learning to walk with canes made me loath to come in at all. How could I take up even a moment of a doctor's time complaining about my allergies when these wounded warriors needed care? So by the time I made it from the parking garage through the lobby to the gynecologist's office, I was already feeling rattled.

In her office, she went through the standard series of questions about my history. Then she asked, "Do you plan to have children?"

I shrugged. "Sure. In a few years, I guess."

The doctor pulled her glasses to the tip of her nose and tilted her head so she could look me in the eyes, quirking her eyebrows up slightly. She didn't say anything, just appraised me quietly for a moment, but I could see what she was thinking: "You're not getting any younger."

I was horrified. 'How dare she!' I thought, 'I'm not even thirty! There's plenty of time!'

Three years later at age thirty-two, remembering that moment, I was plagued with guilt. Had I waited too long? Was it from the deployment? Was it Brian? He'd told me once that he'd stood in front of a piece of radar equipment on purpose right after his divorce so he could never have any more kids. Had it worked?

After a year, we made an appointment to see a specialist. The doctor ran a series of tests on both of us (mine unpleasant and invasive, Brian's a simple variation on a standard and enjoyable activity), and saw no reason that we shouldn't be pregnant—but we weren't. It was time to try interventions. After a series of injections, I went in for an attempt at IUI (intrauterine insemination)—the "turkey baster" method, in which the doctor aimed the payload at exactly the right location at precisely the right moment. Brian held my hand. "This isn't quite how I pictured getting you pregnant," he murmured, kissing my forehead.

I didn't get pregnant.

It was a relatively expensive procedure, and Tricare didn't cover it—they only covered infertility testing, not treatment. The next step, in vitro fertilization or IVF, would be even more expensive, and it wasn't covered either.

I reached out to the VA. At the big conference I'd spoken at, a presenter had specifically said VA covered infertility treatment for women veterans, so I went to my local VA Medical Center. The doctor assured me they did not cover infertility treatments. "Are you sure?" I pressed. She was sure, she said, but would have her nurse look into it. The nurse called to confirm that they didn't.

When I bumped into the woman who had made the presentation a few weeks later, I told her about my experience. She pursed her lips in frustration and wrote down the name of the hospital. Within days, I got a call: "Ms. Williams? I was mistaken. VA *does* cover some infertility treatments."

I contacted the specialist's office, and the billing department said under no circumstances would they take money from the VA. "That doesn't make any sense!" I said. "You're telling me that if the VA sent you a check you would refuse to cash it?" It was baffling, but that was how the system worked. The clinic required an up-front global fee to cover the entire procedure. VA would only reimburse per procedure. I couldn't pay up-front and have VA reimburse me. There was no way to make the system work. I tried contacting other infertility clinics in the area, and eventually gave up in frustration.

"It's just not fair!" I complained to Brian. "We did everything right! We waited until we were ready. We have a house, good jobs. I have a master's degree. We did what we were supposed to do!"

He patted my hand awkwardly. "I'm sorry, honey."

It seemed as if the universe was trying to send me a message: I wasn't meant to be a mother.

———

RIGHT BEFORE CHRISTMAS 2009, I learned that a close relative of mine, Anne, was pregnant and had decided to place the baby for adoption. After thinking about it for a week or so, I couldn't resist calling. "Is it true?" I asked her mother.

She sighed. "Yes. I don't like it, but what can I do? She's made up her mind!"

"Brian and I have been trying unsuccessfully to get pregnant for two years."

"I didn't know that!"

"Well, we didn't tell anyone. I didn't want everyone to ask me if I was pregnant every single time I saw them!"

"I understand that."

"Do you think," I paused, took a breath, plunged on, "do you think she'd consider letting us adopt the baby?"

"You know, I'm not sure," she said. "Let me talk to Anne about it."

Over the next few days, I had a series of conversations with Anne, her mom, and my husband. Brian had been opposed to the idea of adoption when I'd first suggested it; the thought of not knowing a baby's background put him off. This was different—we knew the birth mother, were confident she had a healthy pregnancy. We were warming to the idea, getting used to it. Finally we got the call: "Anne wanted me to tell you that she and the birth father have agreed to place the baby with you and Brian. But you should know: she's being induced in a week."

I sucked in a deep breath. That was much sooner than I'd expected—hardly any time to prepare. That night, I talked to Brian. "I'm sorry to have to pressure you, but we have to decide. Now."

He stared into my eyes for a long moment, then reached out and took my hand. "Okay," he said, "let's do it."

With that, we dove into a flurry of activity: cleaning out a bedroom that had been collecting household detritus, booking plane tickets, finding out what was required legally to bring home the baby across state lines, researching what the process would be to formally adopt him down the road. I was too busy to even fret about the upcoming major change in our lives—there was simply too much to *do* to spend any time thinking. We bought nothing and told no one, afraid that Anne might change her mind. And then we were in Texas. Our hotel was in a dry county, so we couldn't even soothe our nerves with beers. Brian and I spent some time talking to Anne and the birth father, getting to know one another.

The next day we were holding a tiny baby boy in our arms.

Our friends and family rallied immediately to support us when we announced the news. The day we got home from the airport, there were boxes with baby items waiting on our porch. Some of the Honeybadgers rallied to hold a baby shower within weeks. Everything was a blur of diapers and bottles, rocking and swaddling. Kelby barked at us every time Duncan cried for the first two weeks. "Is she angry at him for making noise, or at us for not being able to fix him?" Brian asked.

"I don't know—I'm pretty sure she thinks she'd be able to take better care of him than we are!" I joked.

Zoe flew out for a long weekend. She even put Duncan's bassinet in her room and gave me an incredible gift: two full nights' sleep. While we sat together cooing over my new baby, I almost couldn't believe how much our lives had changed. Six years earlier, we'd been in Mosul together, trying to intercept and translate enemy communications. Now we were both mothers, trying to decode cryptic messages from babies—a whole new challenge. In many ways, war seemed easier, less complicated. You only have one real goal: survival. If you fuck up, you die. But if I fucked this up, an innocent baby would suffer...and there were so many more things that it seemed I might fuck up! I'd met Zoe's kids, and they were both polite, happy, energetic boys. Hopefully, since my best friend—with whom I shared so much in common—was adjusting well to being a mother, I would too.

Throughout those first few weeks, I was wildly grateful that Brian had already been through this once before. Everything about caring for a newborn was terrifying since there had been no time for me to read any baby books. "His poop—it looks like tar! Is that normal?"

"Yep, that's normal."

"Duncan's hair is falling out! Is that normal?"

"Yup, that's normal too."

"What are those tiny bumps on his face?!"

"Baby acne. Don't even ask—yes, it's normal."

Brian was a wonderful father, snuggling Duncan, changing diapers, getting up for midnight feedings. He was more patient than I was during long crying fits. The total responsibility of caring for a newborn drew him—drew both of us—out, prevented the tendency toward self-absorption and introspection. "It's hard to be self-centered when you're worrying about a baby," Brian mused. "Can you believe how even though he's so tiny, he's so much bigger than we are?" I smiled, understanding exactly what he meant. Duncan's whole life stretched out before him, and we had been entrusted with helping him begin it. We couldn't let our pasts bury us—if Duncan needed something, we had to put our own bullshit aside and care for him.

Part of the reason we got Kelby was to help Brian—but it didn't work.[1] Although he'd thought the need to care for her would force him to go for walks, in the end he would just let her out into the yard. But it was different with Duncan. It's impossible to ignore a crying baby. And the love of a baby is like no other—it is offered with no judgment, no conditions, no expectations. It is a gift so freely given that reciprocation is impossible to deny. There was no flattened affect when Brian gazed into the adoring eyes of his son; it softened him, opened him.

Gazing at our son inspired me to get physically active again, too. I wanted to set a good example for him and stay healthy enough to be part of his life far into the future. Lacking the camaraderie and

---

1. I wish we had gotten a trained and certified dog. Several organizations, including http://paws4people.org, specifically prepare dogs to work with veterans struggling with PTSD, and anecdotally it is extremely helpful. When you have a rescue dog with her own psychological problems...not so much.

incentives of staying in shape provided by the Army, I'd been unable to stick with a solid exercise routine. Duncan was motivation, but I needed a goal—so I trained for and participated in a sprint-distance triathlon in our neighborhood. Accomplishing it felt great, and I slowly started getting back into shape.

Not long after we brought Duncan home, Brian had knee surgery to repair an ACL he tore when he took up kickboxing. And weeks later, he started a new job in the Office of Congressional and Legislative Affairs at the Department of Veterans Affairs. I worried that all these major life events piled so close together—surgery, a new baby, a new job—would throw off his routine and send him into a tailspin. But he rallied, adjusting remarkably well to the new schedule. After teasing me for years about going to bed early ("I know you don't like to have fun, Kayla!"), having to get to the office on time—and get up at night to feed a hungry infant—forced Brian to turn in early, too.

Instead of working from home, Brian had to commute to an office—a long process that involved driving to a park and ride, taking a bus to a metro stop, and taking the train the rest of the way into the city. We both worried about how he would handle the bus—but he was able to manage his anxiety. He carried a little vial of Valium religiously, but its mere presence was usually talisman enough to keep panic attacks at bay. Occasionally he had days where it was simply too much to bear, and we would carpool in to my office, where he could pick up a different train. But generally he coped fine. We marveled at how far he had come—for years, the prospect of getting on a bus had been inconceivable. Now it was a daily occurrence.

Brian enjoyed working at the VA, by and large. Rather than pushing for changes from the outside, he was able to work toward them from inside the system. There were other young veterans of OIF and OEF in his office, and they were all equally enthusiastic about making a positive difference for vets. I'd been appointed to the VA Advisory Committee on Women Veterans, and I too gained a window into the system. It was clear that Secretary Shinseki was passionate about improving the department and caring for all veterans. And this wasn't just lip service—as a partial amputee and the former Secretary of the Army, Shinseki was deeply invested in changing the relationship the VA had with veterans and ensuring they were well cared for.

The work was interesting, and Brian's experience working on the Hill at VoteVets meant he already had contacts and knew how the system worked—the learning curve wasn't as steep as he had feared it might be. And the VA was accommodating of service-connected disabilities. There was no discrimination if he needed to take time to handle medical or psychological issues. Rather than being leery of hiring those with war wounds, VA actively sought out disabled veterans.

WHEN DUNCAN WAS ABOUT ten months old, I came down with a nasty cold. Like most kids who go to day care, he seemed to bring home a new bug every few weeks. Trying desperately to control my symptoms, I popped Sudafed constantly.

After a couple of days, something started to tug at the edges of my consciousness. I checked a calendar. My period was late. That never happened.

After Duncan was born, we hadn't started using birth control again, but we also hadn't been actively trying to get pregnant. After trying unsuccessfully for so long, we just assumed it would never happen. I dug out a leftover test kit and peed on the stick. Within minutes the sign was clear: I was knocked up. My first panicky thought was that all the cold medicine might have harmed the embryo. Why hadn't I paid more attention to the calendar?

Brian walked into the bathroom, just home from work. "Hey, honey! What's up?"

Automatically, I hid the stick behind my back. "Uh..." I mumbled.

He squinted at me. "You okay?"

"Um..."

"This is a good thing!" I told myself. "Why are you hiding this?" After trying so hard to avoid pregnancy for so many years, I hadn't quite wrapped my brain around the concept: this was something we wanted. I handed Brian the stick. "Happy birthday!"

"What's this?" my husband asked.

"I'm pregnant."

"Are you sure?!"

"Well, that's what the test says. Are you happy?"

"I'm not sure how I feel. This is so unexpected. And Duncan is still so little..."

We looked at the baby. He was unrolling the toilet paper and giggling.

"But we wanted this, didn't we?" I asked. "I mean, we didn't start using birth control again."

"Well, it's been almost three years since you stopped. I guess I just didn't think it would happen. Let's see what the doctor says. Those tests can be wrong, right?"

It was confirmed: I was pregnant. In a year and a half, we would go from zero babies to two. And this time, I had a full pregnancy to fret about what was coming.

Would we be able to manage it? How would Brian cope when I went into labor? What if he had a panic attack and I had to handle it all alone?

"I'll be fine," he reassured me. "I catastrophize about stupid things, but when it's serious I do fine."

Nervous, I hired a doula. "Just in case," I told him.

After doing a lot of reading, I'd decided to try for a natural childbirth. I hate catheters and wanted the freedom to walk around in case my labor slowed. Choosing a midwife seemed the best way to maximize the chances for a positive experience. Jen had horrified me with part of her birth story: "The doctor didn't warn me he was going to do an episiotomy, just went in there with a scalpel. Seeing the blood spray reminded me of seeing blood splatter when the IED went off in Afghanistan and I almost lost it." I was determined to have a provider who would communicate with me better.

It went remarkably smoothly. Reluctant to get turned away if we arrived too soon, I resisted going to the hospital until Brian put his foot down. "We are leaving. Now." They admitted me immediately. When the time came to push a few hours later, I'd never experienced so much pain or felt more helpless. The knowledge that there was no possible way I could protect myself was nerve-wracking: my body was committed to one thing only, and I was completely dependent on those around me. Brian was fully involved and never flinched; he stayed right by my side and supported me as Alayna entered the world.

When our newborn daughter was placed on my chest, he kissed my cheek. "You did great, honey."

"So did you," I said. "So did you."

EPILOGUE

———— ★ ————

Things had been going well. The feeling of being on edge, waiting for an impending disaster to arrive, started to slowly fade. Then when Alayna was a few months old, Brian started feeling light-headed and nauseated. At first it was just a couple of times a month. Then weekly. Then daily. He was afraid to drive some days, worried he would pass out and wreck, but couldn't bear to get on the bus in case he started vomiting. "I wonder if it's related to the TBI?" he asked. "Maybe the shrapnel shifted or something?"

"When was the last time you got a CT scan?" I asked him.

"Not since I got off active duty. Seven years ago, I guess?"

"Are you serious?!" I was horrified. Part of my effort to back off and be his wife rather than his case manager meant that I was completely disengaged from his medical care. He hadn't been to the dentist in a couple of years either, and other than occasional gentle reminders, I was hands-off this piece of his life. But this news freaked me out—I'd assumed he was getting some kind of regular follow-up care.

"The civilian doctors don't know anything about TBI from blast injuries. They just tell me to go to the VA. But I had such a shitty experience there..."

"Go back. You haven't been to VA for years—they've been improving."

"Yeah, and I work there now. I guess I should."

So Brian called the D.C. VA Medical Center and made an appointment. A whole series of appointments, actually. When he got through to the TBI case manager, she was astonished that he hadn't been getting regular follow-up care for his brain injury or PTSD and arranged for him to see multiple providers during a long intake session. These appointments in 2012 would be the first thorough examination he'd gotten from providers familiar with blast injuries since 2005, when he was being medically retired from the Army. The first appointment was with a physiatrist. "That's what the TBI book said you needed!" I exclaimed. "Remember? And they didn't even have one at Walter Reed!"

At his request, I went with him to his initial appointment. The exam took an hour, rather than the fifteen minutes a typical doctor seems to spend with patients. The physiatrist spent a long time ensuring he understood Brian's history, concerns, and goals. He ordered tests—including a CT scan to ensure there had been no changes. And he made a series of recommendations. "I want you to start taking fish oil supplements. There's strong early evidence that it helps the brain. You need to exercise regularly, that's been proven to help cognition. And you have to cut back on your drinking—alcohol is very bad for people with TBIs. I'd like you to see a psychologist regularly for your PTSD, and follow up with vestibular therapy for your dizziness. We have a recreational therapy program, which I recommend you try. Don't take up kickboxing again—the jarring is not good for someone with your history. And finally, you should quit the fire department. I don't think it's a good idea for you in general, but especially with the lightheadedness you've been experiencing."

Brian walked out with mixed feelings. "I'm glad he didn't just say, 'You're lucky to be alive—there's nothing we can do about your other problems, just be happy.' But I don't know about some of his advice."

"Give it a shot," I said. "What have you got to lose at this point?"

I was pleased that the doctor had asked Brian to drink less and exercise more. And though I knew Brian would miss the camaraderie and service of volunteering with the fire department, I was secretly relieved about that, too. The nights he spent on duty (once a week from 6 p.m. to 6 a.m.) were tough on me, home with both kids. I'd quit when Duncan was born, but Brian had stuck with it. Though I tried to be supportive, it was challenging. This had deepened my empathy for military families—here I was stressing about being on my own with the babies overnight once a week, they had to deal with multiple year-long deployments. It was hard on Brian to quit, though. He held on to his gear for another year before finally turning it in. We stayed in touch with the department, bringing food in on major holidays and trying to support it in other ways.

FOR RECREATIONAL THERAPY, Brian started a golf program. Once a week, he and a group of other wounded warriors would head into the Armed Forces Retirement Home golf course and get a lesson from a professional golfer. "If I finish the whole session, they'll give me a free set of clubs!" he told me.

"Don't you have a set your dad gave you?"

"Yeah, but they don't fit me right. I'm way too tall for them— and they're like twenty years old. These would be used, but much newer and nicer."

I shrugged. It was great that he was enthusiastic, but I'd seen Brian excited about new activities before and wasn't convinced it would stick. His habit of going all in on a series of short-lived enthusiasms had long been a source of friction in our marriage. Brian would try something, enjoy it, and insist on buying a ton of accessories . . . only to abandon the hobby just as quickly.

After our ski trip to Colorado—the one I spent with my leg in a cast—he'd insisted on buying a snowboard. "Can't you just rent one?" I asked. "We don't go very often."

"No! They might not have my size because I'm so tall—and the quality is never good."

And of course it couldn't just be a snowboard—there were boots, a jacket, a helmet, goggles, gloves, stickers, magazine subscriptions— he went all in. After he used the snowboard twice in one season, Brian announced, "The snow on the East Coast sucks for snowboarding," and abandoned it in the corner of the garage.

A couple of years later, he tried surfing during a summer vacation to the Outer Banks. Soon surfing magazines started showing up in the mailbox. The next year he insisted on buying a surfboard the day we arrived at the rental house on the beach. And two wetsuits, short- and long-sleeved. Days later, he took a surfing class. "Can I buy a new surfboard?" he asked me after the session. "This one is the wrong size for me."

"Can you return that one?" I asked skeptically.

"No, it's already been used."

"Then I think it's a really bad idea to buy two surfboards inside a week. You have to make your own decision about this, but financially I think it's a really bad move."

He fussed and pouted, but didn't buy a second surfboard.

I seethed. Why did Brian have to buy so many things, instead of just renting or making do? I wondered if this was a remnant of the TBI—the impulse control portion of his brain had been damaged. Although Brian had gotten better about not buying expensive things without at least discussing it with me first, I supposed there was a chance that his infatuation with trying new activities and buying all the accompanying toys was linked to that.

When Brian had started kickboxing at a local gym, he'd bought shorts, gloves, and wraps, and signed a long-term contract—and then had to abandon it when he blew out his knee. He'd bought a fancy helmet when he got into hockey—then never used it after we went to a rink once and he decided his balance was too off. An expensive bike to replace the cheap one he already had when I suggested family bike rides—hardly ever used. A comprehensive set of equipment for brewing beer—rarely used, though we had gathered an extensive set of pint glasses. Drinking beer—that was a hobby that stuck. I'm pretty sure the first thing Brian said when the doctor confirmed my pregnancy was, "Sweet! Designated driver for nine months!" Everywhere we went on vacation required a trip to a local microbrewery for a tour, a sample—and a T-shirt and pint glass.

He'd even been on a vehicle binge: first he bought a Baja Bug to work on. Then he traded that for a motorcycle. Insisting that wasn't the right size, he bought a Harley. For a while we had two motorcycles in the garage, until I threw a fit and he sold the old one. Sure enough, biker gear started proliferating. He complained that the Harley wasn't the right size and took it apart to make modifications . . . then, when Brian was unable to fix it, it sat, nonfunctioning, in the garage for months.

So this golf thing, I assumed, would be just another hobby that would require the purchase of lots of accessories and an initial investment of time before being cast aside. And sure enough, golf magazines started showing up in the mailbox. Golf books filled the memory of his Kindle. A growing assortment of bold golf pants started to work their way into his wardrobe. I just shook my head, waiting for it to pass.

But it didn't. Brian finished all the sessions, and started going on his own to the local courses. Sometimes he just hit balls at the driving range. Other weekends he would let the course match him up with other singletons to play a game. "You . . . meet strangers?"

I asked. Brian usually insisted I make all the phone calls to arrange appointments and was highly averse to situations where he would have to talk to people he didn't already know. It always surprised me—when he was with friends or drinking, Brian was gregarious, outgoing, expansive, and wildly funny. But if I tried to drag him on a double date, he was reserved and withdrawn almost to the point of embarrassment. The thought of him voluntarily spending hours talking to strangers on the golf course was amazing.

"I almost had a panic attack on the bus today," he said one day after work.

"Oh yeah? Did you take a Valium?" I asked absently, trying to spoon baby food into Alayna's mouth while Duncan threw Cheerios onto the floor.

"Nope. I used a mindfulness technique from golf."

I set the spoon down and turned to face him. "What?"

"I've been reading about sports psychology in those golf books. About how even pros can choke when they're playing. It had some techniques they can use to calm down and refocus. So when I felt the panic attack coming on, I tried it out. And it totally worked!" Brian was smiling, pleased.

It elicited a grin from me in response. "That's amazing! I guess the VA really knows what they're doing with that recreational ther-apy stuff. I kinda thought it was bullshit, but that's awesome!"

I got up and hugged him. Duncan and Alayna insisted on being gathered up for a group hug. It felt good—like we were a real, nor-mal family.

———

AFTER IRAQ, I DIDN'T cry when people died in movies. Well, adults anyway. Babies and dogs dying left me a blubbering mess, but adults? Fuck 'em. We all die. They weren't angels. I'd gotten so used to the prospect of imminent death in Iraq that it just wasn't that big of a deal anymore. I expected to die. It didn't bother me. Shouldn't everyone feel the same way—especially religious people who expect a glorious afterlife? You'd think they'd be actively excited about the prospect.

Around the time when the end of the Iraq war was formally declared, Alayna was about six months old and my son was a little over two. One day, while I was sitting on the floor playing with them, Duncan was being remarkably sweet to his baby sister, leaning over to kiss her repeatedly while she giggled with delight. As I watched them, smiling, it suddenly occurred to me: "When I die, I'll never get to see them again." Tears sprang into my eyes and I gathered them suddenly into my arms, squeezing them until they squirmed to get away. "I don't want to die," I realized.

It felt simultaneously profound and ridiculous. Of course I didn't want to die. But it wasn't until one marriage, two children, and eight years after getting back from Iraq that I was able to truly open myself up to that knowledge.

Loving and caring for children had changed me: it made me feel more affection and empathy for others as well. Yes, I have loved Brian for years. But the love was deeply tangled in a sense of responsibility and fear, shot through for much of that time with threads of anger and resentment. I rarely felt genuine empathy for what he was going through, focusing instead on trying to find solutions or a way for us to get through the results together. And I'd had virtually no sympathy for my parents when I deployed, for Brian's parents when we got home, for military families more generally. We were getting shot at—what were they going through? Knowledge of how safe and secure they were back here obscured from me the different type of suffering they go through.

Looking at my own children now, I try to imagine them grown—and maimed. It's nearly enough to make me want to take to the streets carrying protest signs and marching for peace. Reporters have asked me, "Would you let your daughter join the Army?" And I've answered as honestly as I could: "If it's what she truly wanted to do, I would support her. Same with my son. Because if I didn't, they would do it anyway, and I might lose the ability to be there for them. But do I want either of my children to go to war? Of course not." I bite my knuckles watching them climb on playground equipment worrying they might fall—how do parents take watching their children head off to a combat zone?

I wonder if it's the hormones of pregnancy, childbirth, and breastfeeding—the flood of oxytocin, a hormone that is linked with empathy, trust, and love, thought to facilitate bonding and reduce stress hormones. Is the cause of some of my changed feelings chemical? What about Brian? Research shows that fathers of newborns also experience spikes in oxytocin levels.[1] For years, I had resigned myself to a future with little cuddling, affection, or eye contact—Brian just didn't seem to enjoy non-sexual physical contact and generally didn't meet my gaze. But he snuggled readily with Duncan and was an active, engaged father, staring into Duncan's eyes, talking to him, playing with him. Gradually this spread to me as well; we started holding hands more often, sitting closer together. Was it possible that loving this tiny baby was letting us learn to love each other more deeply? Could it be helping Brian more generally?[2]

Perhaps the mechanism is unimportant. Whether spending time with our babies sparked physiological changes inside our brains or not, it certainly opened our hearts.

---

1. http://www.livescience.com/10784-dads-hormone-boost-caring-baby.html
2. http://www.myhealthnewsdaily.com/608-oxytocin-therapy-psychiatric-illness-101205-.html

THE TEN-YEAR ANNIVERSARY of Brian's injury is coming up. A lot of people in the veterans' community call it their Alive Day. Brian calls it his Phoenix Day—I strongly prefer that term. The imagery of the phoenix arising from its own ashes is powerful. It isn't just about staying alive, it's about renewal. The journey Brian and I have been on hasn't been trying to survive and get back to the way things were before, it has been about forging a new normal—one that is in many ways better than the old.

There's been so much talk about post-traumatic stress, including arguments about whether or not to drop the "disorder" and simply call it PTS, or change the D to an I for "injury" to emphasize that it has a precipitating event rather than being caused by some inherent weakness, as part of efforts to destigmatize help-seeking, particularly among combat veterans.[3] The flip side, post-traumatic growth, has been largely ignored.[4] But that aspect to the aftermath of trauma is just as real. I came home keenly aware of how lucky I am to live in America today, where I have access to health care, electricity, the comforts of modern life—and where the chances of my loved ones dying due to a terrorist attack pale in comparison to the likelihood they will die from diseases caused by overconsumption.

And over time, Brian and I both came to deeply feel our connection to our fellow citizens and be highly conscious of the responsibilities that laid upon us to contribute to society. We are both convinced that having suffered, going through the crucible of war, drove development of our morality. Hermann Hesse said, "Who would be born must first destroy a world," echoing Carl Jung's "There is no coming to consciousness without pain." And so, like a chick hatching from

---

3. http://articles.washingtonpost.com/2012-05-05/world/35454931_1_ptsd-post-traumatic-stress-psychiatrists

4. http://www.nytimes.com/2012/03/25/magazine/post-traumatic-stresss-surprisingly-positive-flip-side.html?pagewanted=all&_r=0

its shell or the phoenix rising from its ashes, rebirth and renewal sometimes only come from wrenching displacements of the world you knew.

Getting to where we are today has not been easy. I liken it to the stock market—a jagged line with lots of ups and downs, but over the stretch of years the upward trend is clear. People have often asked me why I stayed, and I still can't answer that question satisfactorily. My motivations are tangled. I loved my husband, but didn't always like him. I felt an obligation to care for him, one that was mixed up in the military ethos of "Leave no fallen comrade behind." But sometimes the desire to run from that responsibility was so strong that I had to find ways to tie myself to him for fear that I wouldn't stay—getting married, having a public wedding, buying a house: all of these things served as ways I could bind myself, make it harder to leave in a fit of pique. I'm not a religious woman, but in the early years I sustained myself on faith: a steadfast conviction that he would get better, if I tried hard enough, waited long enough, hoped hard enough, he would get better. And he did.

It's made me feel terribly awkward when giving dating advice. When boyfriends treat my friends like garbage, I say, "Leave him!" And they say, "But you stayed. And now look at Brian!" It seems I've lived out the fantasy I shared with so many dumbass girls in high school: if you just love that bad boy hard enough, he'll change! I have to explain, "But Brian had a TBI and PTSD—there were reasons for his problems, and a path to recovery. There's no therapy for asshole."

Early on in our marriage, Brian would accuse me of trying to change him. "This isn't about me changing you," I responded. "This is about the changes that naturally occur when you grow up. Cleaning the house, paying bills, being responsible—that isn't me trying to turn you into someone you're not. That is me expecting you to go through the transition that everyone goes through when they become adults." It baffled me. Shouldn't all this have already happened during his first marriage, or when Sonja was born?

One day he confessed, "Sometimes I feel like ... all the development that was supposed to happen, when I got the brain injury, it just halted. I stopped progressing." But he hadn't stopped—just paused.

During some of the rougher times, two memories helped sustain me. One was a friend of mine from high school, who built a lasting relationship with his girlfriend after they had a daughter together, telling me, "I don't always love her, but I always like her. There are weeks or even months when I'm not that physically attracted to her—I've even felt attracted to other women. But I've always been profoundly interested in her, how she thinks and who she is. And I respect her. I genuinely care about who she is and where she's going."

The other was Anne's mother telling me about her relationship with her second husband. "Whenever one of us comes home from work, we hug and kiss each other first, then the kids. And we make a point of spending at least fifteen minutes a day talking, just the two of us, no matter how busy we are. Because the kids are going to grow up and leave the house, get married, have kids of their own—and we need to still have a relationship when that happens! We are going to be together for the rest of our lives, so we have to invest in our marriage."

Those two conversations helped shape my understanding of what relationships are about and see them as long-term propositions. It isn't about being happy every day. There may be months or even years that are a hard slog. But with a solid foundation of love and respect, with shared values and goals, the investment of sticking together through those tough times pays off in the long run. Perhaps our shared experience of war also helps bind us closer together— certainly it gives us a more visceral understanding of what the other has experienced.

And here we are.

Brian still cycles through periods of depression that come on out of nowhere, leaving him low and joyless for weeks or months, which can only be kicked with a new round of medication. He still has headaches, sometimes short stabbing ones that double him over in agony for just a few minutes, others longer and lower, driving him into bed for hours. And his unpredictable bouts of PTSD symptoms still force him to carry his tiny vial of Valium to ward off anxiety attacks. We wonder if he will be hit with early-onset dementia (common for those with TBIs), if the shrapnel may shift, or if the future holds other physical or mental ailments due to the IED.

Doing research for this book, I tracked down Dr. Armonda, the neurosurgeon who operated on Brian in Baghdad. Brian hadn't been sure the doctor would remember him, but Dr. Armonda recognized him immediately. It was powerfully moving to see him grinning ear to ear at Brian's incredible recovery. It hadn't occurred to me that battlefield surgeons often don't know the ultimate prognosis of their patients, that their secondary trauma might be exacerbated by that lack of closure. While we talked about Brian's journey toward healing, Dr. Armonda congratulated us on our successful marriage: "You know, only 20 percent of TBI patients are still married five years later." The statistic shocked me. I knew the path we traveled had been hard, but had no idea so many other couples didn't make it. Our marriage isn't perfect. But it is solid.

Having children has actually—counterintuitively—improved our sex life. Before we had kids, it was easy to push it off to the next day if one of us was tired or busy . . . and then have the same thing happen again and again until seemingly all of a sudden it had been weeks. Some of the medications Brian was put on decrease sex drive, which could throw us off for months. And some of his symptoms, like the flattened affect, angry outbursts, and negative worldview, also made it much harder for me to feel sexually attracted to him. My hormonally induced shifting sex drive and changing body during and after pregnancy made me much more aware of how factors outside one's immediate control can influence desire, and helped open new lines of communication between me and Brian about sex. We realized that having to juggle all our schedules meant we had to add sex to the mix or it could get lost entirely, so even if we're not both in the mood when opportunities arise, we take them anyway, aiming for twice a week. There's a good chance that the intimacy will spark arousal, and even if the time available or level of passion is constrained by circumstances, our relationship benefits from simply having regular sex—it reminds us that we are husband and wife, not simply parents and household partners.

Sometimes we still wonder what we want to be when we grow up. Neither of us is completely satisfied with where we are or what we do. I contemplate leaving RAND to work more actively in the veterans' community. Brian is considering going back to school. We toss around small-business ideas. But both of us know that our vague itching to improve our lives even further is a clear sign of our profound privilege.

As the kids get older, we want to find new ways to volunteer. Getting involved in projects larger than ourselves and committing to our community has been an important part of our road to recovery, but having two young children has eaten into our available time. We are anxious to find new ways to connect.

Brian and I have sacrificed more than most for this country: a tiny fraction of our peers have served in Iraq or Afghanistan, compared to the large percentages of citizens who signed up to fight in WWII. And though significant numbers of veterans from today's conflicts have come home with some type of physical or psychological wound, few have sustained the type of severe penetrating brain injury Brian suffered.

And yet.

We have lain wreaths on the graves at Arlington. We have seen those who have come home so profoundly injured that they will never be functionally independent. Our sacrifices pale to nothingness beside the grief of those families.

We are living proof that for many struggling with physical and psychological wounds of war, there is a path back from the brink of despair to a meaningful new existence. Though it is a rough road, with the right support it can be navigated. All of us, as citizens, have an obligation to ensure that services are in place for those who need them. Brian and I hope that our example and our efforts ease the way for those still coming home.

We are blessed beyond imagining, being able to look back over the decade we've known one another, assess the ebb and flow of our relationship, and imagine where it will go as we move forward. The wars we fought, both overseas and here at home, may have shaped us, but they will not define us.

APPENDIX

It's been widely accepted that the Department of Defense was not prepared for what would come after major combat operations were over in Iraq, which contributed to the protracted insurgency that developed in the ensuing security vacuum. The same seemed to be true at home: both DoD and VA were not prepared for the influx of troops that came home with severe physical wounds or what came to be known as the "signature wounds" of these conflicts, TBI and PTSD. Brian was injured fairly early in the Iraq war, and that early cohort of wounded warriors was heavily affected by gaps in systems of care, leading to a proliferation of many of the problems we experienced personally: poor care, lengthy and confusing MEB/PEB processes, inadequate case management, unemployment, poor support pursuing higher education, lack of support networks, trouble identifying resources, and more. For some, these barriers proved insurmountable, leading to homelessness, suicide, family dissolution, and other crises.

A series of investigations, commissions, and task forces produced reports identifying a plethora of problems and offering myriad solutions. Among these were the President's Commission on Care for America's Returning Wounded Warriors (commonly known as the Dole-Shalala Commission),[1] numerous Government Accountability Office (GAO) reports including one on "Challenges Encountered

---

1. http://militarymedicine.com/node/77

by Injured Servicemembers during Their Recovery Process,"[2] the well-known and often cited RAND *Invisible Wounds of War* report,[3] an Army Medicine TBI Task Force Report,[4] one from the Defense Health Board on mental health,[5] and many more. Advocates also pressured members of Congress to do more; over time, this led to significant changes. For example, the 2008 National Defense Authorization Act contained a number of provisions to improve care for wounded warriors and veterans,[6] and the Post-9/11 GI Bill dramatically increased education benefits for today's veterans. In addition, a vast number of nonprofit organizations have stepped up to help fill remaining gaps. Those who come home today are far more likely to find proper care and services. That does not, however, mean that the system is perfect or that no work remains to be done.

At events around the country, people regularly ask me, "What can I do?" Sometimes, these are wounded warriors or families still struggling to find the support they need. Often, the question comes from civilians who want to help, but don't know how. Below, I offer some suggestions. Note that these are *highly personal*—I urge you to use them only as a starting point. Many organizations are local, state, or regional. There are variations in purpose or direction that may be a better fit for you than for me (for example, I'm not drawn to faith-based groups but that may be right for you). I can't claim to know about all good programs. And it's always a good idea to do your own due diligence—a nonprofit I mention or ignore now may have changed focus or leadership, for better or for worse, by the time you read this.

---

2. http://www.gao.gov/products/GAO-07-606T

3. http://www.rand.org/pubs/monographs/MG720.html

4. http://www.armymedicine.army.mil/r2d/tbitfr.html

5. http://www.health.mil/dhb/subcommittees-MHTF.cfm

6. http://www.fas.org/sgp/crs/misc/RL34371.pdf

The most important message I would offer to anyone struggling is *Don't give up*. There is compelling evidence that treatment works for mental health issues, but that doesn't mean the first counselor you try will be the right one for you. You may not want to be medicated—if not, try a psychologist, social worker, or group therapy. Or yoga, or kickboxing, or volunteering. Don't isolate, stagnate, or quit. If you bought toothpaste and didn't like the flavor, would you swear off brushing your teeth forever? No, you'd pick a new variety. Apply that same principle to picking a mental health provider or an organization to volunteer with: if the first one doesn't work out, try another until you find a good fit.

SERVICE MEMBERS, VETERANS, AND WOUNDED WARRIORS

Veterans in crisis can call the crisis line at 800-273-TALK (8255) twenty-four hours a day. They also have online chat sessions and more. Memorize the number and share it.

Department of Defense (DoD)

Compared to when Brian and I were on active duty, DoD has a huge number of new or dramatically expanded resources.

- Military OneSource (www.militaryonesource.mil) offers everything from financial counseling to disaster resources to non-medical counseling.

- inTransition (www.health.mil/intransition/) provides coaches to maintain continuity of mental health care and more during times of transition.

- The Real Warriors campaign (http://www.realwarriors.net) is a multimedia public awareness effort to encourage troops (as well as vets and family members) to seek help.

- The Defense Centers of Excellence for Psychological Health and Traumatic Brain Injury (http://www.dcoe. health.mil) offers a tremendous number of resources on those issues.

- The Sexual Assault Prevention and Response website (http://www.sapr.mil) has lots of data for those hoping to learn more about MST, as well as links to resources for those personally affected.

Department of Veterans Affairs (VA)

You earned your benefits—use them. VA (http://www.va.gov) is a somewhat complicated beast: it's important to remember that VA is comprised of three entities—the Veterans Health Administration (VHA), Veterans Benefits Administration (VBA), and National Cemetery Administration (NCA)—and they're fairly disconnected. You may qualify for health care even if you don't qualify for disability (for instance, medical and mental health care for conditions related to military sexual trauma is provided to veterans regardless of type of discharge or benefit claim status). So you may have to spend some time figuring out what you need and how to get it. Get signed up and learn what you qualify for.

Veterans' health care may have a bad reputation in many quarters, but that's outdated: independent researchers have found that VHA patients receive higher-quality care on many measures.[7]

---

7. http://www.rand.org/pubs/research_briefs/RB9100/index1.html

There are also options: innovative developments like a smart-phone app for PTSD and remote "telehealth" counseling sessions. Vet Centers (http://www.vetcenter.va.gov) may meet your needs for non-medical counseling better than a traditional VA Medical Center—they're usually smaller, there's very little paperwork, and the care can seem more personal. Note that while VHA generally cannot help active duty personnel, there are exceptions for those who have sustained certain types of serious injuries (such as spinal cord), and Vet Centers are also authorized to help AD troops in some cases.

Especially for women veterans, it's also important to go to VA for health care to send the right demand signals—if we don't show up in sufficient numbers, they won't be pressured to increase services specifically designed to meet our needs. Due to the growing number of women veterans and our changing needs, VA can cover care for newborns for the first seven days after birth for eligible women veterans getting VA maternity care, and has been testing child care pilot programs at several sites.

VBA can certify you for a VA-backed mortgage and clarify your educational benefits. If you have service-connected problems, fill out a disability claim—and remember, your lungs may seem fine now, but documenting exposure to burn pit smoke now may matter if you have problems down the road. If possible, submit a Fully Developed Claim electronically for faster processing.

And make sure your family knows about the burial and memorial benefits you've earned; NCA could be a tremendous help to them during a terrible time.

Community Resources

The National Resource Directory (www.nrd.gov) lists well over 10,000 national, state, and local resources. You can search this huge database of vetted organizations to find one that meets your needs, or find a way to get involved. See what the best fit is for you!

- Federally chartered Veterans Service Organizations (VSOs) are approved by the VA to assist veterans with filing claims—so if you are worried about getting your paperwork done right, this is a good place to start (learn more at http:// www.va.gov/vso/). These include, but are not limited to, Disabled American Veterans (http://www.dav.org), Veterans of Foreign Wars (http://www.vfw.org), and the Wounded Warrior Project (http://www.woundedwarriorproject.org). They all have other missions as well.

- A suite of wellness resources—including online assessments, a library of resources, and workshops—is available at www. afterdeployment.org.

- The Mission Continues (http://missioncontinues.org) awards community service fellowships to post-9/11 veterans.

- Team Rubicon (http://teamrubiconusa.org) is made up of veterans who respond to natural disasters, using skills developed in the military to serve in a new capacity.

- Student Veterans of America (http://www.studentveterans. org) has communities on college campuses so vets going to school now have better support systems in place than when Brian and I first hit the books again.

- The Pat Tillman Foundation (http://www. pattillmanfoundation.org) offers scholarships to veterans.

- The Bob Woodruff Foundation has a public education wing (http://remind.org).

- The USO (http://www.uso.org) supports troops abroad and troops and families at home.

- Not Alone (http://www.notalone.com/site/Default.aspx) provides programs, resources, and services to warriors and families impacted by combat stress through a confidential and anonymous online community.

- Service Women's Action Network (http://servicewomen. org) focuses primarily but not exclusively on issues that disproportionately affect women troops and veterans, such as military sexual trauma.

Family Members

Many—but not all—resources available to service members and veterans also include their families, so review the previous section. Note that although the VA generally cannot help family members, Vet Centers now offer both family counseling and bereavement counseling.

- Blue Star Families (http://www.bluestarfam.org) is an organization dedicated to supporting, connecting, and empowering military families.

- Fisher House (http://www.fisherhouse.org) provides housing for military families close to loved ones during hospitalizations.

- Tragedy Assistance Program for Survivors (http://www. taps.org) helps the families of all those who have made the ultimate sacrifice (including suicide survivors).

Civilians

Some general advice: Be thoughtful about what you say to veterans and military personnel—some like being thanked for their service, others find it discomforting.[8] Remember time and place—a combat veteran newly returned from Afghanistan may not want to tell you "what it's really like over there" at your cousin's wedding—she may want to just relax with family and friends instead of having questions bring to mind horrible experiences. This isn't to say you should not ask your best friend what he went through, of course. But rather than pushing them to tell you about what happened downrange, let friends or colleagues who are veterans know that you're there and willing to listen if they want to talk. If they seem to be struggling, offer to help them find or navigate resources, which can be confusing. Or just let them know by your consistent presence that you're still there, that you still want to hang out—and consider getting out to do something active instead of just sitting around drinking. As much as many of us enjoy doing that when we first get back, it isn't always the best coping mechanism.

If you want to give time or money, use the NRD to search for local or national organizations that are a good fit for your values and interests. Consider using a resource like Charity Navigator[9]

---

8. http://usnews.nbcnews.com/_news/2012/11/11/15079818-your-thank-you-to-veterans-is-welcomed-but-not-always-comfortably-received?lite

9. http://www.charitynavigator.org—however, note that there are concerns about how these ratings are developed; see, for example, http://articles.latimes.com/2012/apr/30/opinion/la-oe-shakely-charity-rating-Kahneman-20120430.

to ensure that the one you pick is a responsible steward of your donation.

Perhaps most importantly, get involved in the national conversation and political process. The single best way you can thank a veteran for their service is by using the right to vote that military personnel were willing to die to preserve for you. Tell your representatives that you care how veterans are treated and watch how they vote on important issues.[10] We as a nation elected politicians who chose to send troops off to war—now we as a nation must hold elected officials accountable for ensuring that the systems are in place to care for veterans when they get home.

---

10. IAVA (Iraq and Afghanistan Veterans of America) does a Congressional Report Card: http://www.veteranreportcard.org.

ACKNOWLEDGMENTS

Although I alone am responsible for any errors or flaws in this book, many people contributed to its strengths and enabled it to be published. They all deserve thanks.

If it weren't for Dr. Rocco Armonda, along with medics and other medical professionals, Brian likely would not have survived—he certainly would not have recovered to the extent he did. They all have our most profound gratitude.

I'm grateful that George Greenfield at CreativeWell and Jason Corliss at Verbatim Lecture Management helped me get speaking engagements—for that put me in front of many people who said, "You should write another book." That encouragement convinced me to tell this story. Then, my agent Sydelle worked hard encouraging W. W. Norton to take a chance on my second book, and my editor Alane (along with the rest of the consummate professionals there) brought this dream to fruition. Without the flexibility afforded me by the RAND Corporation, I would never have found the time to do the actual writing. And the loving providers at Kindercare gave me the ability to focus on working while knowing my children were well cared for.

I also appreciate that the VA responded positively to my criticisms and reached out to include me at local and national levels, which helped me better understand the source of gaps in services and the steps being taken to fill them. I'm grateful to the numerous nonprofits and advocates dedicated to helping wounded warriors, troops, veterans, and military families; civilians who have not forgotten us even as the wars have dropped off the media radar; those few dedicated journalists who have continued to report on these vital issues; and everyone doing research to allow treatment and programmatic changes to be evidence-based and scientifically sound.

Several people generously gave me their time: Stephanie, Danielle, and Jennifer gave invaluable input on early drafts of each chapter; Dr. Armonda, Dr. French, Matt Haney, Kenny Donovan, Rudy Cervantes, Nadean, Zoe, and Lauren all let me interview them to fill in gaps in my memory or knowledge; Bobby wrote down his memory of what happened on the bus; Peggy wrote down her memories of when they learned of Brian's injuries and first saw him; Terri Tanielian at RAND reviewed the appendix for tone, and others suggested resources.

Myriad people also provided less tangible but no less important forms of support along the rocky road to recovery and also the cathartic process of writing the book: my parents, Darby and Chris; Brian's parents, Peggy and Gene; our siblings Frank, Gretchen, and Shanna; Padi and Jim; Lynne and Greg; our wonderful friends Nadean, Stephanie, Amber, Tia, Casey, Josh, Vic, Chico, and Angel; Brian's colleagues who helped him reintegrate into the workforce: Todd, Peter, Brandon, Jon, Joan, and Stacy; and of course the HBC, Carolyn, Meg, Danielle, Jen, Rachel, Heather, and the rest. Others who have provided support via social media or over beers throughout this process are too numerous to list, but the kind words and encouragement have helped me push through difficult times.

Most of all, I am grateful to Brian for being my partner in all things, coparent, supporter, brewer and buyer of delicious beer, and a phoenix who has never given up. You continue to give me hope and inspire me. I look forward to many more years with you full of gentle bickering, laughter, and love.